ILLEGAL ENCOUNTERS

Illegal Encounters

*The Effect of Detention and Deportation
on Young People*

Edited by

Deborah A. Boehm *and* Susan J. Terrio

NEW YORK UNIVERSITY PRESS

New York

NEW YORK UNIVERSITY PRESS
New York
www.nyupress.org

© 2019 by New York University
All rights reserved

Chapter 1 was previously published in *The Land of Open Graves: Living and Dying on the Migrant Trail*, by Jason De León. University of California Press, 2015. Reprinted with permission.

References to Internet websites (URLs) were accurate at the time of writing. Neither the author nor New York University Press is responsible for URLs that may have expired or changed since the manuscript was prepared.

Library of Congress Cataloging-in-Publication Data
Names: Boehm, Deborah A., editor. | Terrio, Susan J. (Susan Jane), 1950–   editor.
Title: Illegal encounters : the effect of detention and deportation on young people / edited by Deborah A. Boehm and Susan Terrio.
Description: New York : New York University Press, 2018. |
Includes bibliographical references and index.
Identifiers: LCCN 2018012214| ISBN 9781479887798 (cl : alk. paper) |
ISBN 9781479861071 (pb : alk. paper)
Subjects: LCSH: Illegal alien children—Government policy—United States. |
Illegal alien children—United States—Social conditions. | Juvenile detention—
United States. | Deportation—United States. | Mexicans—Legal status, laws, etc.—
United States. | Central Americans—Legal status, laws, etc.—United States.
Classification: LCC JV6600 .I55 2018 | DDC 364.1/370830973—dc23
LC record available at https://lccn.loc.gov/2018012214

New York University Press books are printed on acid-free paper, and their binding materials are chosen for strength and durability. We strive to use environmentally responsible suppliers and materials to the greatest extent possible in publishing our books.

Manufactured in the United States of America

10 9 8 7 6 5 4 3 2 1

Also available as an ebook

CONTENTS

Introduction: Encounters with Illegality 1
Deborah A. Boehm and Susan J. Terrio

PART I. IN: CONFRONTING ENFORCEMENT,
DETENTION, AND DEPORTATION 15

1. Risky Border Crossings 19
Jason De León

2. Social Citizens and Their Right to Belong 32
Tobin Hansen

3. Illegality and Children's Power in Families 45
Joanna Dreby

REFLECTIONS: Entering Multiple Systems 58
José Ortiz-Rosales and Kristen Jackson

REFLECTIONS: Surviving Detention 66
Williams Guevara Martínez

PART II. THROUGH: NAVIGATING LAWS AND
LEGAL SYSTEMS 73

4. The Post-1996 Immigrant Underclass 76
Susan Bibler Coutin

5. Youth on Their Own 89
Nina Rabin and Cecilia Menjívar

6. Immigration Courts 102
Susan J. Terrio

REFLECTIONS: Representing Unaccompanied Children 114
Wendy Young and Megan McKenna

REFLECTIONS: Judging Children 123
Dana Leigh Marks

v

vi | CONTENTS

PART III. OUT: RESPONDING TO "ILLEGALITY"   131

7. Youth Negotiate Deportation   135
   Lauren Heidbrink

8. Youth Activism   147
   Carolina Valdivia

9. Dreaming across Borders   159
   Deborah A. Boehm

   REFLECTIONS: Looking Forward   171
   Abel Núñez and Rachel Gittinger

   REFLECTIONS: Still Dreaming   181
   Margarita Salas-Crespo

   Commentary: The Best Mankind Has to Give?   189
   Jacqueline Bhabha

Acknowledgments   197

Notes   199

Bibliography   213

About the Editors   231

About the Contributors   233

Index   241

Introduction

Encounters with Illegality

DEBORAH A. BOEHM AND SUSAN J. TERRIO

Fleeing violence in their home nation of Honduras, young Diego and his mother, Wendy Osorio Martinez, came to the United States seeking asylum. They were apprehended by US Border Patrol agents and transferred to Berks County Residential Center in Pennsylvania, one of three US immigration detention centers that hold women and children. They were ordered released after being held for nearly two years—654 days—in the facility, during which time Diego, three years old when he left detention, had learned to walk and talk.[1]

* * *

In February 2017, twenty-one-year-old Juan Manuel Montes Bojorquez was deported from the United States, despite his status as a recipient of Deferred Action for Childhood Arrivals (DACA), and although he migrated with his family as a nine-year-old and had spent most of childhood in the country. A brief interaction with law enforcement—a US Border Patrol officer asked Juan for identification as he was walking in Calexico, California—resulted in his deportation later that night. Today he lives in Mexico, far from family and friends.[2]

* * *

When Guadalupe García de Rayos went for her annual check-in with US immigration officials, US Immigration and Customs Enforcement (ICE) agents took her into custody while her husband and two US citizen children waited outside. ICE later announced that Guadalupe would be deported. Although her children and a group of immigrant advocates tried to block the van transporting her, ICE deported Guadalupe to Mexico, the country from which she had migrated more two decades earlier, as a child herself, at the age of fourteen.[3]

* * *

In each of these cases, young people faced distinct circumstances, had diverse experiences, and held different immigration statuses, and yet collectively these encounters demonstrate similar patterns in the ways that children and youth interact with government agents and institutions. This book's main intent is to track and understand how young people encounter, move through, and/or are outside of a range of legal processes, including border enforcement, immigration detention, federal custody, courts, and state processes of categorization. Even if young people do not directly enter state immigration systems—because they are US citizens or have avoided detention as undocumented immigrants—they are nonetheless deeply impacted by the invasive reach of government in its many forms.

Thus, this book's title, *Illegal Encounters*, highlights our focus on young people's interactions or encounters[4] with the different legal systems that regulate immigration. Scholars from across disciplines have made "illegality" a focus of their work, considering the ways in which individuals are subject to laws that mark them as "illegal" in a range of contexts,[5] especially through state actions that are tied to immigration status.[6] Research about the "legal production of migrant 'illegality'"[7] problematizes "illegality" itself, showing how categories assumed to be natural are in fact created by laws, lawmakers, and government bodies and agencies that carry out immigration enforcement.

Throughout this volume, we consider children's and young people's many encounters with illegality, deportability,[8] and deportation—those who migrate as well as those who are affected by the migration of others. We examine the impact of legal systems and discourses that construct legal categories on the everyday lived experiences of young people and their families, paying particular attention to the contradictions that occur when the state serves as both the body enforcing immigration law and the entity ostensibly tasked with providing a humanitarian response to crisis and suffering.[9] To illuminate the circumstances that young people currently face when they move to and from the United States, the following chapters and reflections consider and prioritize on-the-ground consequences. In what ways do political, legal, social, educational, and other systems shape children's experiences of immigration, and how do young immigrants and immigrant families negotiate the increasingly restrictive state actions of immigration control and policing?

In the United States, millions of children and youth are undocumented migrants or have family members who came to this country without authorization. In this context, the unique challenges faced by young people—from new arrivals to long-term residents with a range of immigration statuses and citizenships—demand special attention. The media stories, reports by nongovernmental organizations (NGOs), and occasional documentary films on this subject provide only a partial view of this complicated set of circumstances. This volume takes a comprehensive and systemic approach by following children and youth as they cross the border, suffer apprehension and detention by immigration authorities, go through removal proceedings in immigration courts, lead lives in the shadows outside of legal systems, and witness the migration experiences of their loved ones. We turn our attention to how these processes unfold within specific local, national, and transnational contexts—in the United States and across the Americas, especially Mexico and Central American countries—as people migrate across the US-Mexico border and as the US government enacts policies and laws aimed at controlling and restricting such movement.

In the following pieces, then, contributors focus on the challenges that young migrants from the Americas face within and/or outside of the purview of overlapping criminal, immigration, and child welfare systems, whether in the United States or in their countries of origin. Children and youth who migrate to this country find themselves curiously situated both within and outside of different systems, and often betwixt and between different frameworks, institutional responses, and laws. For example, children may be treated as adults in immigration courts; criminalized and held in secure facilities even if very young; caught up in immigration enforcement aimed at their parents; granted temporary legal status (or not) as young people raised in the United States; and/or subject to government policies and practices but without the constitutional rights granted to citizens. The paradoxical and perplexing positionality of children vis-à-vis immigration and other state regimes is the result of a combination of factors and aspects of identity, including age, citizenship, family relations, race, gender, and class position, among others. We maintain that children, youth, and young adults uniquely grapple with these contradictions, because of their categorization as "minors" or as members of the next generation, and because of the particular ways in which they are perceived socially, culturally, and within institutions. We therefore focus on precisely this positioning of young people in, between, and outside of legal systems and institutions.

The book provides new perspectives on immigration debates and discussions taking place in the academy, among policy makers, and in the public sphere. It is unique in that the contributors privilege the voices and everyday experiences of immigrant children and youth themselves.[10] Some of the following chapters and essays provide first-hand accounts of the experience of immigrating as children or as teenagers to the United States, including those whom the US government categorizes as "unaccompanied alien children" and those who migrated at a young age with family members. Many of the pieces are written by advocates and service providers who have years of experience working directly with young people and who draw on these interactions to provide specific policy recommendations. Still other contributors are researchers whose work focuses on the everyday lives and experiences of young people as understood from their own viewpoints. By combining these different perspectives, the book presents ethnographically rich accounts that also have policy implications, are of theoretical importance to academics, and convey the outlooks of young people themselves—views of immigration that are generally missing from the public arena but that can contribute to informed debates and policy reform.

This book, then, is innovative in the way that it combines writings by academics, practitioners, and migrant youth. We bring together work by scholars, including ethnographers from anthropology, education, sociology, and legal studies; practitioners such as social workers, attorneys, and judges; authors at different stages of their careers, including senior and junior scholars, graduate students, college students, and recent graduates; and most important, those who immigrated to this country as children themselves. Our primary aim is to bridge disciplinary and professional divides in order to bring different perspectives into productive dialogue and to highlight the connections and/or gaps between theory and practice.

The volume also highlights the range of experiences that young people have in the context of immigration—whether they themselves or their loved ones are immigrants (or both). Some children migrate with undocumented parents or other family members while others make the journey alone or with hired smugglers to reunite with parents who previously migrated to the United States. After growing up in the country, some undocumented and US citizen children may follow deported family members to countries they left as children or remain in the United States on their own, with relatives, or in foster care or state institutions.[11] Among children living in the United States, many have such strong ties to the nation that they may not even be aware of their unauthorized status until they apply for a driver's license or a job.[12] Still others migrate alone, often fleeing violence in their home country, and are apprehended by immigration authorities. Some are immediately deported, while others may be detained, placed in deportation proceedings, and released to sponsors.[13] Countless young people live in the shadows for years.

By underscoring the ways in which young people encounter or avoid legal systems, this book problematizes the very policies, laws, and legal categories that shape so much of daily life for immigrants in the United States. By following children and youth as they navigate US immigration policies, we complicate the supposed binary of "legal" and "illegal" in their lives—that is, the notion that such categorizations of migration can be neatly defined and separated. The volume highlights the ways that young people (1) enter *in* government systems, (2) move *through* legal processes, and/or (3) are forced *out* of the nation or resist unjust institutions that attempt to define immigrants as outside of the national body. Certainly, these stages—in, through, and out—are not easily delineated, and a primary aim of this book is to show the overlapping and blurry character of young migrants' encounters with, and challenges to, the very illegality that is thrust upon them by state action, policy, law, and practice.

Mapping Illegality in the Lives of Young People

From the nation's founding until today, US immigration laws and policies have emphasized restriction, exclusion, and control. Contemporary immigration and deportation policies are a legacy of long-standing ideas about race, imperialism, and state power. Late nineteenth-century legal doctrine, for example, established the government's right to expel foreigners[14] and held that deportation is not punishment,[15] a finding that still applies today. During the same period the Supreme Court distinguished civil detention from criminal incarceration,[16] holding that jailing pursuant to a civil proceeding against a potential deportee was permissible. The view that immigration detention differs fundamentally from penal imprisonment has persisted even as the number of adults, youth, and families in detention has skyrocketed.

During the late twentieth and early twenty-first centuries until the contemporary moment, the US government has expanded the category of "illegality," ushering in further restrictions on immigration and criminalizing immigrants,[17] including migrant youth and even very young children. Immigration and antiterrorism laws, such as the Illegal Immigration Reform and Immigrant Responsibility Act of 1996 and legislation passed after September 11, 2001, placed a heightened emphasis on security and containment. These statutes curtailed existing personal freedoms, gutted due process protections, gave unparalleled enforcement powers to immigration authorities, blurred the already tenuous boundary between immigration and criminal law, and limited judicial review of detention and deportation decisions. This legislation also expanded the categories of deportable offenses to include nonviolent misdemeanors, applied them retroactively to include acts committed "at any time" in a person's life, and eliminated the exercise of discretion by immigration judges in most deportation cases.[18]

The conflation of immigration and criminal laws and the increased reliance on enforcement have had an adverse impact on young people, ranging from infants to young adults, specifically as members of families. Because of the militarization of national borders, there are growing numbers of families that extend transnationally and have members with mixed legal statuses. Illegality and deportability disrupt and reconfigure immigrant families in profound ways.[19] Divided families result when, for example, family members are forcibly separated while in federal custody at the US border, undocumented parents of immigrant or US citizen children are detained or deported, or unaccompanied child migrants are removed at the border or held in federal custody after apprehension by immigration authorities. Indeed, it is precisely in the sphere of family life that children often encounter legal systems and the state actions that limit or define their status as children, as immigrants—or as those who are related to immigrants—and as members of families, communities, and social networks.

And, as several of the pieces in this volume underscore, migrant children themselves are at constant risk of confronting the coercive power of government systems of apprehension, detention, and deportation. Unaccompanied child migrants from Central America and Mexico who seek refuge, family, work, and education in the United States may be caught in federal detention systems or deportation proceedings. If they are apprehended by immigration authorities, child migrants enter a labyrinthine system (see Guevara Martínez, this volume) that may include Border Patrol stations, ICE detention centers, subcontracted facilities and jails, and proceedings in state and federal courts. And, as several contributors to this volume show, US citizen children are also affected by the immigration status of loved ones as parents and other family members move in and out of legal systems.

Undocumented children and youth who grow up in the United States have the same aspirations and abilities as their US citizen peers but are often socially and economically marginalized. Many are permanently stymied by the cumulative disadvantages of lacking citizenship, and, despite educational and other opportunities in the United States, they may end up in the same structural position as their undocumented parents and significantly disadvantaged compared with their peers.[20] The persistent effects of illegality limit social mobility and constrain social networks.[21] By adulthood, illegality can become a "master status" that pushes them to the margins.[22] Exploitative jobs, missed opportunities, and accumulated frustrations exact a significant toll on the physical and psychological well-being of young people.[23] And all children with ties to immigrants—regardless of immigration status or citizenship—can be deeply impacted by "illegal" statuses and restrictive immigration laws.

This volume examines the impact of evolving immigration policies, especially those that regulate entry, produce unauthorized migrants and illegality, and redefine potential citizens. On the one hand, the authors explore how children and youth are marginalized within and across borders, and how legal frameworks and state power disadvantage them. On the other hand, the pieces also examine youth empowerment movements and civil disobedience initiatives through which youth challenge public policies on enforcement and deportation and shape legislation on citizenship, family security, and immigration. In this sense, young people interact with, are coerced by, and/or challenge systems of "illegality" and "legality," as well as the spaces in between. Although we outline agency on the part of individual children and youth, above all, the pieces in the volume demonstrate the structural power of state-based and supranational forces that constrain and limit young people and their family members as they move across borders.

Law and Policy as Everyday Experience

Multiple factors have coalesced to produce this complicated legal backdrop to the immigration of young people and their family members, including a patchwork of existing laws as well as the absence of laws that could address certain aspects of immigration. Restrictive immigration laws, intensified enforcement at international borders and in the country's interior, as well as executive actions and federal programs such as those overseen by the US Department of Homeland Security (DHS) clearly influence the everyday lives of young immigrants and young people in immigrant families. In addition, government agencies and laws that do not specifically address immigration—for example, in the spheres of education, child welfare, and social services—also play out in the lives of children and youth. Finally, the absence of laws, especially decades without comprehensive immigration reform, shapes daily experience for millions of infants, children, and teenagers in the United States.

There are currently more than 11 million unauthorized migrants living in the country, more than 2.5 million of whom are young people.[24] Among the most vulnerable of migrants are unaccompanied minors who flee violence in their home countries and are apprehended after dangerous crossings at the US-Mexico border (see De León, this volume). Since 2012, a total of 231,416 children and youth have migrated alone to the United States,[25] and, after apprehension by immigration authorities for unauthorized entry, have entered a complex system of detention and immigration courts. Federal regulations in place since 1997 mandate the humane treatment and prompt release of detained children and youth to approved sponsors. Nonetheless, numerous problems have persisted: long periods of detention with no set end point; the overuse of secure facilities; rigid behavioral management programs; the use of a detention model organized by security level; the intensive scrutiny of sponsors, including parents and close relatives; a shortage of therapeutic facilities; and the long-standing trend of locating facilities in remote areas to reduce costs and access to voluntary attorneys, as well as to keep children close to the border and ready for deportation if ordered.[26]

Whether they migrate alone or with family members, undocumented immigrant children and youth have no right to government-appointed counsel or child advocates in family, district, or immigration court proceedings, and they face extremely limited avenues of legal relief under US immigration law.[27] If they are in immigration court proceedings, they must find volunteer or pro bono representation on their own, a daunting challenge given the high demand for and critical shortage of free legal services for immigrants (see Young and McKenna, this volume). Even with competent legal representation, young immigrants must defend against removal by proving eligibility for forms of relief designed almost exclusively for adults (see Marks, this volume), and their cases are often heard in accelerated immigration court hearings or "rocket dockets" (see Terrio, this volume). Many of those who enter the United States without authorization or have no qualifying relative may never be able to regularize their legal status.[28] Others may wait for years to have their asylum cases adjudicated in backlogged immigration courts, hit statutory limits on available humanitarian visas such as Special Immigrant Juvenile Status (SIJS),[29] or apply for other temporary statuses such as Deferred Action for Childhood Arrivals, an executive order issued under the Obama administration.

On September 5, 2017, the Trump administration announced that DACA would be terminated. As of that date, nearly 800,000 young people had qualified for this status.[30] Because of DACA, immigrant youth were able to come out of the shadows to pursue higher education, employment, home ownership, and more. DACA provided temporary work authorization, the possibility to obtain a driver's license or to travel internationally through Advance Parole (see Boehm, this volume), and, most significantly, a deferral or suspension of deportation.[31] But, from the beginning, those with DACA were in a tenuous position in that a deferral of removal is temporary and can be revoked at any time. The Trump administration's termination of DACA made the future legal status, and future trajectories, of DACA recipients that much more uncertain. As many as 1.8 million young people who have grown up in the United States would qualify for legal status and a path to citizenship if Congress were to pass a form of the Dream Act,[32] underscoring the ways that the *absence* of sound policy impacts young people currently living in the United States.

Children and youth also face US immigration enforcement when they cross the border with family members. For example, in 2014, the Obama administration responded to the arrival of 61,000 undocumented families—largely mothers and young children—with aggressive enforcement policies[33] designed to deter potential asylum seekers by building new detention facilities specifically intended to hold women and children.[34] These "family reception centers" have been the subject of repeated allegations of due process violations, unsafe conditions, mistreatment of children and parents, woefully inadequate medical care, and deliberate misinformation about the possibility of release.[35] Despite a Ninth Circuit Court ruling ordering the government to release all children in family detention in 2016,[36] the US government continues to detain them in inhumane conditions for prolonged periods.[37]

Finally, an estimated 5.1 million children and youth—both US citizens and undocumented immigrants—are living in mixed-status families within the United States.[38] Many undocumented children in mixed-status families cross the border undetected, live in stable households and safe communities, and build lives in this country. Indeed, many undocumented immigrants brought as children to the United States grow up knowing no other home. They enroll in public schools, form strong social networks, interact with different systems and government agencies (see Ortiz-Rosales and Jackson, this volume), connect with community organizations (see Núñez and Gittinger, this volume), engage in advocacy efforts (see Valdivia, this volume), and become members of the United States even if not legally recognized as citizens (see Salas-Crespo, this volume). In some cases, living in the shadows also means living outside of the most coercive of government systems—such as detention centers and immigration court systems—and out of the reach of certain US immigration laws and policies.

Still, young people with diverse legal positions, citizenships, national memberships, and immigration statuses are subject to the effects of US immigration laws every day. For example, the vast majority of those in mixed-status families—79 percent, or 4.1 million—are US citizens,[39] demonstrating the profound impact of US immigration policy on children and youth regardless of their citizenship or immigration status. These figures underscore the limitations of US immigration law and the few possibilities for reuniting families across borders or allowing family members to change their immigration status through loved ones—even as US immigration law is ostensibly based on family reunification.[40] And when families extend transnationally, financial and emotional strains take a toll on caregivers and children (see Dreby, this volume), both in the United States and in countries of origin.

Thus, young people with a range of statuses experience US immigration enforcement and laws in diverse ways. Youth and young adults may be deported as "unaccompanied minors" (see Heidbrink, this volume), after coming to the United States with family members (see Coutin, this volume), or after encounters with the criminal justice system (see Hansen, this volume), even in cases when they have lived most of their childhood in the country. Immigration laws pose serious structural obstacles for all children affected by immigration, including those who live on their own (see Rabin and Menjívar, this volume), those who reunify with parents after long periods of separation, and those in blended or mixed-status families. And, both US citizen and immigrant children often live with a constant fear of being found and/or having family members apprehended,[41] experience detention firsthand or through others when loved ones are detained, and find their lives altered after deportation, whether their own deportation or that of their parents, siblings, or other family members.[42] In sum, the reach of US immigration laws extends to children and youth of all ages and impacts those in a wide range of circumstances and with diverse immigration histories and trajectories.

Navigating Legal Systems: In, Through, and Out

Against this backdrop of laws, policies, and government actions, children and their family members must navigate systems that are both opaque and increasingly coercive. We have structured the book around three guiding themes—in, through, and out—while recognizing that there is considerable overlap among them. Part I, "In: Confronting Enforcement, Detention, and Deportation," traces young people's path as they enter, often through force, into multiple legal systems associated with migration. In part II, "Through: Navigating Laws and Legal Systems," we see firsthand the encounters between young people and multiple government agencies. Finally, part III, "Out: Responding to 'Illegality,'" follows children and youth who are outside of legal systems, whether they are formally expelled through deportation, out in the sense of claiming their immigration status as a tool for organizing, and/or on the margins due to unjust laws that limit opportunities for a change in status. Each part includes three chapters and two shorter essays. The book concludes with a commentary by Jacqueline Bhabha about children's international legal and human rights in the current moment. Together, the pieces underscore the complexities of diverse encounters with the state, and the circumstances of being within, moving through, and living outside of immigration categories and processes.

This movement is not linear, and young people can be in, between, and/or outside of different systems simultaneously. For example, migrants and their loved ones may at times be closely controlled by legal institutions, such as when detained at a federal facility, and yet at other times—including when crossing borders clandestinely or building lives in new destinations despite unauthorized status—migrants may not formally interact with government or judicial agents. Some who go into immigration systems may come out with a changed immigration status, and even those who would not seem to be the likely targets of immigration policy, such as US citizens, can be caught within systems. Being *in* legal systems can result in youth being deported and formally expelled outside of the nation. After being in detention, for example, youth may choose to leave or "self-deport," despite eligibility for legal status, because they can no longer endure separation from their families. Being *out* can mean living in the nation without legal status. Finally, those entangled with government bureaucracies may also overtly challenge them from the outside, as "Dreamers" and DACA recipients have done. In this case, youth have come out of the shadows, even as they continue to be confined by immigration laws with limited possibilities for a path to citizenship.

INTRODUCTION | 13

The legal immigration regime under President Obama was focused on enhanced enforcement and deterrence. Nonetheless, current federal immigration policies are that much more restrictive, and few could have predicted that the hyperbolic statements on "illegal immigration" made by candidate Trump would become federal public policy just weeks after his inauguration. For example, the DHS memos of February 17, 2017, vastly expand the definition of "criminal aliens" and the priority categories for deportation, propose new detention facilities, call for thousands of additional immigration enforcement agents, discourage asylum seekers (in violation of US and international law), enlist local police as federal enforcers, redefine who counts as an "unaccompanied alien minor," propose the prosecution of parents who pay smugglers to bring their children to the United States,[43] and, ultimately, aim to speed up deportations.[44] The immediate and future effects of these actions on young people cannot be overstated, and will, without question, shape their lives in the months and years to come.

We end this introduction as we began—by highlighting specific cases and narratives of young people as they contemplate their future, but this time from our individual and collaborative research. Referencing the limited period of eligibility for deferred action, one DACA recipient told us, "I live my life in two-year increments." Now that DACA has been rescinded, young people with approved applications face an even more uncertain future. Although she is a US citizen, another young woman similarly described the uncertainty that defines her everyday life; as she completes her undergraduate studies and prepares for medical school, her otherwise very bright future is shaped by fears that her undocumented immigrant parents might be deported to Mexico. And, when we interviewed a fifteen-year-old from Colombia who came to the United States as an unaccompanied minor, he was perplexed by the anti-immigrant sentiment expressed during the 2016 presidential election:

> I don't understand why Americans feel this way about immigrants. This is a country made by immigrants. They came from another country as we did. They are the same as us. This country is full of different cultures and people. If we expel them all, then they will not see how big and beautiful this country is. Donald Trump says he wants to make America great

again, but I would tell him that if America was not great, no one would want to come here. And I wouldn't be here.

Despite different circumstances, migration trajectories, and nations of origin and citizenship, these young people—and the many others described throughout the volume—share the experience of living in the United States during a period when encounters with illegality are commonplace for millions of children, youth, and their loved ones.

This volume is intended to make visible the burdens, hopes, and potential of a population of young people and their families who have been largely hidden from public view and are currently under siege. We write at a time when the issue of the nation and its newcomers is sure to guide federal, state, and local politics moving forward. The United States and its residents collectively face an uncertain future, and this new reality makes it all the more urgent to follow young people as they move into, through, and out of the complicated and often bewildering systems and institutions that characterize the United States—laws, policies, and state actions that influence the lives of so many within the country but also impact countless people in countries throughout the world.

PART I

In

Confronting Enforcement, Detention, and Deportation

In this part, authors consider the systems that young people enter as immigrants—systems through which the state controls, apprehends, detains, and deports foreign nationals—but also the way that young people enter or are *in* systems even when not obviously so. Looking at cases at the border and in the nation's interior, the pieces show the particular effects of border controls, legal systems, and categories of "illegality" more generally on young people. Young people may enter into, become caught within, or find themselves firmly situated in immigration and criminal justice systems that can result in deportation and being forced outside of the country.

Paradoxically, children and youth are likely to be rooted in the nation even if not recognized as members of it; enter into systems and institutional procedures even if not formally so; are subject to US immigration laws and policies even if not directly; and might need to navigate government bureaucracies even if outside of or on the margins of the nation. As the contributors in this part show us, young people are in systems that construct and monitor "illegality" as they cross the border (De León); enter into and are then defined by the criminal justice system in the United States and may be deported as a result (Hansen); go into federal custody and immigration detention (Guevara Martínez); are caught within overlapping systems (Ortiz-Rosales and Jackson); and find themselves governed by immigration laws and practices whether or not they formally interact with government agencies (Dreby). Indeed, the reach of the state places far more individuals in immigration regimes than those who are actually immigrants themselves.

In chapter 1—which aptly opens part I—Jason De León uncovers the coercive intent behind the federal border control policy known as Prevention Through Deterrence. As a result, migrants are pushed into remote desert and mountainous areas characterized by extreme environmental conditions. This policy has failed to deter border crossers while successfully turning the rugged terrain of southern Arizona into a killing field. Apprehensions while trying to cross the border are among the most violent ways young people find themselves placed *in* US immigration systems and deportation regimes. The border zone is a liminal space where migrants are positioned both inside and outside the nation. If they lose their way, are abandoned by smugglers, or are weakened by hyperthermia, their only hope may be rescue by Border Patrol and, ultimately, expulsion. Too often this brief incursion into a hostile landscape ends in death, the erasure of bodily remains, and the impossibility of migration to the United States or return to one's homeland. The threatening space of the US-Mexico border that De León describes poses particular threats to children and youth who are attempting to cross, especially when doing so without adult family members. Guides and smugglers typically facilitate the movement of young people, or—which is equally dangerous—children increasingly attempt to cross alone or with groups of other young people. As children and youth are apprehended trying to enter the United States, they also enter a complicated system of immigration enforcement and detention.

In chapter 2, Tobin Hansen centers on migrants who were brought to the United States as children and who grew up in the country. Over time, children become embedded within US communities, developing personal histories and social bonds as they reach adulthood. However, many of the young men Hansen interviewed found themselves caught up *in* criminal and immigration enforcement systems that are difficult to exit. As undocumented youth, they may be labeled as "criminal aliens," a racialized practice that confines and expels young people despite their strong connections to families, communities, and the nation. Focusing on memories of apprehension, detention, and "removal" or deportation among men in Nogales, Sonora, Mexico, the chapter demonstrates how, over time, multiple structures of social, economic, and political marginalization in the United States result in the expulsion of Mexican nationals who identify as US social citizens.

Dreby's chapter complements Hansen's focus on the powerlessness of deported Mexican men by examining the relative experiences of power among Mexican girls with different immigration and citizenship statuses who live in transnational families, some in Mexico and others in the United States. Dreby shows how all members of families may find themselves *in* legal systems: migrant children are affected, but so too are nonmigrants, both those whose parents migrate without them and those born to migrant parents in host countries. The specter of illegality within a family changes children's roles and concrete responsibilities, as well as their feelings related to these changes. Dreby's focus on mixed-status families examines the ongoing challenges children face when they enter the state's system of categorization—directly or indirectly—as some siblings are marked as "illegal" while others stay in Mexico or are US citizens. Dreby shows the impacts that regimes of illegality have on families and especially on children and youth.

The piece written by José Ortiz-Rosales and Kristen Jackson illustrates how as young migrants enter the United States, they also enter a complex landscape that may include legal, educational, child welfare, and health care systems. Youth can be *in* systems and yet outside of social communities and on the margins. These systems intersect, overlap, or diverge depending on the circumstances that bring young people to the United States, as well as their family networks, access to legal representation, the availability of health care services, and their educational environment, among other factors. Focusing on the experiences of three young people, Ortiz-Rosales and Jackson show how different factors converge to create a range of outcomes that may or may not serve the child's interests. The authors underscore the fact that legal status—while a potentially powerful step in changing one's circumstances in the United States—is not necessarily sufficient for ensuring security for children and youth. They advocate powerfully for an intersectional approach that can better serve young people as they move into, but also through and out of, intersecting systems.

In the final piece in this part, we hear directly from a young man, Williams Guevara Martínez, who recounts his motivation for leaving his home in El Salvador, his journey to the United States, and his experiences in federal custody and after release. He charts his personal attachments, educational opportunities, work experience, and commitment to build a productive life in the United States and to help others like himself. Guevara Martínez left El Salvador in search of safety, but he was soon placed in a complex detention system that included a new set of violations and insecurities. Migration north can entangle youth in detention and other legal regimes that shape their lives even after they have been held in federal custody for a relatively short period. Now having graduated from high school and gained US legal permanent residency, Guevara Martínez looks back to explain the challenges of youth who enter the country alone and without authorization, those who find themselves *in* systems that have an immediate impact but also unanticipated effects after release.

1

Risky Border Crossings

JASON DE LEÓN

On April 3, 2013, fifteen-year-old José left Cuenca, Ecuador with two cousins, thirteen-year-old Felipe and nineteen-year-old Manny.[1] Their trip lasted several months but was relatively uneventful. After leaving Guayaquil by plane, the three of them crossed multiple borders by car and bus. After less than two weeks of travel they arrived in Mexico. Once in Mexico City, the cousins were sent to different safe houses where they then spent forty-five days waiting for transport to Nogales.[2] Unable to leave their houses, they tried to keep themselves busy. They mostly watched TV and paced around a small courtyard. The house where José was kept had Internet, and he was able to periodically log on to Facebook when his smuggler let him (for a fee of course).

Finally, after a month and a half of being cooped up indoors, José's cousins were loaded into the luggage compartment of a passenger bus, given a bucket to urinate in, and told not to make any noise. For two cramped days Manny and Felipe laid quietly under the bus while dozens of unknowing passengers sitting above them snoozed, read magazines, and stared out their windows at the northern Mexican countryside. Although the details of how José got to Nogales are currently vague, it was likely a trip similar to what his cousins experienced. When they finally reached the border, the three boys were reunited and taken to a safe house where they waited, along with dozens of other migrants, for their guide to tell them when it was time to try their luck. Ten days after arriving in Nogales, a car showed up one night and drove them to the edge of the desert.

> FELIPE: We left the house in Nogales at night and were dropped off underneath a *puente* [bridge or overpass]. It only took like twenty minutes in the car to get from the house to the *puente*. Everyone was

carrying a black backpack and their one bottle of water. A gallon of water. Some bottles were white and some were painted black. . . . José was wearing black Air Jordans with black pants, a black sweatshirt, a black shirt, and black hat with red letters on it. Everyone had black clothes on.

MANNY: José had a rosary, a prayer card, and a chain with an owl on it that his girlfriend gave him. He was wearing a belt that had phone numbers written on it. It had his dad's cell phone and house numbers. He had no identification.

FELIPE: We crossed a fence and then started walking. We were traveling with two guides. There were around forty people in our group. One of the guides was named Scooby. I don't remember the other one's name. . . . We climbed a hill and at the bottom we crossed another fence. When we climbed the first hill we could see the city of Nogales, and then it disappeared. We walked all night and then rested near a *rancho* around 4 or 5 a.m. We slept in an abandoned house there. In the morning we started walking again.

MANNY: We left from the *puente*. We walked a little bit and then climbed a mountain. After the mountain it got flat, and then there was a road with a house on it. After we crossed the road, there was nothing, just mountains and mountains. We walked past a tall mountain that had two blinking antennas on it. They had red blinking lights. The guides called it *la Montaña de Cerdo* [Pig Mountain].

FELIPE: Our group separated that next day. Me, José, and Manny stayed together with Scooby. . . . We would climb a hill and Scooby would be waiting at the top for people. On the second day of walking we got to the start of the hill at about 6 a.m. and rested. José's shoes were starting to fall apart. The soles were coming unglued. José kept stopping to sit and drink water. We were giving him water so he could keep going. We then climbed a hill and dropped down to a flat area where there wasn't any shade or trees. It was impossible to hide there.

MANNY: We had rested at the bottom of a hill for ten minutes when my cousin José started to sleep. He didn't want to get up. Every time we stopped to rest, he would try to sleep. The guide would say, "We are going to rest and catch your breath and then we are going to start walking again. Don't sleep." Well, José started to sleep. It was the heat.

The heat will get you. It robs you of energy. We really didn't have much to drink. José had water in his backpack, but he needed more. He started to drink a lot of water. He was just getting thirstier and thirstier. We had brought *sueros* [electrolyte solution] and gave them to him. He finished everything. He couldn't control himself.

FELIPE: He stopped walking around 7 a.m. He couldn't go on. José fell down and Scooby started kicking him. Scooby was saying, "Get up or I am going to keep kicking you." José's leg gave out, and he just slumped down on the ground. He said that he'd had enough. Scooby was yelling, "You need to get up or I'm going to beat you." José was sitting on the ground looking dazed [makes woozy head movements], and Scooby just kept kicking him. He tried to get up but fell with all his weight. He was falling on bushes and the branches were breaking. He fell three times and the last time he couldn't get up. He was very sleepy and his eyes were half open. We were all kind of like that but José also had the flu. When we left Nogales he was sick. He said he was going to turn himself in. He told me, "I can't go on, but you should."

MANNY: His feet wouldn't let him go anymore. He was on the ground and said, "I am going to turn myself in." Immigration was all around at this point. Where we left him there was Border Patrol everywhere.

FELIPE: There were helicopters around because, the day before, they were catching a lot of people in our group. We told José we were going to keep going, and we left him sitting at the bottom of the hill. He was in a spot where there was no place to hide, no trees or anything. José had food and a little bottle of water that I gave him. We walked to the next hill where Scooby was waiting. That was the last time we saw him.

A day and half after leaving José behind, the cousins and their guide were spotted by Border Patrol and chased into the mountains. It was at this point that Scooby abandoned them. They were now alone, lost, and out of food and water. To compound issues, thirteen-year-old Felipe was dehydrated to the point that he began coughing up blood. At daybreak they started walking until they stumbled upon a lagoon and were able to fill their bottles with murky liquid. That morning they somehow found their way to Arivaca Road, where they were quickly picked up by Border

Patrol. As the crow flies, they had walked almost thirty miles through multiple mountain ranges.

When they finally spoke to their families from federal detention days later, Manny and Felipe reported that José had stayed behind. Despite the fact that they left him in an area with heavy Border Patrol presence, José never turned himself in. At the end of our first interview Manny remarked to me, "I don't know why he didn't turn himself in at that moment. Maybe he kept walking. I'm not sure what happened."

Prevention through Deterrence

In July 1993, the Immigration and Naturalization Service (INS) promoted Mexican American Border Patrol agent Silvestre Reyes to chief of the El Paso Sector. Reyes was brought in during a moment of crisis when a series of lawsuits and claims of human rights violations had been brought against the Border Patrol in the region. Two of the major grievances lodged against the agency were that legal Latino residents were subjected to unfair racial profiling and harassment, and that the consistent pursuit of undocumented border crossers through neighborhoods was a dangerous and abusive practice.[3] The majority of El Paso residents who lived along the border were Latino, which made it difficult for *la migra* to figure out who was "illegal" without directly interrogating people. Locals were tired of law enforcement questioning them about their citizenship while they were going about their daily business. In response to these complaints, Reyes came up with a radical new enforcement strategy that would fundamentally change how the border was policed. Timothy Dunn describes what happened on September 19, 1993, when Reyes launched Operation Blockade:

> The emphasis of the operation was to deter unauthorized border crossings in the core urban area between Ciudad Juárez and El Paso by making a bristling show of force. . . . This took the form of posting 400 Border Patrol agents (out of 650 total in the sector) on the banks of the Rio Grande and adjacent levees in stationary, ubiquitous green and green and white patrol vehicles around the clock, at short distance intervals (from fifty yards to one-half mile) along a twenty-mile stretch between El Paso and Ciudad Juárez. This mass posting of agents created an imposing line, if

not [a] virtual wall, of agents along the river, which was supplemented by low-flying and frequently deployed surveillance helicopters.[4]

Prior to this strategy, the standard operating procedure had been to try to apprehend border crossers *after* they had crossed the boundary line. The circus-like atmosphere created when dozens of people at a time jumped the border fence while agents in green uniforms chased after them like Keystone Cops was ludicrous. Comedian Cheech Marin even built his film *Born in East L.A.* around this border-wide phenomenon. These daily scenes exemplified the difficulties of trying to seal the border. Reyes's mass deployment of agents in and around the El Paso port of entry was thus an effective public relations move that seemed to satisfy local residents. This "show of force," however, didn't stop illegal immigration. It mostly frustrated migrants accustomed to crossing in urban zones and forced them to move toward the edge of town, where they could easily hop the fence in depopulated areas.[5]

In addition to funneling traffic away from downtown, this strategy also made migration less visible and created a scenario in which the policing of undocumented people occurred in areas with few witnesses. Out of sight, out of mind. Despite the fact that this "deterrence-displacement" strategy only made border crossers harder to see,[6] some politicians soon touted it as a success.[7] The operation's effects were felt along much of the US-Mexico border during the 1990s when it was adopted in Southern California (Operation Gatekeeper in 1994), Arizona (Operation Safeguard in 1994 and 1999), and South Texas (Operation Rio Grande in 1997). When Reyes set Operation Blockade in motion, he intended to shift traffic away from the city and "put [migrants] out in areas where they're on [Border Patrol's] turf."[8] Little did he know that this approach would soon evolve into a large-scale policy that would strategically use the natural environment and subsequently become the foundation for border security in a post-9/11 world.

The logic behind Operation Blockade was straightforward. Placing heightened security in and around the downtown urban port of entry in El Paso would force undocumented migrants to attempt crossings in more rural areas that were easier for law enforcement to monitor. Although this initial strategy in El Paso had been neither officially sanctioned nor fully evaluated by INS, it immediately garnered media and political attention and was soon adopted as a part of a new federal project. Less than a year after Operation Blockade, INS published its Strategic Plan,[9] which essentially repackaged what Reyes had done informally into a national program: "The Border Patrol will improve control of the border by implementing a strategy of 'prevention through deterrence.' The Border Patrol will achieve the goals of its strategy by bringing a decisive number of enforcement resources to bear in each major entry corridor. The Border Patrol will increase the number of agents on the line and make effective use of technology, raising the risk of apprehension high enough to be an effective deterrent."[10] One of the primary components that structured the new strategy of Prevention Through Deterrence (PTD) was the recognition that remote areas along the border (e.g., the Sonoran Desert) are difficult to traverse on foot and hence can be effectively used by law enforcement. This, however, was by no means a recent epiphany, as noted by historian Patrick Ettinger: "From their earliest work enforcing the Chinese Exclusion Acts [enacted in 1882], immigration authorities had discovered that the desert and mountain wilderness could be made effective allies in the fight against undocumented entry. Desolate routes deprive migrants of access to food and water. Only along well-defined roads or on railroads could immigrants obtain the necessary resources for travel, and it was along those routes that immigration patrols might be best stationed to capture undocumented immigrants."[11] As one federal agent testified in 1926, the goal of border enforcement was to "at least make attempts to cross the border dangerous and hold illegal entry down to small proportions."[12]

The acknowledgment that the desert, as well as the other extreme environments crosscut by the border, could strategically be used to deter migrants from illegal entry on a large scale was not, however, formally laid out in policy documents until the start of the official PTD era, after 1993. The initial Strategic Plan memorandum was among the first to refer to environmental conditions as a potential resource for securing the geopolitical boundary: "The border environment is diverse. Mountains, deserts, lakes, rivers and valleys form natural barriers to passage. Temperatures ranging from sub-zero along the northern border to the searing heat of the southern border effect [*sic*] illegal entry traffic as well as enforcement efforts. *Illegal entrants crossing through remote, uninhab-*

ited expanses of land and sea along the border can find themselves in mortal danger" (emphasis added).[13]

Although policy makers have written extensively about PTD for decades,[14] only the earliest documents associated with this strategy articulate a clear vision of the role that officials imagined the environment playing in enforcement: "The prediction is that with traditional entry and smuggling routes disrupted, illegal traffic will be deterred, or forced over more *hostile* terrain, less suited for crossing and more suited for enforcement" (emphasis added).[15] Prior to PTD, the dominant enforcement practice emphasized catching people after an illegal entry had been achieved and then processing them through the *voluntary-departure complex*, whereby apprehended migrants were permitted to waive their rights to a deportation hearing and returned to Mexico without lengthy detention.[16] Many have described this as a relatively useless process that individuals become familiar with, and less afraid of, after repeated apprehensions.[17] PTD was a direct reaction to the ineffectiveness of this previous disciplinary practice.

In the 1994 Strategic Plan, the use of the word "hostile" suggests that this new form of boundary enforcement was intended to be more aggressive and violent (and thus more effective) than previous programs. The word choice is also interesting given that the architects of the Strategic Plan not only involved the Border Patrol but also included "planning experts from the Department of Defense Center for Low Intensity Conflict,"[18] experts who had previously been charged with developing strategies for quelling insurgencies in the developing world.[19] The great irony is that some of the migrants whose movement these defense experts were working to stop were fleeing violence in Central America that US interventionist policies had sanctioned and supported.[20]

After this initial report was issued, the words used to characterize the desert environment would be gradually changed from "hostile" to "harsh," "inhospitable," and the like.[21] This shift in tone reflects but one of many bureaucratic attempts to sanitize the human costs of this policy. For example, although actual desert conditions are a linchpin of this enforcement strategy, relatively few public documents focused on PTD describe them or comment on the correlation between the strategy and migrant fatalities.[22] In addition, despite showing numerous photographs of agents both on patrol and "rescuing" people in the Sonoran Desert, the 2012–2016 Border Patrol Strategic Plan makes no mention of this landscape or its key role in deterring migration. This hostile terrain is now camouflaged in policy memorandums.

* * *

In 1994, it was predicted that PTD would push the migrant experience beyond simple apprehension and deportation. The architects of the Strategic Plan relied on a number of key assumptions, including the fact that "violence will increase as effects of strategy are felt."[23] "Violence," however, was poorly defined in this document and probably too blunt for some people's liking. Later policy briefs substitute this word for euphemisms such as "costly." A congressional report written just three years after the Strategic Plan stated: "The southwest border strategy [previously known as the Strategic Plan] is ultimately designed to deter illegal entry into the United States. It states that 'The overarching goal of the strategy is to make it so difficult and so costly to enter this country illegally that fewer individuals even try.'"[24]

Although no public record explicitly states that a goal of PTD is to kill border crossers in an attempt to deter other would-be migrants, the connection between death and this policy has been highlighted by both academics and various federal agencies charged with evaluating Border Patrol programs.[25] An excerpt from a 2010 report to Congress reads: "'Prevention Through Deterrence' . . . has pushed unauthorized migration away from population centers and funneled it into more remote and hazardous border regions. This policy has had the *unintended consequence* of increasing the number of fatalities along the border, as unauthorized migrants attempt to cross over the inhospitable Arizona desert without adequate supplies of water" (emphasis added).[26]

This comment that the increasing number of migrant fatalities is an "unintended consequence" of PTD is misleading and ignores previous evidence suggesting that policy makers were well aware of the role that death would play in this enforcement strategy. For example, as one of the "Indicators for Measuring the Effectiveness of the Strategy to Deter Illegal Entry along the Southwest Border," a 1997 report by the Government Accountability Office (GAO) identifies the "deaths of aliens attempting entry." Concerning the "predicated outcome if AG's [the attorney general's] strategy is successful," the same report claims that it "depends on how enforcement resources are allocated. In some cases, deaths may be reduced or prevented (by fencing along the highways, for example). In other cases, deaths may increase (as enforcement in urban areas forces aliens to attempt mountain or desert crossings)."[27] I had to read the foregoing quote several times before I fully grasped its message. It clearly and publicly states that one way for the government to measure the efficacy of PTD is via a migrant body count. In some ways this is merely a sanitized version of the many anti-immigrant comments that accompany online articles about border crosser deaths; for example: "As long as the immigration numbers are declining . . . I can live with the border death numbers."[28] The sector of the American public that attributes a low value to the lives of migrants seems to mirror the federal government's perspective.

The statement from this official document suggests both that early on in the planning of this policy the migrant death rate was considered a useful metric to gauge the program's effectiveness (i.e., "violence will increase as effects of strategy are felt") and that the Border Patrol clearly understood that fatalities would rise as "enforcement in urban areas forces aliens to attempt mountain or desert crossings." This report was published prior to the spike in deaths that occurred in the Arizona desert starting in the early 2000s.[29] As early as 1997, however, evidence clearly showed that the body count associated with PTD was primarily caused by "environmental exposure (falls, hyperthermia, dehydration)."[30] Rather than shooting people as they jumped the fence, Prevention Through Deterrence set the stage for the desert to become the new "victimizer" of border transgressors.

Perilous Terrain

After weeks of planning I am finally able to arrange for José's mother, Paulina, and José's two cousins to speak by phone with members of the Border Patrol's Public Information Office and its Search, Trauma, and Rescue team (BORSTAR). The hope is that if Manny and Felipe can remember enough about the crossing and where they left José, we can retrace their steps in the desert and narrow down a survey area to look for him. I am the first person to phone in. I strike up a conversation with several agents who are participating on the conference call:

JASON: Just to give you guys a warning, everyone is holding out
that he is still alive. So they are gonna have questions. Some of
Paulina's questions are gonna be like, "Is it possible that he is in
detention somewhere and he just hasn't been identified with his
proper name?" These are things that I have tried to reassure her
are highly unlikely after so much time has passed, but she is still
going to ask.

AGENT: We will do our best. Uh, I'm not sure if we would be able to
answer a whole lot of questions. We are going to try and gather as
much information as we can to be able to assess the situation to see
if it's possible to conduct a search for some human remains of this
young man.

Paulina, Manny, and Felipe call in. Thirteen-year-old Felipe is the
first to be interviewed, and it doesn't go well. He is unable to provide
many specific details that would be of use and is also understandably a
bit nervous during the process. After less than five minutes one of the
BORSTAR agents starts to get audibly frustrated:

FELIPE: We crossed under a *puente*. Then we climbed a hill. We climb
up this entire hill and then passed a fenced. From there we started
walking north.

BORSTAR AGENT: Could you see Nogales?

FELIPE: Yes, we could see Nogales from the hill.

BORSTAR AGENT: Was it east or west?

FELIPE: I don't know. We could see the city, though. From there we
kept walking for like an hour, and then we found a small house that
was under construction. We went inside for a little bit and then kept
walking again. . . . We were in Tucson because we passed a ranch
where they had horses. We passed that and got to the road. It was just
me and Manny because José stayed behind.

BORSTAR AGENT: No, no, no. What I want to know is *when* you
crossed because I can't . . . [annoyed]. When you say "this house" or
"this *puente*," you were in Mexico, right? Look, I don't know Mexico.
I only know what is in the United States, so I need to know at what
point in your trip you crossed from Mexico to the United States. Am
I clear? How did you know you crossed the border?

FELIPE: There was a fence that we crossed. It was a barbed wire fence. The coyote said that we had passed into the United States. . . . We crossed the border between Mexico and the United States during the day. We crossed the border more or less around 5 p.m. in the afternoon.

BORSTAR AGENT: How was the terrain near the fence?

FELIPE: It was an area full of mountains. There was a hill where the fence was. We climbed it and in the middle of the hill we crossed the fence. Then we kept walking up hill. There were a lot of trees . . .

The interview drags on for over an hour. Manny and Felipe have conflicting accounts regarding how many days they spent in the desert, and their memory of details such as landmarks and the cardinal directions they walked are vague at best. This is not surprising given their age, unfamiliarity with the region, and the fact that they spent a great deal of time walking under the cover of night. They focus on telling the agents about the "large mountains with blinking antennas" and the flat and denuded area where a very sick José was last seen. After an hour of listening to them tell their stories, you can hear the aggravation in the voice of the BORSTAR agent who isn't getting the details he wants. Finally, Paulina gets on the line, and one of the more sympathetic agents sitting in on the call asks if she has any questions.

PAULINA: I don't have any questions. I only ask that you help me find him.

AGENT: We are very sorry. I know that this is very difficult for you and your family. All I can tell you is that we are going to analyze the testimonies of these guys and communicate with Mr. De León about possibilities of how we might proceed in this case. I know that this is not something that is going to really help you in this moment, but unfortunately the reality is that this is a big area. Uh, well, it's a very difficult terrain, so we need to talk here and see what we can do.

PAULINA: I don't think that José would have gone back to Mexico from the desert, because he spent like a month there. The last day in Nogales he called us to tell us that he was going to leave. He was really happy because he was finally getting out of there and was going to be with us [cries]. There were other calls he made that day. He has a girlfriend in Ecuador. She got a call on her cell phone that was a lot of numbers. She checked the call and it said that it was from a different country.

AGENT: Was this before or after he crossed?

PAULINA: This was later. At the end of the month there was another phone call. My sister answered it there in Ecuador, and she is sure that it was José because he called out her name and then hung up the phone.

BORSTAR AGENT: So you think he might have gone back to Mexico and at one point called Ecuador?

PAULINA: Yes.

BORSTAR AGENT: [in a condescending voice] Ma'am, let me get this straight. You guys are saying that in the best case, after all of this, after they left him in the desert, you think that he has made some phone calls saying that . . .

PAULINA: Yes. Yes, I think . . . [ten seconds of uncomfortable silence]

Before the BORSTAR agent can say anything else, one of his colleagues cuts him off and then hits the mute button. We wait quietly for almost a minute before they come back on the line. One of the agents quickly tells us that they will see what they can do, and then the call ends. Twelve days later I receive the following e-mail:

Dear Mr. De Leon,

I would like to personally thank you for contacting us regarding the disappearance of José Tacuri. We appreciate your patience and the facilitation that you provided with the interviews of Manny and Felipe.

After spending many hours and days analyzing the provided information and conducting interviews of our own, it became apparent that the circumstances in this particular case would not sufficiently provide for any additional Border Patrol searches for José. However, we fully understand his family's wish may be to continue to search for José through a different means. As such, I would like to share with you our perceptions of where José may have crossed and traveled. It is likely that he crossed the international boundary east of Sycamore Canyon, south of the Atascosa Mountain range. The "antennas" referenced in the interviews are most likely to be those on Atascosa Peak. José likely separated from his cousins on the west side of the Atascosa Mountains, probably northwest of Atascosa Peak. His cousins then continued their journey northward, eventually being apprehended somewhere east of Moyza Ranch Road and south of Arivaca Road.

We in the Tucson Sector strongly sympathize with his mother and family during this difficult time. José's story is a tragic and sobering reminder of the dangers faced by so many undocumented migrants who undertake the journey to enter the United States through rough and perilous terrain.

2

Social Citizens and Their Right to Belong

TOBIN HANSEN

Gabriel and I shared a sliver of shade on a scorching street corner in northern Mexico one sluggish afternoon in August 2014.[1] At that moment, there were no cars for him to wash. Gabriel recounted, in adept English, growing up in the United States and his deportation to Mexico. He was born in the Mexican state of Sinaloa in 1987. When Gabriel was six months old, his family migrated without authorization to Phoenix, Arizona, where his mother worked at a fast-food restaurant and his father in construction. He described some childhood memories: drawing, spending time with neighborhood friends, and running with squirt guns on summer days. Beginning at age eighteen, he learned metal fabrication, tile installation, and light-frame construction through on-the-job training. He told me: "I'm a hard worker. [My previous supervisor] knows I busted my ass up there. . . . I still call him and he says, 'Whenever you want to come back, you have your job here.'" In Phoenix, Gabriel worked full-time and also shared child care duties with his partner for their young son and daughter—dropping them off at school was a favorite part of Gabriel's day.

A run-in with law enforcement in 2009 led to a short stint in the Maricopa County Jail and triggered an Immigration and Customs Enforcement (ICE) detainer, a document requesting that the jail hold Gabriel until an ICE officer could come to investigate. Gabriel was shocked to be taken into ICE custody. He recounted his conversation with the agent: "I said to him, 'You're deporting me? I lived here my whole life. How can you deport me?' And the ICE agent was like, 'You're a wetback. Why didn't you fix your papers?' I didn't know I needed to. I mean, I knew I was a wetback, but I was like, 'I went to school here, I did everything here. I didn't know I needed to fix any papers.' And he goes, 'Well, you're getting deported.'"

SOCIAL CITIZENS AND THEIR RIGHT TO BELONG | 33

Gabriel never anticipated that an arrest would trigger deportation. As someone who had "lived here my whole life" and done "everything here" over decades in the United States, Gabriel had not imagined himself susceptible to deportation. And Gabriel was not the only one who seemed to recognize his social and cultural embeddedness in the United States. The ICE officer's inquiry into why Gabriel did not regularize his immigration status suggested an assumption that Gabriel—an English-speaking "American," even if not "legally" so—*does* belong in the United States, save for his immigration status. Like Gabriel, many longtime residents sense the potentially devastating ramifications of the specter of deportation,[2] even as they may not think of themselves as susceptible to removal because of their long-term ties to the United States.

Gabriel's life in Mexico since 2009 has reflected the repercussions of deportation. After he spent a few months in his home state of Sinaloa, trying to connect with family he had not seen in years and many of whom he had never met, some cousins told him of construction work in the faraway border state of Coahuila and asked if he wanted to join them. Gabriel worked for two months at a Korean maquiladora, building heavy-duty aluminum tables for machinery repair. It was good work, but temporary. And his employer did not pay him almost US$200 from his last paycheck—wage theft of nearly half the total amount he had earned.

Next, Gabriel moved to Nogales, on the border, so that he could be closer to family. His partner and two children, who live three hours up the freeway in Phoenix, try to visit each Christmas and when they can at other times during the year, but family visits are infrequent because Gabriel's partner is busy working long hours at McDonald's and cleaning houses, leaving the children with his mother while she works. Gabriel's contact with them occurs mostly through text messages and video chats. He shares an apartment with his uncle, who was also deported after many years living in the United States, and they run a small parking lot two blocks from the thirty-foot, bollard border fence, charging to park by the hour and selling cigarettes within eyesight of craggy, Arizonan hilltop neighborhoods. In Mexico, Gabriel ruminates over the chances of successfully "getting papers," perhaps in the form of a resident visa, sometime in the future. Or he wonders whether he should return clandestinely and risk federal incarceration: "If I get the illegal reentry, then maybe I won't be able to get my papers. Right now I don't have any felonies. But I don't want to wait so long. My kids are little."

Gabriel's experience reflects how an intensified focus on identifying noncitizens and deporting them results in permanent exile for some childhood arrivals from the only home they have ever known. For longtime residents, deportation is particularly punitive. Noncitizens who arrive as children and become longtime US residents face the unique risks of physical, legal, economic, and social exclusion from the United States. During adolescent development, childhood arrivals create trenchant local and national bonds.[3] Despite their status as noncitizens, they develop a form of *social citizenship*—a concept of belonging I draw on here that conceives of membership emanating from interpersonal ties, cultural orientation, and personal narratives formed over time.[4] Social citizenship is thus one aspect, along with recognition of a legal right to presence, of full community membership.[5] Interviews I conducted with adults deported to the northern Mexican cities of Nogales and Puerto Peñasco, both in the state of Sonora, after migrating to the United States at age twelve or younger illuminate how some childhood arrivals become entangled in US crime control and immigration control regimes.[6]

This chapter suggests the ways in which the US government's expanded deportation authority intensifies the overlapping vulnerabilities of many social citizens, such as the people with whom I work. As working-class men of color, they have disproportionately high levels of contact with the criminal justice system, and as legal noncitizens they face a perpetual threat of removal. Finally, once deported, they experience both a displacement from home in the United States and relegation to unfamiliar receiving communities in Mexico.

Historically entrenched labor, migration, and social patterns result in countless child migrants from Mexico, like Gabriel, growing up and making their homes in US communities. It can be complicated or impossible to change their legal status as Mexican citizens who are unlawfully present in the United States, if they even know they are unlawfully present. And for legal permanent residents, gaining naturalized citizenship is also costly, even if they meet the requirements. Because many legal permanent residents are unaware that they can lose this protected status, they do not consider obtaining US citizenship to be a priority. "I thought permanent meant *permanent!*" said one deported legal permanent resident. Many of the deported men who participated in my research were not eligible for temporary protection under Deferred Action for Childhood Arrivals (DACA). Many were deported before the order took effect, did not meet the educational or military requirements, or were disqualified by the narrow criminal history restrictions. In contrast to DACA recipients who have been described sympathetically in public discourse, many research participants worked low-wage jobs, and some joined gangs or were convicted of serious crimes. Thus, their belonging in the United States derived not from the social capital that accrues through achievement in school, high-status work, or privileged class and racial identities but from participation in alternative, oppositional, and often stigmatized spaces—yet they are very much US social citizens.[7]

Ties That Bind

The experiences and learning that form beliefs, shape everyday actions, and create connections with others are especially important during adolescence, for the ways that social and cultural identifications are carried into adulthood. Schools, families, neighborhood streets, churches, and other vibrant domains socialize people into shared ways of life. For Martín, the places and people of his Mesa, Arizona, neighborhood were critical to the way he has come to understand his orientation to the world. I met Martín in Nogales in 2017. He rents a room by the week in a pumpkin orange building perched on a hill a few blocks from downtown. One day we chatted on his small balcony, near his meditation mat, after he had returned from work at a call center selling home plumbing and appliance warranties to US residents. He was wearing a lime green polo shirt tucked neatly into blue jeans. He came across as self-possessed, as usual, flashing white teeth easily. Martín, who was born in Chihuahua in 1978, told me:

> That's where my grandparents were from. Down between Cuauhtémoc and the capital. I went to kindergarten down there. We moved up to Mesa [Arizona] when I was like six. I should've gone into first grade, but since I didn't speak English, they put me in kindergarten. So I started over again there. I lived up in the US for over thirty years. . . . I went to school there my whole life. Well, I dropped out my sophomore year. I still regret

that. . . . I grew up in a rough neighborhood. I was the oldest, so I had to take care of my little brothers and sisters. I did a lot of chores. I helped my mom with everything—I cooked and cleaned a lot. Then, I dropped out of school because I was going to do the family thing. I was getting married and everything when I was sixteen. . . . And it didn't really work out with my first wife.

Martín worked hard in Mesa, and despite his unauthorized status, he felt that he had gotten his life on track. He earned his own delivery route at a medical supplies company, which took him around Phoenix and to Tucson and other cities. He enjoyed working out and reading about religion. And he laughed with me—as we chatted on Mexico's patriotic celebration, Independence Day on September 16—about celebrating the "Americanized" Cinco de Mayo holiday every year in Mesa.

But Martín described his relationship of the last ten years with his wife as the anchor in his life: "She's a great woman. I love her. I'm really lucky to have her. Well, we're lucky to have each other. I believe that God does everything for a reason. We got married three years ago, by law, through Maricopa County. But we saved up to have a nice wedding [ceremony]." Martín carefully pulled from a plastic bag a stack of four-by-six wedding photos. He explained each shot as I flipped through. Martín was beaming while showing me the photographs—each frame included his wife, work companions, and childhood friends and showed Martín with his hair freshly buzzed and wearing an impeccable black suit and red tie. "We did it right. We had all our friends there. A couple people in my family went. But that was it—and she didn't have any family. Since my wife's Asian, my family doesn't accept her and her family doesn't accept me, because of our ethnicity."

Strong bonds are created when lives become entwined and when people share in quotidian activities, create physical and emotional intimacy, and develop mutual aspirations. For Martín, the most acute agony of deportation has been precipitated by separation from the most important person in his life, his wife, Li. He has struggled over the years with his family's rejection of his choice to marry an Asian American woman: "It's tough. We just have each other. We're our family [pause], we rely on each other." Martín's pain is compounded by the part of his life that is missing without his wife: "My wife worked at the Y[MCA] as her second job. And I would go with her to work out. We would go together in the mornings. And also sit at Starbuck's. When we weren't working, we could sit there for hours."

Only months after their marriage ceremony, however, ICE apprehended Martín during a traffic stop. The arrest and detention that separated Martín and Li left them disoriented and emotionally raw. As he described:

> When I got picked up, it was right after we got married! My wife was devastated. It hit her so hard. She was absolutely devastated. And I felt so bad. She would drive to Florence [an immigration detention center one hour from Mesa] like twice a week to visit me. That's the only thing that kept my spirits up. If I wouldn't have had her, I know I would've gotten in trouble. I don't mean drugs or anything like that, I just mean I would've gone to a dark place. . . . She's what's got me through this. She's a special, special person. . . . I'd never been locked up like that.

Since Martín's deportation to Nogales several months ago, the couple has struggled to make sense of their situation. Li, who is a US citizen, has consulted with lawyers in Phoenix to look into options for adjusting Martín's status. They are hoping a lawyer can help them decipher Martín's deportation paperwork. It is especially murky to him because the space designating the period of legal exclusion from reentry—generally a ban of a certain number of years, or for life—was left blank. In addition, Martín's health has been a concern. He told me, "Being down here, I get jittery. I just get nervous and I feel a lot of pressure. I've gone to emergency a few times. I'm taking my blood pressure every day. Sometimes it's 155/95. I'm taking medication, but it's hard [and] it makes me drowsy. But I have to take it."

Fortunately, Martín has landed a coveted call center job, which pays about US$400 a month—well above the mean local income. But it is not nearly enough to split the rent and bills with his wife, as they always had, for their Mesa apartment. Martín has applied for a weekend job as a convenience store cashier. Li drives for Uber in Mesa as a third job to contribute to their collective income. Most important, Li makes the three-hour trip to Nogales most Saturday nights after work and drives back Sunday night. The cost in time and money is overwhelming, but the couple is getting through it by considering their situation temporary. As Martín explained:

> The whole reason I'm here [in Nogales] is because I feel close to her. I could've gone back to Chihuahua. My grandparents died, but that's where my family is. But I'm here for my wife. I love her. We're working to stay together no matter what. But if I was down there, she couldn't go visit me in Chihuahua. When I was locked up, she went to Cibola [New Mexico] to visit me! But she can come down here [to Nogales] on the weekends. Here it feels like home because of my wife.

Confusion

As Martín's story suggests, the apprehension, detention, and adjudication process is unsettling. Navigating the complex legal landscape is overwhelming, and unresolved questions sometimes linger after a person is shepherded through multiple detention facilities and immigration court appearances. The life-altering outcome of deportation itself, particularly for longtime US residents, magnifies the turmoil of the experience. Alfredo, for example, was left feeling that his deportation was arbitrarily rendered, the result of a happenstance run-in with police on a bad day, an arcane series of judicial actions meant to "mess with your head," and a final decision by a judge that has radically shifted the course of his life. Less than two months after his arrest in the Phoenix neighborhood where he had lived since he was only a few months old, Alfredo was in Mexico, deported. His time in immigration detention and during court hearings, four years earlier, remains a blur. And although he tries not to, he sometimes cannot help but continue to brood about it, not understanding the legal circumstances of his deportation. I met Alfredo in Nogales in 2014, and we have spent many mornings at the taco stand that he owns and operates, and afternoons on street corners or at his house. On a chilly November afternoon outside a car wash, we talked over the sounds of passing cars and the whistles and shouts of bustling sidewalks. Alfredo was wearing a long-sleeved, gray T-shirt—still covered by his olive green work apron—and loose-cut jeans.

SOCIAL CITIZENS AND THEIR RIGHT TO BELONG | 39

Alfredo was born in Ciudad Juárez, Chihuahua, in 1987 to parents from a rural Chihuahuan town. Alfredo's father went to work in Phoenix when his mother became pregnant with him. Alfredo was less than a year old when he and his mother reunited with his father in the United States. Through his father he became a legal permanent resident. Growing up, Alfredo had an active social life and loved watching movies and professional basketball games. As we spoke, he laughed when thinking back on his eclectic childhood experiences in South Phoenix. He was outgoing and liked to ride bikes and trade football cards, especially for the San Francisco 49ers. Alfredo had a role in a third-grade Shakespearean adaptation and, in class, learned all the lyrics to the songs from *Mary Poppins*—including "Supercalifragilisticexpialidocious."

Maricopa County sheriff's deputies detained Alfredo in 2013, yet he does not know why. Alfredo had started using drugs recreationally and was high when a police officer handcuffed him in the street outside his house. But he was never charged with a drug possession crime. Days and weeks later, and even today, Alfredo's immigration custody, his legal rights, and the reason for his deportation remain unclear to him.

> ALFREDO: I remember it like it was yesterday. It was the day that *World War Z* came out and we saw it in the theater. And after that I got high with my girl. . . . When the sun was coming up and everything, we got in a [verbal] fight. We were yelling and I told her, "Call the cops! Just call the cops. I don't care." And when the cops were there, I told one of them I was drunk. I said, "Arrest me. Just take me in, take me to Mexico!" I don't know, I was just steamed. And they took me down to Durango [a Maricopa County jail].
>
> TOBIN: What were you arrested for?
>
> ALFREDO: That's the thing! They never told me what I was arrested for. They never read me my rights, they never gave me a paper, never took me to no court, nothing! They just put me in jail. And they sent me into this other little room with [an] immigration [agent]. . . . He put these papers down in front of me. It was my voluntary deportation [Voluntary Departure]. And I was like, "Just send me to Mexico, just tell me where to sign." . . . And he told me, "Don't sign. Read the papers, whatever, but don't sign this now."

Alfredo believes that the officer was genuine in trying to give good advice, perhaps imagining the potential implications of any decision that Alfredo would make. Yet Alfredo himself was very mistrustful at first; he did not know if he was obligated to sign, or what consequences might result from a decision either way. He heeded the officer's recommendation to wait, while also remaining unsure about having made the right choice. He still felt that he had little information and, without legal counsel, no support for figuring out the options available for him. Alfredo continued:

ALFREDO: They sent me to Florence that day. I was there for forty-five days before I saw the judge. . . . And they didn't tell me my rights or nothing in there.

TOBIN: Did you ever have a lawyer, or any legal representation?

ALFREDO: No, there was never a lawyer to talk to or nothing. And the whole time you're in there, they're like pushing you and pushing you. Everyone's pushing you to sign, to self-deport. It's like everyone creates these illusions in your head. The COs [corrections officers] and the other people in there are all like "Are you gonna' sign? Are you gonna' sign?" It was crazy, it's like everything is working for you to sign.

TOBIN: You felt like everyone was pressuring you.

ALFREDO: Yeah! Because they tell you, "You're gonna' be in here for nine months or a year." I was like, "I shouldn't even be in here. I'm not supposed to be here! I'm not like everybody else in here." And when I went before the judge, my family couldn't be there or anything. . . . And the judge was like, "Well, what you want to do?" And I told him, "I want to voluntarily deport. I just want out of here." The judge was surprised. He looked like he was about to sign my papers or something. And so he just said, "Are you sure?" I was like, "Yeah. I just want out of here. Send me to Mexico." I hate to even think about it [signing a Voluntary Departure]. . . . And they didn't give me any papers when they deported me. Not one paper. They didn't give me nothing. They mess with your head in there.

Alfredo felt isolated and uninformed throughout the detention and immigration court process. He perceived himself as "not like everybody" in detention—self-conscious of his difficulties expressing himself in Spanish and of his unfamiliarity with his "country of origin." Although the visits from Alfredo's parents and sisters provided relief, his arrest and deportation happened without any of them understanding the timing of his deportation, the consequences of signing a Voluntary Departure order to escape the pressure and "just get out of here," and the implications of not having legal representation.

Social Citizenship and Constructing Belonging

As the experiences of Gabriel, Martín, and Alfredo reveal, childhood arrivals who grow up in the United States orient their lifeworlds to their home communities and nation. In the United States, they become proficient in everyday ways of living, inhabit local social landscapes, and make sense of their selfhood as belonging to a place. People imbue places with specific meanings and construct their worlds within them. Unique interconnections develop over time and bind together people, places, and ways of life. Some of these relationships with people and place are readily identifiable, such as Martín's anguish over the separation from his wife. Others, however, are ephemeral, more akin to a feeling, a sense, or a perception, and when talking, deported people often grope for words to express their sense of connection. In Nogales, deportees explained to me in detail the personal meanings and importance of their neighborhood streets, favorite mountain walking trails, corner hangouts, shoe stores, and the sounds and smells of the Fourth of July—and, of course, their children, spouses, parents, and other loved ones—all back home in the United States.

Simultaneously, most people I interviewed expressed pride in their "Mexican" heritage and identity. This putatively national label is at once an ethnic/cultural heritage and a legal/political identity that many proudly ascribe to themselves. Nevertheless, the label is situationally deployed—as many often call themselves "American" or "like an American" as well—and in all cases people construct themselves in opposition to "the Mexicans down here" or those who grew up in Mexico, recognizing fundamental social and cultural differences. They also are persistently aware in Mexico of being marked as "pochos," or "Americanized" outsiders.

People understand their connections to the nation in other ways as well. Javier, deported in 2011, spoke of a heritage connection, and his family members' legal citizenship marked his personal narrative. Of his four grandparents, three were US citizens, born in rural Arizona towns in the 1920s and 1930s. His parents lived and worked in the United States but also lived in Mexico for short stints. Javier was born in Nogales in 1974. Javier moved back with his family to Phoenix at the age of three as a US legal permanent resident. His memories of childhood include playing blacktop basketball and skateboarding with other kids in his predominantly Mexican American and African American neighborhood. Despite his family ties, the drug possession crimes he was convicted of and that led to his deportation leave him no legal recourse for regaining status in the United States. His mother is a US legal permanent resident, and his father, a naturalized US citizen, passed away years ago. Although his brothers, sisters, cousins, mother, and children make the six-hour round-trip drive from Phoenix a few times a year, contact with family—as they celebrate birthdays, holidays, and graduations; get jobs; and join the military—occurs primarily through Facebook.

Today, social and cultural connections to the United States carry less weight in determining noncitizens' right to presence than they did in previous decades when racialized, ethnic, and class identities engendered marginalization yet still conferred social inclusion within the nation. But, beginning in the 1980s and 1990s, noncitizens' vulnerability to deportation intensified substantially. The consequences of this tough-on-crime approach to immigration enforcement were unique for longtime residents because, as immigration policing intensified in the interior, protections from deportation for those with strong connections to the country were simultaneously weakened. In the 1970s, an interagency "non-priority program" recommended de-emphasizing the deportation of certain noncitizens. Nonpriority status was even granted, for example, to "aliens who have committed serious crimes involving moral turpitude [and] drug convictions."[8] In fact, criteria listed for determining deportation priorities included "many years presence in the United States" and "Family situation" ahead of "Criminal, Immoral, or Subversive . . . conduct."[9] Subsequently, the 1990 Immigration Act barred judges from making "judicial recommendations against deportation," effectively eliminating most forms of discretionary relief from deportation.[10] And the Illegal Immigration Reform and Immigrant Responsibility Act of 1996 prohibited "criminal aliens" from appealing their deportation based on social or cultural ties.

The intensified enforcement focus of the Trump administration expanded the category identified as "criminal aliens."[11] This focus, however, ignored the fact that in 2015 roughly one-third of deported "criminal aliens" had only a previous conviction of illegal entry, and another 17 percent were deported for drug possession, while only one-fifth were deported for assault, burglary, weapons offenses, robbery, or sexual assault combined.[12] These statistics, coupled with criminological data that suggest that noncitizens commit crimes at lower rates than US citizens,[13] refute popular notions of immigrants as prone to criminality or of all deportees as serious criminals. Admitting the fact that non-citizens are generally law-abiding denizens of local communities and the nation certainly challenges the viability of current policy approaches to immigration. But such facts also discredit paying the high costs— vast resource expenditures and social anxiety—associated with intense immigration enforcement, particularly given the long history between the United States and Mexico of circular migration, direct labor recruit-ment, and economic policies that exacerbate wealth disparities.

Dispelling the myth of an inherent immigrant criminality illuminates the potential benefit of moderating enforcement approaches that are almost exclusively focused on lawbreaking—starting with a reconsid-eration of noncitizens' social membership. And a shift away from the frenzied focus on criminality raises critical questions. When should the criminal convictions of noncitizens—lawful permanent residents, other visa holders, or undocumented people—trigger deportation? For what crimes? And when should social citizenship matter? Public safety and the public good are among the overt objectives of state immigration en-forcement practices. But in what ways might public safety be compro-mised by harsh immigration policing tactics and outcomes?

Many of the men I interviewed described being confused by their deportations or, like Gabriel and Alfredo, feeling blindsided by the fact that they could be deported in the first place. They grew up thinking that they belonged in US communities, their lives enmeshed in shared everyday activities, mutual understandings, social connections, ways of communicating, and webs of cultural values. Everyday connections with community and nation anchor people's selfhood. Recognizing social citizenship can reconfigure the moral calculus of rigid enforcement. The lives of childhood arrivals who become longtime residents reveal the problem with ascribing people to the narrow categories of "legal" or "illegal."[14] Gabriel's simple question—"How can you deport me?"—provides an evocative starting point for interrogating legal exclusions and their disproportionate effect on those labeled "immigrants," "aliens," or "illegals"—the many people whose full, expansive, and complex personhood is reduced to a legal status.

3

Illegality and Children's Power in Families

JOANNA DREBY

> ANDREA: I sometimes translate for my mom in the hospital or some-
> where else.
> JOANNA: Do you like doing that?
> ANDREA: No.
> JOANNA: You don't! How come?
> ANDREA: Sometimes I don't understand some words, or how to say
> them, or I don't know what they mean.
>
> Interview with ten-year-old Andrea

The turn toward restrictive immigration policies and practices in the United States, and around the world, has brought to the fore a body of scholarship documenting the detrimental impacts that regimes of illegality have had for families and especially for children and youth.[1] Children have been shown to be particularly vulnerable when detentions and deportations target their parents, experiencing a multitude of negative emotional, sociodevelopmental, and health impacts.[2] As other chapters in this volume illustrate, border crossings and immigration controls shape children's lives in unique ways as young people move within and outside of legal and deportation systems. The threat of deportation may be most salient for the least powerful members of families.[3]

Rather than emphasizing the direct impact of immigration enforcement, this chapter turns to the unintended consequences of policies for children in families. Their experiences show the ways that families cannot escape immigration control, even if they are not formally *in* government enforcement regimes. Specifically, it explores how the specter of illegality within a family shapes daughters' roles and responsibilities and, as a result, their relationships with adults. Although the roles and responsibilities of both boys and girls may change as a result of enforcement regimes, girls' experiences illustrate most acutely the intersections between immigration regimes and power differences related to age and gender.

This chapter draws from the experiences of daughters living in Mexican migrant families. Although international migration processes are complex and highly contextual, 40 percent of children in US immigrant households have a Mexican-born parent, and estimates suggest that approximately half of unauthorized migrants are Mexican.[4] As such, the case of Mexican migration is a good one for exploring the potential magnitude of children's experiences with illegality. In what ways do immigration laws and policies shape young girls' everyday roles and responsibilities in their families? How do girls in Mexican migrant households interpret these experiences of changing power relations with adults? This chapter addresses the oft obscure ways that public policy potentially alters the organization of family life.

The Daughters of Mexican Migration

International migration alters family relationships and may be an important source of generational conflict.[5] Following Barrie Thorne's 1987 call for child-centered research,[6] recognition of children as autonomous social actors during international migration has increased. Childhood experiences shape long-term trajectories of social mobility among immigrants.[7] And children's access to resources may vastly differ from that of their parents in mixed-status families.[8] Immigration controls may also alter both families' access to resources and children's social mobility over time. And yet family migration stories are complex, giving rise to varying pathways and outcomes in the lives of the daughters of Mexican migration.

To show how immigration regimes often function in ways that intersect with gender inequalities, I focus on the stories of girls living in three different types of migrant families.[9] First, consider the experiences of girls in transnational families, like Flor, who was living with her maternal grandparents in Oaxaca, Mexico. I met Flor after her parents had migrated without authorization to work in Nevada. Illegality underpins the experiences of the majority of children like Flor who are separated from their parents due to migration. This is primarily because legal restrictions govern parents' decisions to separate from children. Parents feel apprehensive about undertaking a dangerous unauthorized border crossing together with their children; risks are especially high for young women crossing the border, and the costs of securing a safe passage for children are more often than not prohibitive.

Anticipating the precariousness and costliness not only of the crossing but also of adjusting to life in the United States as an unauthorized migrant—of finding work and adequate housing—prompts many parents to leave children with relatives for a time until they can either return to Mexico or send for their children. During periods of separation, parents' lack of legal status is a significant barrier. It restricts parents' freedom of movement, preventing them from regularly visiting children. Moreover, lacking a legal status, most parents work in low-wage jobs and struggle economically to both provide for themselves and send income home to cover children's living expenses. Saving money for a reunification, either in Mexico or in the United States, is a difficult feat. While parents are away, daughters like Flor must adjust.

Second, some Mexican migrant children are unauthorized migrants themselves, like Marjorie, who was born in Monterrey, Mexico, but came across the border with her mother when she was a baby. Children who undertake an unauthorized border crossing may be aware of the precariousness of the crossing to varying degrees, depending on their age at the time of the journey and the type of passage their parents are able to secure. In Marjorie's case, she does not remember the border crossing but has grown up constantly aware of her lack of authorized status in the United States. Indeed, legal status has a profound impact on children's development. Some children feel relatively secure in the communities where they are raised and "awaken to the nightmare" of illegality as they age into adulthood, seeking employment or higher education.[10] Others, like Marjorie, who first lived in Texas but whose childhood memories are rooted in New Jersey, where I met her, are acutely aware of the importance of legal status at decidedly earlier ages. Children as young as age five, for example, talk about not having papers.[11] Although they may not fully understand the intricacies of immigration law, they understand that having or not having papers differentiates them from children born in the United States. They may hide their legal status from peers, keeping it a secret from all except their closest friends.[12]

Third are the nonmigrant children born in the United States to unauthorized Mexican parents like Eloina, a native of New Jersey whose mother and father are unauthorized migrants from Oaxaca. As Eloina's experiences show, even US citizen children cannot escape US immigration controls. Indeed, parents' unauthorized status has been shown to have a series of negative impacts on child development.[13] Many of these impacts are related to the economic instability of parents who experience especially high poverty rates as undocumented workers.[14] Moreover, children in poor households may lack access to important social services if their parents are unauthorized.[15] Applications for various types of assistance programs, even for nongovernmental charity programs like Toys for Tots, may require—or parents may think they require—a Social Security number. Other impacts are less tangible. For example, parents may be less involved in children's schooling, whether because their work schedules prevent it or due to fears of calling too much attention to themselves.[16] At the time of our interview, for example, Eloina's mother worked an evening shift; thus, she was asleep when Eloina woke up in the morning and away at work when Eloina returned home from school. Mother and daughter barely saw each during the weekdays.

In what follows, I detail some of the complexities evident in the experiences of Flor, Marjorie, and Eloina by drawing on interviews and observations with both parents and children in these three families. Their experiences are also representative of themes I found in research with members of more than 120 Mexican migrant families.[17] Taking seriously the roles and responsibilities of children, or the "work kids do" in immigrant households, reveals the disproportionate power relations between generations in migrant families.[18] Children act as translators and interpreters for their parents and also "broker" parental adaptation to US society by taking on child care duties or intervening in school-based settings.[19] Taking on adultlike responsibilities is, however, a double-edged sword. On the one hand, young girls may relish greater autonomy in relations with adults through brokering activities; they gain symbolic power in their families.[20] Flor, Marjorie, and Eloina all seem to be aware of their maturity and, to some extent, accept their responsibilities in their families. On the other hand, children may be disadvantaged when they are increasingly responsible for the work that is fundamental to household maintenance.[21] As their stories show, all three girls have mixed feelings about these grown-up responsibilities.

Considering the work daughters do in each of these three types of families also shows how illegality heightens and complicates generational inequalities in families by altering children's roles and responsibilities. As their stories indicate, various factors are at play in young people's lives. Yet, due to the specter of illegality in their families, all three young women contribute significantly to the maintenance of their respective households. All three are cognizant of the economic difficulties their families face due to their parents' unauthorized migrations. They experience mixed feelings about their roles in their families. These changing roles may bring children closer to their parents but also may lead to tension and conflict with caregivers and siblings.

Flor

Flor, aged sixteen, her eighteen-year-old sister Nelva, a twelve-year-old brother, and an eight-year-old sister had been living with her maternal grandparents, Fernanda and Bernardo, for nearly a year when we met. Fernanda and Bernardo, like others in the small town of about 2,600 residents in the highlands of Oaxaca, are part of a farming family. As I approached the house set back away from the street, I walked by four cows milling about the property, along with two donkeys and a handful of chickens and turkeys. Yet none of the couple's eight children has been able to make a living by farming, a condition true of others in this town where internal migration within Mexico and external migration to the United States are quite common. Fernanda and Bernardo's three sons live in Mexico City; all five daughters, including Flor's mother, work in the United States as unauthorized migrants.

Flor's mother was never able to make ends meet in their hometown. Six years and three children into her marriage, economic constraints became too great; she and her husband migrated to Nevada, where others from their small town had also gone. Flor explained, "At first they went together and that was because there was no work. They both went for that reason. But then my mom came back, but my father stayed there." Recalling that time, Flor said, "The truth is I felt really sad." She and her siblings lived at first with her father's parents, and Flor was relieved when her mother came home. When Flor's mother left again a year later, the children moved in with Flor's maternal grandparents, Fernanda and Bernardo. Flor's sister Nelva explained that their mother planned for this in advance: "She decided to go for it to be much better, so that she could help . . . she said to me if I can help take care of my siblings and if she could count on it she would go. I told her 'yes.' And also my grandmother committed to watch us so that she could go work over there." Flor also seemed to better understand her mother's rationale for being away, commenting, "This time I am not so sad, maybe because I am used to living without her."

Yet not all is well with Flor and her siblings; Flor explained that "it's not the same" with her grandmother and that they have "small problems. . . . I talk with my mom and I ask her for advice. She gives me advice about what to do." In a separate interview her grandparents also spoke of family tensions. According to Bernardo, "The word of their mother or father counts, not ours. These girls ask for permission from them over there [abroad] and then they leave." And Fernanda explained, "My husband and I talked about it this past December because we were a bit mortified at how they went out to the dances." Each December, migrants return from Mexico City and from the United States for the holidays, and parties are plentiful. Bernardo sat his granddaughters down for a talk, encouraging them to wait for their parents before they start dating "so that they can be married in white dresses."[22] He also struggled with his grandson, who "does what he wants."

Economic difficulties compounded emotional struggles. Fernanda explained that it is sometimes hard to feed the children; the US $200 she typically receives once or twice a month is not enough. But Flor said that her parents will not be coming home soon "because they have various goals that they have not yet met . . . they need to put up the bricks for the house and build the fence." Flor stopped going to school last year. She recently started to work at a taco stand in the town center in order to have spending money. She explained, "For food we are never lacking. Not for clothing either. But sometimes if we want something, we don't have it." Her sister Nelva confirmed that money is an ongoing problem. In fact, Nelva had been feeling guilty about the extra expenses associated with her education and stopped attending until the school secretary convinced her to continue her studies. As she said, "What happened is that also because my mom has plans and I think that the money is not enough, I thought I should work and help out."

Unauthorized migration can be slow in yielding economic results. In the meantime, this family's arrangement hinges on each member taking on new roles and responsibilities. Fernanda and Bernardo love their grandchildren and want to help their daughter, but they are somewhat reluctant caregivers. "I am not used to battling with these children again," explained Fernanda. As for the children, Flor reported that her older sister, Nelva, is "in charge of the rest" of the siblings, saying, "She is the one who reports on how we are doing here." Yet because Nelva travels daily to high school in a neighboring town, Flor's role at home has expanded. According to Nelva, "My sister is the one who does most of it because I am studying. She is the one who is in charge of getting [our siblings] ready for school and looking after them." Flor has many responsibilities. She told me: "I take their lunches to school, first to the elementary school and then to the middle school. Then I come home and I do the chores. . . . My grandmother cooks for us all. . . . I wash my clothes and those of the younger two, and my sister washes her own clothes." Flor said that her sister is in charge of disciplining their younger brother, yet the boy does not seem to acknowledge that anyone has authority in this transnational family situation. According to Flor, "No matter what we say, he doesn't listen."

Marjorie

Marjorie, who will soon turn fifteen, answered the door of the basement apartment in the suburbs of a midsize city in northern New Jersey. Her mother, Gladys, works an afternoon shift and so was not home when I came to interview Marjorie and seven-year-old Agustin. A few days earlier, Gladys had explained in her somewhat husky voice accompanied by a bright smile that the cramped apartment with the miniature bathroom suited her because she herself is so short. Having just showered and changed for work, Gladys told me her story while completing her midday routine, preparing a dinner of bland chicken tacos to leave for Agustin at her mini stove. Gladys is not officially divorced but has been separated from her husband for the past four years, ever since he was incarcerated for a drug offense. At the end of his jail sentence, he was deported to Mexico. Because their marriage had been an abusive one, Gladys does not miss her husband, but she sorely misses the economic stability she enjoyed while married. She had been a stay-at-home mother until her husband went to jail, at which point she began to work full-time. Gladys continually struggles to make ends meet, having moved eight times over the past four years before landing in this two-bedroom basement apartment with a hallway as a kitchen.

In our interview, Marjorie explained how her life had changed dramatically after her father's arrest: "My mom started working when I was in fifth grade. So I've been pretty much taking care of my brother since." She added, "It was a lot harder for me 'cause I never really experienced my mom going to work. She was always like a stay-at-home mom and everything." Marjorie's daily routine includes waking up at 5:50 a.m. to catch the 6:50 bus to school, where she eats breakfast. Her return bus drops her off around 2:50 p.m., at which point she rests until it is time to pick up her brother at 3:30 p.m. Then, she told me, "We'll just hang out here and then we'll do our homework and then we'll watch TV or like have a snack. 'Cause I don't really like giving him his dinner right away 'cause then like later he's still hungry and stuff. So then I'll give him his dinner like later around like six." Because Marjorie's mother, Gladys, gets home around 8:00 or 9:00 p.m., Marjorie does not see her much during the week.

When we first met, Marjorie was not participating in any extracurricular activities, although she mentioned that she likes softball: "Last year I did it for the township because my best friend's dad, he was like the coach, so he gave like my mom a discount and everything." Although Marjorie worked out the extra expense with help from her friend, the time commitment was not easy. "Last year I would have practices during like weekdays," she explained, "so I would bring my brother with me sometimes. And he would just like watch me." Before her father left, Marjorie did cheerleading. As she told me, "'Cause my mom didn't work, I had time."

As her comments reveal, Marjorie is acutely aware of her family's economic difficulties. She explained, "I guess it's like hard for us. Because, um, like my mom can't really get like an official professional job or whatever. So I guess like, not trying to sound negative, but like we're probably gonna have like money problems most of the time. Maybe like until I can work or something." Marjorie harbors mixed feelings about her increased responsibilities. On the one hand, she feels very close to her brother. She told me, "Even though like we argue and stuff, we're still pretty close 'cause like, like we, I don't know, we depend on each other a lot. So I guess it's good."

On the other hand, Marjorie felt different and somewhat resentful at not having the same sort of childhood as many of her American friends. "I've noticed that like many Hispanic kids, they grow up faster than . . . white kids and everything. . . . So we usually have to grow up faster than usual kids do." Marjorie went on to explain that she often translated for her mother, something that started after her father left, since he spoke English well. "So I would know like more than I was supposed to when I was younger. . . . I wish it wasn't like that."

Marjorie told me that she wants to be a child psychologist and that she is interested in helping children like her brother in the future, children who are similarly disadvantaged by their family situation. However, like her mother, Marjorie is unauthorized. She was born in Mexico and came to the United States with her parents at the age of two. Marjorie and I kept in touch throughout her sophomore and junior years and again after her high school graduation. At first Marjorie hoped to attend a four-year state university, and she had good enough grades to do so. But she was dissuaded by the financial aid application process: she would have had to pay out-of-state tuition, and so she opted to attend community college instead. But when she received a work permit through the Deferred Action for Childhood Arrivals (DACA) program, she decided to attend college part-time at night so she could work full-time to help support her mother. Together they can now afford a two-bedroom apartment in a decent neighborhood.

Eloina

Eloina was cooking dinner when I arrived to interview her. Her house is located about a half hour drive from the midsize city in central New Jersey where she and her mother used to live, along with many others from the region of Oaxaca where her mother was born. I was impressed at how she busied herself in the kitchen making tacos. I sat with her mother, Ofelia, who was at the kitchen table with her youngest child, a ten-month-old baby. I took turns interviewing the mother and daughter while Eloina's other half siblings, aged five and three, played in the other room with their father.

"I came in '97," explained Ofelia, telling her migration story. "My idea was to come here because almost all the people there came here and they talked about '*el norte*' this and '*el norte*' that. I worked in Mexico City, and I always said I wanted to go to *el norte*." Ofelia was born in the highlands of Oaxaca and started migrating for work when she was just thirteen, dropping out of school at the age of her daughter Eloina at the time of our interview. "We were very poor," she explained, her own mother was a widow. Ofelia traveled back and forth between Mexico City and her hometown until she married a classmate who also migrated for work. They came north together as unauthorized migrants when Ofelia was twenty-one. Their daughter, Eloina, was born less than a year later, and Ofelia split up with Eloina's father shortly thereafter.

Ofelia mostly raised Eloina on her own, as a single working mother. "I was hardly at home with her. I always was leaving her somewhere in the early morning and picking her up in the afternoon." Now that Ofelia has moved in with her new partner and has three young children, she said that she is much more aware of how hard it is to be a mother. Ofelia is home with the children in the daytime and leaves for work for an afternoon shift at 3:30 p.m. As she told me, "At first I couldn't get used to it . . . now it is Eloina who wakes me up in the morning." Eloina interrupted her mother for instructions on what to add to the tacos, adding, "I also cook in the mornings. When I don't have school I make pancakes." She described her morning routine: "[My siblings] wake up early. I let them play and my mom sleeps. I do my homework. Then I wake up my mother. I play with them. Then I help her . . . we do it all together."

Indeed, mother and daughter seem exceptionally tight. Ofelia recounted her story in front of Eloina, who seemed to have heard it before. "Sometimes I translate," Eloina explained, although often her mother's partner does. "When my mom and I are alone, I have to read it all for her." She added, "I help out a lot with my siblings." "Yes, she helps me a lot," confirmed Ofelia. According to Eloina, "I wash the dishes, I clean the table. Sometimes I sweep the entire house. I clean my room and make my bed. But sometimes I am busy with homework."

Despite her home responsibilities, Eloina's schoolwork takes priority. Eloina changed schools recently, when they came to live with Ofelia's partner less than a year ago. When I asked her how things have changed, she explained, "I like it better now." She does not have to translate all the time for her mother because her mother's partner helps out. Also the new school seems better. In the city school, "they criticize you a lot, they make fun of you for what you are wearing." Eloina is doing well, getting mostly As and Bs, and she recently started to stay after school for a rock-climbing program. She explained that when she grows up she wants to be a chef; she was making tacos that night to learn how to cook from her mother.

Although mother and daughter have a close relationship, Eloina is not always happy about her living situation. She explained, "Sometimes I want to stay with my mother, and sometimes with my father. Then I miss my mother, or I miss my father. Sometimes I get mad at my brothers and sisters, then I say to my mom, 'I don't want to live here.' And I do want to live here, but I just get mad at my siblings . . . then my mom gets sad and angry. Or sometimes she tells me I should go. And since she is mad, I get even more sad."

Aside from preoccupations related to being a teenager of divorced parents, Eloina worries quite a bit about immigration. She said, "Because we see it in the news that a lot of people are caught. Getting them at random. Just took them. That really scared me that time." Eloina told me that she doesn't know what she would do if something like that happened in her family. Earlier in our interview, Ofelia explained that she has property in her hometown she would return to, "in case one day they kick us out. One never knows, right? We would have to go . . . hopefully it doesn't happen, because my children are used to living here." Even though Eloina is a US citizen, she feels the situation is acutely unjust and ended her interview with a message for the president: "It is not fair that Americans have more rights than Hispanics. . . . I want to tell him that those who are here should get papers."

Illegality in the Lives of Mexican Daughters

Illegality shapes the lives of children living in Mexico and in the United States, and of both migrant and nonmigrant children, drawing them "into" systems that may even be geographically distant. Above all else, unauthorized migration alters the roles of girls with their siblings. Older daughters living in Mexico take over many household responsibilities, particularly in the care of younger siblings. And so do daughters living in the United States who end up helping mothers who juggle housework and child care around the nontraditional work schedules common to low-wage workers.[23] Daughters have mixed feelings about these changing roles, which have differential effects on family dynamics depending on where children live.

Children living in Mexico may agree to help their parents with household responsibilities during parental absences, in a sense buying into parental goals of international migration as a means to improve the well-being of the entire household.[24] They may feel valued and important for their active participation in the migration strategy. And yet taking on these adult roles, young girls, like Flor and her sister Nelva, are also well aware of the economic pressure facing the family when hardships continue and the remittances parents send are not enough. Their own interests, in furthering their own education, for example, may take a backseat to the family's needs. Similarly, some girls may find it difficult to discipline younger siblings for whom they feel responsible, and yet they struggle with their own feelings of abandonment. Like Flor, they may not accept the authority of substitute caregivers and may cede authority to migrant parents who are not present to supervise them on a day-to-day basis.

Daughters growing up unauthorized in the United States may also take on adultlike responsibilities in their families, particularly if an enforcement action has altered the family structure, as was the case for Marjorie, who viewed her father's deportation as the impetus for her role changing in the family. Because of ongoing financial difficulties, growing up means joining parents as low-wage workers rather than pursuing their own career goals and interests. In Marjorie's case, receiving a work permit ironically did not break her out of this relationship of mutual dependency with her mother. Marjorie chose work over education, a situation she so acutely observed just a few years earlier as differentiating her from her peers by having her join the world of adults faster than normal.

For children with US citizenship growing up with unauthorized parents in the United States, supportive roles in families may be similar, with daughters like Eloina helping out significantly at home. And yet these increased responsibilities may not require them to put their own interests on hold to the same degree as they did for Marjorie, who was unauthorized like her mother. Rather, US citizen children may enjoy the benefits of helping in terms of the bonds it creates with parents and the skills they learn from parents, like Eloina's cooking experience. More so than unauthorized children, US citizen children may share these household responsibilities with others, like Eloina's stepfather, in order to take advantage of opportunities outside of the home. And yet the threat of immigration enforcement does not disappear. Instead, it manifests in the fears of children like Eloina, who worried that her family would be separated if her mother were to be deported.

Immigration law, specifically family reunification legislation, purports to allow families to migrate as a unit.[25] Indeed, past scholarship typically describes families as engaging in international migration projects together, as a cooperative household unit.[26] Even when family members are transnationally divided, they maintain significant relationships with each other.[27] And yet, women and men do not experience international migration on equal playing fields.[28] Power relations between men and women are both challenged and reproduced through acts of international migration.[29]

Similarly, restrictive immigration policies do not impact adults and children equally. Children face unique challenges that are simultaneously connected to, but independent from, those of adults. Illegality alters children's roles and responsibilities in families due to challenges related to parents' unauthorized immigration status. On the one hand, children gain power in relationships with adults, feeling they grow up more quickly than other children. On the other hand, the stress of adultlike responsibilities often outweighs the benefits children experience in terms of tighter bonds with parents and siblings. These effects are especially salient for daughters and for children with siblings, who are disproportionally impacted.

In conclusion, to fully consider how the reality of illegality shapes the lives of families and children over time, it is important not only to examine the devastating impacts on child health and well-being but also to consider children's changing roles and responsibilities in their families. Paradoxically, illegality both challenges power relations between adults and children in families and reinforces the inequalities that dependent children feel somewhat powerless to control, as Marjorie put it, because they have to "grow up too fast."

REFLECTIONS

Entering Multiple Systems

JOSÉ ORTIZ-ROSALES AND KRISTEN JACKSON

As complex as the immigration system is in the United States, it would be easier to navigate if immigration were the only pressing concern in a young person's life. When we hear the term "undocumented youth," we easily imagine that these children will encounter only the immigration legal system in the United States. However, they have distinct vulnerabilities that make involvement with other systems necessary. Youth often arrive in the United States with educational needs, language challenges, and unaddressed trauma on top of their lack of lawful immigration status.

To understand better the lives of undocumented youth, we must explore their complex maneuvering through various systems, including child welfare, education, juvenile justice, behavioral health, and social systems, among others. Many times, it is these systems' interactions and their overlap with the immigration system that shape young people's experiences and decisions. Accordingly, in this essay we examine systems' intersectionality and the importance of cross-system collaboration. In doing so, we share real-life examples of immigrant children. We—a social worker and an immigration attorney working at Public Counsel, a nonprofit law firm in Los Angeles—incorporate our experiences and those of our clients.[1] Their stories show how systems converge in young people's lives and how young people need adults who are willing to work together across them.

Systems, Intersectionality, and Collaboration: Essential Concepts

Systems may sound ephemeral, but they exert highly concrete influence. They are composed of people, places, and environments that interact with youth and can serve as resources or barriers. When one system is impacted, it affects other systems in a child's life. For example, when youth feel like outsiders in homes with younger US citizen siblings and perhaps have not lived with a parent for many years, concentration at school can diminish along with their motivation to stay in the United States. Recognizing the intersectionality of the lives of undocumented youth is paramount even when an attorney's or social worker's primary goal is to secure lawful immigration status. Indeed, it has a deep ethical dimension. It is critical to examine systems holistically "instead of reacting to specific parts, outcomes, or events and potentially contributing to the further development of unintended consequences" that may work to a youth's detriment.[2]

Moreover, collaboration across intersecting systems—by adult stakeholders such as parents, attorneys, social workers, therapists, and teachers—is key. Unfriendly systems viewing undocumented children as "alone" or "others" without support may treat them as vulnerable and expendable. But when stakeholders work together across systems in a youth's interest, these adults are more accountable and have a more complete picture of the barriers a young person faces. For instance, when social workers visit a school and learn that it does not provide English Language Development classes, they can advocate that youth receive language support to ensure academic success and social integration. And young people are better able to make informed decisions—including about their immigration cases—and to use resources available outside the legal system. Leveraging resources can make progress easier as stakeholders know they can count on outside services, benefits, or policies to support their goals and objectives.

Stakeholders benefit from working with each other, but they must also work in partnership with young people to fulfill young people's own goals and objectives. Collaborating with young people includes involving them in decision making, ensuring that they understand their legal obligations and opportunities, and supporting them to meet different systems' expectations. By exploring their motivations, stakeholders can identify young people's priorities and the best approach to keep them engaged. For example, a young man experiencing homelessness in Los Angeles may opt to move to his grandmother's home in Utah rather than enter the child welfare system because his top priority is having family support and a place to stay—even though he knows he may lose his longtime immigration attorney in the process. Undoubtedly, working with undocumented youth often requires creativity and forging new partnerships in the systems that young people actively choose to engage. Children are actors, not simply passive characters upon which systems act.

Mario: An Interdisciplinary Approach to Maneuver a Series of Systems

Mario's story is like that of many Central American youth. His mother migrated to the United States years ago, leaving Mario and his siblings in Guatemala while they were still very young. When Mario was fifteen, gang members killed his brother. That tragic event triggered Mario's own migration to the United States. During his journey from Guatemala, he experienced labor trafficking as he entered the United States. US Customs and Border Protection (CBP) apprehended Mario at the US-Mexico border, providing his first encounter with the immigration enforcement system. CBP placed Mario into removal proceedings in immigration court and turned him over to the federal Office of Refugee Resettlement (ORR), the agency tasked with holding undocumented minors who are apprehended in the United States without a parent or guardian. ORR eventually reunified Mario with his mother in Southern California in 2013 and provided a case manager whose role was to assist Mario during his transition.

Fortunately, Mario had mental health services, access to an education, two case managers (including a human trafficking case manager), and legal representation in his removal proceedings. He obtained a T visa, which is a form of immigration relief for trafficking survivors that creates a path to permanent protection in the United States. Yet life remained difficult for Mario. He still had a hard time adjusting to a new home and addressing the complex trauma he experienced before, during, and after his migration. In the United States, he was sexually abused and suicidal, cut himself repeatedly, and struggled with substance use. Importantly, however, his county-appointed social worker, case managers, immigration attorney, therapist, and mother worked as a team to support Mario in facing these grave challenges.

Because of the sexual abuse, the county removed Mario from his mother's home. Mario's life thus intersected with the foster care system—in addition to the juvenile justice system, the criminal justice system, and the immigration system. At that critical point, it was of utmost importance that all stakeholders met with Mario to clarify their various roles. Through a strengths-based approach, Mario was able to assess his own skills and competence, as well as his needs. Stakeholders emerged with a fuller picture of Mario that helped them better understand how he behaved and made decisions. In collaborating with Mario, the team took into account his language challenges, culture, limited formal education, and history of trauma. A competent Spanish-English interpreter was part of the team during all meetings to ensure that all team members understood the discussion and that Mario could participate fully in the decision-making processes affecting him.

It is no surprise that each of the systems Mario encountered had its own priorities, which often conflicted with one another. For example, the juvenile justice system prioritized his staying in line with the law at peril of his arrest, while the behavioral health system, of which his therapist was a part, prioritized treatment rather than criminalization of substance use. These differing, and at times conflicting, priorities made stakeholder collaboration even more important. In particular, it was essential that Mario's immigration attorney, his social worker, and his therapist—all of whom had an intimate understanding of the history that influenced his behavior—advocate for Mario with actors in the more punitive systems, such as probation department officials.

This interdisciplinary team's advocacy humanized Mario and altered these officials' views of his conduct and the consequences he should face. His team's work took into account his life context, including his history as well as his current circumstances. And it allowed various stakeholders to communicate directly with one another, thus making their collective efforts with Mario more effective. The collaboration among the stakeholders underscored the reality that each entity influenced the outcomes that Mario experienced across the different systems.

Diego: The Complexity of Family Dynamics for Immigrant Youth

Unlike Mario, Diego migrated to the United States to flee his parents rather than reunite with them. Diego grew up in El Salvador and lived with his maternal grandparents for the first fourteen years of his life. During that time, his grandfather beat him mercilessly, leaving bruises and scars. Seeking a way out, Diego planned to kill himself. He went so far as to set up a rope with which to hang himself. Diego did not go through with his plan and instead moved in with his parents, but they too inflicted physical and emotional abuse. To escape this mistreatment as well as extreme gang violence, Diego made the journey to the United States alone in search of his paternal grandmother.

Diego did not make it directly to his grandmother, however. Instead, CBP captured him at the border, then placed him into removal proceedings and turned him over to ORR. His paternal grandmother stepped forward to sponsor him, and ORR, fortunately, released him into her care. Living with her in Long Beach, Diego thrived for the first time in a healthy environment. He had his own bedroom, attended school, began to learn English, saw a doctor, and received critical mental health services. However, even in his grandmother's home he was not entirely safe. Diego's uncle assaulted him and then pressured Diego's grandmother to kick Diego out of her home, which she did.

After leaving his grandmother's care, Diego continued to experience his family system as unsupportive of his goals. Diego lived with various aunts and uncles, bouncing around from home to home. His housing was unstable because he did not have a job. He prioritized going to school, but his family expected him to earn money so he could contribute financially to the household. Diego eventually gave in. Despite his social worker's advocacy with family members, Diego stopped going to school and attending therapy so that he could work and maintain stable housing with an older cousin. Unfortunately, this stability was short-lived; it ended when Diego's cousin moved to Northern California.

Diego could have followed his cousin to Northern California, but doing so would have jeopardized his immigration case. Had he moved, he would have lost the Public Counsel attorney and social worker with whom he had developed a relationship. They were working to prevent his removal by securing him Special Immigrant Juvenile Status (SIJS), a form of immigration relief for abused, abandoned, and neglected children. Diego decided to stay in Southern California to avoid losing this valuable legal representation—there was no guarantee an attorney in Northern California could take his case. Essentially, Diego gave up stable housing and a support system to be able to fight his immigration case. His social worker assisted Diego in locating a short-term shelter. There, he was able to stabilize his housing by eventually entering that shelter's transitional housing program.

While Diego originally had the support of multiple intersecting systems (including family, school, and mental health), his family system breakdown became a barrier to his other supports. Diego's family ultimately failed him in the United States, just as it had in El Salvador. This heightened Diego's vulnerability because there was no opportunity for interdisciplinary collaboration—his family system effectively shut out his valued school and mental health systems. Once Diego faced homelessness, his social worker's actions were critical to his ability to continue working on his immigration case. Without the social worker's intervention to engage a new system—supportive housing—Diego's trajectory would likely have ended differently. Once housed, Diego was able to focus on addressing the anxiety and low self-esteem caused by the trauma he had experienced. Diego now has a safety net of interdisciplinary support, and he is enjoying increased independence in the secure, supervised living environment of his transitional housing program.

Leslie: An "American" Child Encounters Juvenile Justice and Immigration Systems with Devastating Consequences

Unlike Mario and Diego, Leslie came to the United States as an infant. Born in Mexico, she grew up in California. In Leslie's early years, her grandmother alone provided love and affection. Her father was largely absent. Her mother terrified her by withholding essential care and abusing her terribly—including during three years Leslie spent back in Mexico, where her mother failed to feed her, tied her to a chair, and attacked her with cables and scalding spoons. Leslie returned to the United States at age seven. Yet years later, Leslie's US roots did not prevent the harsh blows dealt by the overlapping juvenile justice and immigration systems.

As a teen, Leslie entered a juvenile justice system where overt hostility toward immigrant children doomed her.[3] Though Leslie spoke fluent English and attended local schools, the Orange County Probation Department (OCPD) targeted her for immigration enforcement. Ignoring California's confidentiality laws, OCPD turned over sensitive material to US Immigration and Customs Enforcement (ICE) while Leslie was in juvenile hall.[4] As a result, ICE promptly prioritized Leslie for deportation. OCPD need not have turned on Leslie. In other counties, juvenile justice systems work with immigration attorneys toward immigration *relief*, not deportation, for children.[5]

Collaboration between Leslie and her legal teams, however, shielded her from some harm. The Orange County Public Defender's Office, along with Public Counsel, sought SIJS in juvenile court, but the judge refused based on his own "policy considerations."[6] Pulling in additional partners, Leslie and Public Counsel collaborated with the Immigrant Rights Clinic at the University of California, Irvine—as well as the Immigrant Legal Resource Center and the Young Center for Immigrant Children's Rights—to prevail on appeal. Leslie not only received SIJS but also helped youth nationwide through the first appellate decision to address this status when youth are in delinquency. She is proud of that role.

Even after she secured SJIS, however, Leslie suffered immigration prosecution. OCPD turned Leslie over to ICE, who passed her off to ORR. ORR detained Leslie for months, exacerbating her disconnection from her only caregiver and from her everyday life. US Citizenship and Immigration Services (USCIS) refused to grant Leslie Deferred Action for Childhood Arrivals because of the confidential records OCPD gave to ICE. Nonetheless, Public Counsel succeeded in closing Leslie's immigration court case. Yet after detention, Leslie struggled with her trauma history and her fear of continued involvement with the juvenile justice system. Without the consistent, effective support of her grandmother, case manager, or therapist, Leslie lost touch with her legal team. Though USCIS granted Leslie's SIJS visa, it denied her green card application after she missed her interviews. Leslie was so close to permanent residency, but it remained out of reach.

Leslie's trajectory shows legal advocacy's limits in a highly complex web of intersecting systems. Though her legal teams repaired some damage wrought by hostile juvenile justice actors, they alone could not achieve Leslie's goals. Social work support at Public Counsel—not available until recent years for youth like Leslie—and positive juvenile justice interventions might have made a difference. If Leslie's probation officer had worked with ORR staff more willingly, ORR may have released Leslie more quickly. If Leslie had had more mental health support, she may have weathered her immigration process more easily. If an adult had arranged and traveled to meetings with her, Leslie may have obtained her green card. Leslie's legal case spurred both legislation and a successful effort to serve Orange County immigrant youth,[7] but Leslie herself remains in limbo. Still without a green card or work permit, she struggles with adult criminal charges, and her own child is in foster care. Leslie needs collaborative allies across systems now more than ever.

* * *

As Mario's, Diego's, and Leslie's stories show, the lives of undocumented youth in the United States are multidimensional and intersect with complex systems. Their lives cannot, and should not, be reduced to their attempts to obtain lawful status in the United States within the immigration legal system. Instead, we should understand their full range of challenges and achievements, recognizing that lawful immigration status is one of many elements supporting long-term stability in this country. It is necessary, but not sufficient. It may ease some of youth's interactions within systems, but it does not immediately transform them.

An interdisciplinary team approach holds promise for meaningful work with undocumented youth. Ideally, it offers young people a range of adults with whom they can develop trusting relationships as they enter, move through, and eventually exit intersecting systems. It is a hallmark of trauma-informed practice—taking into account a child's history and working with individual clients to build on strengths while addressing history's effects on the present. Within a team, each adult need not become an expert in the other systems in which a child engages. Indeed, ideally their varying expertise is complementary rather than duplicative. Youth who do not benefit from an interdisciplinary team approach must face each complex system without the support of other advocates. They often miss opportunities to make progress as systems' priorities compete or conflict. To best support undocumented youth, adults must partner with them and collaborate with others in their lives.

REFLECTIONS

Surviving Detention

WILLIAMS GUEVARA MARTÍNEZ

I came to America in 2012 when I was seventeen. I'm going to tell what actions ended up bringing me here. I'm from El Salvador, and I used to live with my father. I worked with him from the time I was eleven years old. My father is a strict person, and he used to beat me when I didn't work fast enough. He used ropes and belts. I still have scars on my left hand from one time when he hit me with the back part of a machete.

At home I was always hungry because we didn't have much money. He made me work from 6:00 to 12:00 every morning and then I had to walk an hour to middle school. In high school he made me work night shifts, and I couldn't eat lunch because I had no money. I was so tired, hungry, and scared, and I failed school twice. In my last year of school, I failed all my classes because my dad used to make me work the night shift taking care of the chickens that we would sell. My father beat me for that too, even though he didn't want me to go to school.

My dad fought in the civil war in my country in the 1980s, and this affected him deeply. He used to have flashbacks about the war, and when he was drunk it was normal to hear him talk about the war. He became really aggressive when he was drunk, and his addiction to alcohol was so big that he used to drink three to five times per week. He always used to beat me when he was drunk, and my mother could never stop him. We were a very humble family, and we lived almost solely from what we cultivated ourselves. My brother would help us when we needed to buy something for the farm, but a lot of times there was no money because my father spent our money on alcohol and women. I am the last of nine children in my family. They left home before they turned twelve to go to work so they could have a better life.

At home I got beat a lot of times, but I can say that there are two times I always remember. The first was when I was about one or two years old. I don't know why my father hit me. My mother was at church and he was drunk, and I did something that bothered him. He took his belt, and he started to hit me so hard that my back started to bleed. The second time was more recently, when I was sixteen. My sister got into trouble with my father because she didn't have permission to have a boyfriend. One day she got home late after school, and he was a little drunk, and he assumed that she was with someone and he got really mad. He took off his belt, and he was going to beat my sister, but I got in the way. I told him, "Don't hit her." That just pissed him off more, and he beat both of us.

That was so normal at our house. Why did I leave? Because of the relationship that I had with my father, the limited options that I had in education, to be someone with a stable job was going to be so hard. The economy in my country was getting worse and worse, and the gang activity was growing so fast. All that pushed me to leave. My sister is in the United States too. In 2012 my sister returned to El Salvador to visit. She stayed one month. She was working in the United States and told me all about it. After my father hit me with the machete, I just couldn't take it anymore. My mother contacted my brother Alan in Maryland, and he sent the money. I think that we paid half up front and the second half after I crossed. My father didn't care and didn't pay anything.

On August 20, 2012, I decided to leave my country on my own. I left with a small group of people and a coyote. There were three girls, one guy, and me. Most were between twenty and twenty-five years of age, one was thirty-three, and I was the youngest. I said good-bye to my mom in the morning. My dad didn't really care about me leaving. The same day we got to the border of El Salvador and Guatemala. We crossed a river, and someone helped me because I don't know how to swim. After that we walked for about three hours through big hills, and a van picked us up and we traveled a couple of hours until we got to Guatemala City. We went to a motel and stayed for a couple of hours, and they woke us up at 3:00 a.m. I was really tired by that time, and we spent almost the whole day in the van until we got to the border between Guatemala and Mexico. The place we stayed was called Gracias a Dios—

thanks to God. We stayed there for about a day, and the next day we had to climb a mountain. By that time a lot of people wanted to go back to their home countries.

After that we crossed a forest, and the border with Mexico was really close, and a pickup truck came to get us. We had to run to catch it, and there were a good many people in there. After that we got to a big house where a van was waiting, and they told me to get under the seats. We traveled like that for three to five hours. Later we got to a motel where I finally took a shower, and there were a lot of people in the room, so I had to sleep on the floor with only a blanket. I don't know how long I was asleep, but the next morning they put three people in the backseat, and they decided to make the rest of us take the freight train—the Beast—so we could move faster to another place. That train is scary because you have to hold really hard to the train to not fall off. I almost fell, but a man held me and helped me. After a couple hours on the top of the train my initial group got back together. It was around 5:00 p.m., and we walked for almost seven hours in the desert of Mexico. We got into a truck trailer and spent the rest of the night there. We couldn't sleep at all that night because the road was so bad. There were deep holes that made the truck bounce all over. We finally got to Reynosa, and we stayed for five days in a house near the US border. Every day we ate the same thing.

We woke up at 3:00 a.m. to cross the Rio Grande at around 5:00 a.m. There were around eighteen people going to cross the border. We had inner tubes. I remember that there were two women with babies. We tried to hide in the trees. We stayed there under the trees because we heard a helicopter. After we crossed, we got a ladder and climbed over a wall. We walked a few minutes on the US side until we saw a pond. Then we saw the cars of immigration and some agents got us.

The immigration agents were really abusive. They forced us to get in trucks and go to a station. They made us sit in rows and took our [personal] things and our papers and threw them away. I was worried about what was going to happen after that. They took me to a detention center and did all the paperwork. I am not sure what you call it, but it was a place with no windows. We were put in a big cell, with benches and one bathroom. It had an open toilet in the corner. There were cameras inside. We were confused, and we couldn't tell if it was night or day.

There was one guy in our group. The guard asked him questions and made him say he was older than eighteen. The guard wanted to deport him and they did. When he came to me, he wanted me to say the same thing. I said, "Why would I say that? I am not eighteen." We knew that you get sent to a shelter if you are under eighteen. So I had to stay in that place [Border Patrol station] for five days. It was awful. Everything was bad. The juice, the bread, and the ham. The burritos were cold. Our clothes were wet, and we were so cold. Later they took us to a shelter in Los Fresnos, Texas.

We were really scared because they didn't tell us anything. What would happen next? Where would they take us? We did meet a person there, and he knew that they would take us to a shelter. He explained how it would be. Later we did meet other kids who had been through the same thing. I remember driving to the shelter. We went in a car. There were two guys and a girl who was twelve years old. A man drove. We all took care of her 'cause she was so scared. We were four in all. The guys were so excited to go there. When we got there, we had a shower and they gave us clothes to wear. They took us to a big room where we picked out clothes that looked like they would fit. There were jeans and T-shirts and they said, "Go find some clothes to wear! Go find the right size." Then they put the kids in alphabetical order. Boys were the first part of the alphabet and girls were from Q to Z. There were six in each group, two groups to a house. They were duplexes.

There were a lot of rules. There was no pushing, no touching, no handshakes, no hugs. We could play soccer at certain times. There was a party on Independence Day—September 15—for my country. They had a dance and other parties. For every three kids there was a worker to watch us. The workers were mostly women. They had to make sure that there were no fights and that we stayed in order when we left our rooms. There was no messing around. We had to get up early, all together, to wash and brush our teeth. We had three minutes to do that. We had to stay with the group and be on time. We went together to the cafeteria to eat. We went to class in the morning. There were four classes and they ended at 11:00 a.m. We studied English there. Then we had lunch and we played soccer or something else. Then dinner and back to the house at 7:00 p.m. We could play cards until lights out at 9:00 p.m.

We couldn't fight, have "sexual touching," or say bad words. One kid ran away, and they caught him. Most kids stayed for a couple weeks, but I knew one kid who stayed there for more than a year. We got really homesick. We could go and talk to the counselor. But we weren't allowed to use electronic devices so we couldn't send messages and write using the Internet. At the beginning, I didn't want to be there. I didn't know anybody. I didn't know the length of time I would stay there. I was so homesick and I missed my family. I didn't have friends.

Right away they talked about family reunification. They asked if I had family in the United States and if I had a phone number they could call. I explained that I have a brother and he could take care of me. So they sent him the papers and all the information. The state agreed with the process. They asked for proof that he is my brother. Then he filled it all out and it was approved. It depends on the family, how long it takes them to do the papers. It takes more or less time. My brother was fast. He did it in two weeks. It was weird because I wanted to stay when it was time to leave. I had made friends. Even now I stay in touch with those friends through Facebook. I have one friend in Silver Spring that I know from the shelter. We talk but not about legal status.

I stayed at that shelter for twenty-four days, and on October 24, 2012, I finally saw my brother. At that point I was finally safe, and I lived with him in Maryland. Because I had to go to immigration court, my brother found out about the law clinic Esperanza in Baltimore. We contacted the head of the office. She helped me. I needed a guardian. My older brother became my guardian. I met Scott Rose, who is a lawyer, and he helped me. I went to court, and I told my story, the whole story, to the judge. I got a Special Immigrant Juvenile visa, and after two years I got my green card.

When I came to Maryland I just wanted to work, not go to school. My brother said, "No work. You are going to school." I didn't want to go. I wanted to make money. That's why I came here. I was so excited. But I went to Parkville High School in Maryland and I had to start in ninth grade because I didn't know English. It was really hard to learn because the classes in El Salvador were equal to tenth grade here. When I came to school I saw other kids who skipped class and would go outside to smoke weed. I wanted to skip school. But I stayed there because I want to learn. My first year was stressful. My situation then was bad. I was anxious all the time. I had a breakdown. My world history teacher, Mr. Burns, was nice but hard. He was always trying to help me, but I didn't pass the class. So I took it again and I passed. I had a really good math teacher, and I got an A, B, and two As. When I was in El Salvador, I always felt tired because I had to work and sometimes I slept in class. Finally, in senior year in the American high school it was OK. I knew enough English and I had a friend from El Salvador. He came here and did not have a strong case. He was about to turn eighteen, and his birthday was only three weeks away. I told him about the juvenile visa and helped him to find a lawyer through the same clinic in Baltimore.

Did I imagine my life would be like this? No, I never thought so. At home I was surrounded by gangs. I was not into that. I don't use drugs. My father taught me not to use drugs or alcohol. That is really ironic coming from him. I want to bring my ma here to live. I have three sisters in the United States: Carmen has a boy who is three years old; Raquel also got SIJS [Special Immigrant Juvenile Status]; and Ruby has a six-month-old baby and a daughter who is six years old. I have two grandmothers back home. My mother's ma is ninety-three years old. She still works and she does well. She does not even use a cane. She is a weaver in the village back home.

I got my green card in 2014, and I am on track to become a US citizen. I am doing well in school, and I am active in my church. My older brother took care of me great. He gave me food and clothing and everything else that I need. He helped me with my homework, and I had my own bedroom in his apartment. He was my guardian until this past summer, when he died. We were at the beach, and he had an accident in the ocean. He saved my nephew from drowning, but the ocean was too strong and my brother could not get back to shore. I am really happy that I live with my sister now. I also help her because she is dealing with the same things I am because my father also tried to kill her with a machete.

I testified at the Maryland Assembly and helped with a bill that expanded eligibility for that Special Immigrant Juvenile visa from eighteen to twenty-one years of age. I will start college in the spring of 2017, and I will go to the Community College of Baltimore County. I want to work as an electrical engineer.

What did I learn from the experience of migrating? We are innocent when we leave home. We don't know what to expect. We can get lost and have very strong feelings. That is what happens. I would tell kids who are thinking about leaving home and coming here that it is really hard to make it all the way here, but it is worth it because it is way better here. Everything was really hard, but the American Dream is in my hands and I'm pretty sure that I will make it come true.

PART II

Through

Navigating Laws and Legal Systems

In part II, the contributors examine how the actions of institutions and immigration policies play out on the ground in the lives of young people. As children and their loved ones directly confront restrictive immigration policies and move through government systems, they negotiate US immigration laws (and the absence of laws), legal proceedings, and the effects of current politics at local, state, and national levels. Here, contributors outline how children and youth move *through* various systems, as young people and their family members who are caught within government systems must navigate complicated processes and procedures.

When young people enter the United States and become subject to US immigration controls, their movement through immigration systems is often marked by contradictions and unpredictability. For example, if children and youth enter the court system, their trajectories are often stalled by multiple challenges, including inadequate legal representation (Young and McKenna), overloaded court dockets and confusion about legal processes (Marks), and threats to due process (Terrio). Young immigrants must also maneuver through processes of legal categorization as they apply for a status adjustment (Coutin). Navigating multiple systems in schools, communities, housing, and more (Rabin and Menjívar) can result in forms of uncertainty that are likely to increase in the years to come.

In chapter 4, Susan Bibler Coutin shows how young people who immigrate to the United States from Central America and move *through* US legal systems are at risk of becoming an immigrant underclass, that is, a set of individuals whose life opportunities are powerfully constrained by legal status. Immigrants who arrive as children face multiple challenges, ranging from violence, poverty, and racism to difficulties and hardship that are specifically linked to immigration status, including family separation across borders, few or no opportunities for legal relief or work authorization, challenges as they pursue higher education and careers, and the daily threat of deportation—whether it is their own or that of a family member. This chapter underscores the contradictory processes that converge to place child migrants in an underclass, forcing them to linger in a space of legal nonexistence rather than to move out of systems of immigration control.

In chapter 5, Nina Rabin and Cecilia Menjívar consider the experiences of youth—both immigrant youth and the US citizen children of immigrant parents—living on their own in the United States as a result of immigration enforcement. They outline the complex family structures and living arrangements of youth, ranging from siblings raising siblings and young high school sweethearts rapidly becoming domestic partners to couch surfing. These diverse circumstances capture the varied and often heart-wrenching decisions immigrant families must make about where young people are most likely to thrive. Some young people describe a precocious sense of responsibility for their parents' futures, while others express their longing for the parental comfort and love that other relationships could not fulfill. The wide range of experiences and emotions that the interviewed youth voiced captures the complex reality of young people in immigrant families as they move *through* legal and other systems after deportation.

Susan J. Terrio's chapter examines federal immigration courts and the challenges immigration judges face. Operating with a small fraction of the budget allocated for enforcement agencies—just one-sixtieth—the courts are plagued by staff shortages, huge backlogs, lengthy delays for cases to be heard, and negative press regarding judicial training. Stress on adjudicators and court staff has been heightened with the creation of fast-tracked hearings for juveniles and backlogged cases that now exceed 500,000; dramatic reductions in the proportion of juveniles with legal representation; and negative national press following the testimony of a senior immigration judge who claimed that legal representation is not necessary for juveniles because US immigration law can be taught to "children as young as three years old." Immigration judges comment on the toll their work exacts through repeated exposure to persecution stories, heavy caseloads, intrusive administrative oversight, negative press, and increased pressure to complete cases. Terrio highlights power imbalances that favor the government and threaten both fairness and due process as children go *through* an enforcement system where immigrants lack basic legal protections.

As Wendy Young and Megan McKenna write in their contribution, the lack of due process specifically for unaccompanied children creates a significant gap in the US immigration system—a system that treats these children as "little adults" with nominal recognition of their unique needs and vulnerabilities. The unprecedented increase in the number of children coming to the United States, which peaked in the summer of 2014, sparked changes in the system and resulted in more access to pro bono representation, but also new challenges as an increasingly political spotlight was placed on the US treatment of these children. More than two-thirds of unaccompanied children in deportation proceedings lacked representation in 2014, demonstrating the lasting effects on those who have already moved through detention and immigration proceedings and the challenges that children continue to face today. This piece outlines the history of the US government's approach to unaccompanied children and the ongoing challenges to full representation that persist as children move *through* US legal regimes.

In her piece, Dana Leigh Marks explores everyday challenges faced by noncitizen youth in trial-level immigration courts. Because the stakes of these proceedings are so high, they have been analogized to death penalty cases, yet they are conducted in settings more closely resembling traffic courts. No attorney representation is guaranteed, despite the fact that immigration law is considered by higher courts to be second only to tax law in its complexity and dramatically misaligned with many state laws with which it intersects. Other challenges include the impact of cultural differences and misunderstandings such as those caused by interpretation issues or implicit bias, and the reality that many in these proceedings suffer emotionally and psychologically from post-traumatic stress. Here, young people move *through* a court system that may be difficult to understand and even more challenging to navigate.

4

The Post-1996 Immigrant Underclass

SUSAN BIBLER COUTIN

In 2008, I had the opportunity to do interviews in San Salvador, El Salvador, in the offices of Homies Unidos, a transnational organization that formed in the 1990s to address urban violence and the transnationalization of gangs. One of the individuals I met was Lorenzo Gómez,[1] who was receiving assistance from the organization, and who had been deported to El Salvador after growing up in the United States. Lorenzo's account of his experiences sheds light on how individuals who migrate as children navigate laws and institutions as they move through multiple countries, often being regarded as outsiders by both their country of birth and the country where they were raised.

Lorenzo had entered the United States in 1978, when he was eight years old, when his family immigrated for economic reasons. He recalled his early life in the United States: "As a child, when I was growing up in elementary, I started to notice . . . that I was in love with the English language at that point. You know? And I was so fascinated with it that, I became a little book worm. I would grab books, go through them, and read them." Lorenzo was proud of his language skills. During our interview, which was conducted in English, he imitated different accents, showing how New Yorkers speak in Brooklyn and in the Bronx. Yet, Lorenzo's life took a dramatic turn when he fell in with kids who were involved in gangs. As he told me:

> I can never forget this, it was what really switched my whole world around to be a child with a lot of dreams and expectations in life, to become from the 'hood. I made that decision when I was in junior high. That's when I started to meet the homies. . . . And I was a fool, myself! I started to run around with those guys in the 'hood. And that lasted for a good eight years, then I realized that was not a way of life, not for me. And I decided

THE POST-1996 IMMIGRANT UNDERCLASS | 77

to get out the 'hood. And it's like they say, you can get outta the 'hood, but you can't get the 'hood outta you.

Lorenzo became a lawful permanent resident in the United States in the early 1980s, and he thought that later, when his father naturalized, he too had become a US citizen. After completing a jail term in 1989, he held various jobs, including his favorite, an AT&T operator. Lorenzo reenacted this job for me during the interview: "'OK, where do you want to place your call?' 'The Florida Keys.' 'OK ma'am, this is the area code, and who do you want to call?' Stuff like that. It was fun!" Then, in 1996, after the Illegal Immigration Reform and Immigrant Responsibility Act expanded the list of crimes that made noncitizens deportable and applied this definition retroactively, Lorenzo was picked up for speeding and was told that he was not a US citizen and that he was deportable.[2] Deportation proceedings were initiated, but Lorenzo missed a hearing. In 2000, Lorenzo was convicted of drug possession, and he learned that he had been ordered deported. Lorenzo explained, "Immigration came back in for me and said, 'You know what? We're gonna go ahead and deport you back to El Salvador.' 'Wait a minute. I'm supposed to see a judge.' 'No, you're not eligible to see a judge, because you've been deported in absentia [without being present]."[3]

After being deported to El Salvador in 2000, Lorenzo immediately rejoined his family in Los Angeles. In 2002, he was apprehended for driving without a license and was deported a second time. He returned to the United States again, a journey that was filled with horrors, which he described as follows:

I got mugged on the way over there. I saw people that fell off the train. . . . They get chopped up. I saw that! One of my buddies. . . . And then we bought the newspaper the next day to see if we'd see something, and we sure did. His limbs were everywhere. His head was just cut off. It was horrible! And a lot of the women get raped. Because they have a lot of gang members. . . . I was sleeping and they mugged me, and they grabbed me by the neck. "Wake up!" And I had a machete right here [motions toward stomach]. "All right, just run up all your money, that's all we want." . . . People die every day on that train.

In 2004, Lorenzo was apprehended in Texas, and this time he was prosecuted for unlawful reentry and sentenced to four years in a federal prison. He had been deported a third time in 2008, shortly before our interview. He described his situation:

> I don't believe that what they're doing to me is fair at all. I'm just here running around. I don't know anybody in this country. No friends. No family, no support. I live in the streets. I'm homeless. If I could keep my clothes clean it's because some guy is helping me out where I can wash my clothes and shower. But other than that, I don't have a place of my own. I'm going through an extreme and exceptional hardship.[4] It's what I told the judge! "Sir. This is what I'm going to go through. Please, help me." They don't want to listen. They think everyone can go back home and live happily ever after. It doesn't work like that! I have my daughters back home. My mom, dad, brothers, sister, and I'm the only one here. So I would like to go back home. I really would.

At the time of our interview, Lorenzo was desperate to return to the United States again but also was fearful of additional prison time. He told me:

> I'm scared. Because if I get busted crossing, I'm going back to the BoP [Bureau of Prisons] for reentry again. This time, I'm gonna get double time. Eight years. So I really don't know what to do. I'm so confused. I need time. I miss my family so much! I'm really hurt! For some time, I was drinking a lot here in Salvador, because I was so hurt and confused. I don't understand why this happened to me! Why? Why? Why? But, I'm still here, I'm still going through the hardship. An extreme hardship.

Lorenzo's narrative reveals that US immigration policies are producing an underclass of individuals whose lives are not viable anywhere. Due to the young age at which he immigrated, Lorenzo identified with the United States. It was the country where he had grown up, learned English, developed an intimate knowledge of different neighborhoods—such as the Bronx versus Brooklyn—gone to school, worked, become a lawful permanent resident, and had a family of his own. Unfortunately, it was also where he went through the US criminal justice system and acquired a criminal record, one that stripped him of his US residency and made him deportable. In El Salvador, at the time of our interview, he had no job and was living on the streets. He could not return to the United States legally. If he returned illegally, he risked the same fate as his friend, who was decapitated after falling off the top of a moving train. And even if he succeeded in entering, he would be at risk of being imprisoned for eight years and then deported once again. How are people such as Lorenzo supposed to exist?

Lorenzo is not alone. In fact, children who immigrate to the United States from Central America or other countries are also at risk of joining an immigrant underclass, that is, a set of noncitizens whose life opportunities are powerfully constrained by a lack of legal status. For example, though US citizens who are impoverished or are members of racial or ethnic minority groups also experience criminalization, a US citizen convicted of a minor offense faces only jail time or probation, whereas noncitizens can actually be deported. Child arrivals, as those who immigrate to the United States before turning sixteen have come to be known, may experience a number of adverse circumstances, including violence in their country of origin, lengthy family separations, the challenges of immigrating without authorization, being undocumented in the United States, a lack of work authorization, challenges in pursuing higher education, poverty, racism, the threat of removal, no opportunity to regularize permanently, and a deep disjuncture between legal and social experiences of belonging.

Furthermore, civil immigration laws have become more punitive, subjecting noncitizens to detention and deportation, whereas criminal prosecutions of immigration violations, such as reentry following a deportation, have skyrocketed.[5] The 2012 Deferred Action for Childhood Arrivals (DACA) program provided important protections until it was rescinded by the Trump administration in 2017. Some local or state measures have allowed undocumented students to qualify for financial aid and/or pay in-state tuition, yet these remedies remain limited, and the possibility of deportation looms large under intensified Trump administration enforcement policies.

This chapter is based on semistructured interviews conducted between 2006 and 2010 with forty child arrivals who were living in Southern California, forty-one child arrivals who were deported to El

Salvador, and twenty-five advocates who worked with youth in either country. I met interviewees through colleges, universities, community organizations, and word of mouth. Interviews lasted one to two hours and examined child arrivals' lives in El Salvador, immigration experiences, future plans, and returns to El Salvador. Approximately half of the Southern California participants were reinterviewed after one to two years. Half of the US participants were women, whereas, due to the overrepresentation of men in deportation to El Salvador, all the deportees who were interviewed were men. Analyzing this material makes it possible to detail the borders that potentially place child migrants in an underclass, confining them to spaces of legal nonexistence.

An Immigrant Underclass

The term "underclass" refers to a social stratum of people who experience persistent poverty and marginalization due to structural conditions such as unemployment, the denial of access to public benefits, and discrimination.[6] In the case of immigrants—and as shown by the experiences of Lorenzo—this underclass may have transnational dimensions in that its members may be excluded from multiple societies and social spaces.[7] Government policies are key in producing this class. In particular, reforms that were adopted in the United States in 1996 expanded the definition of an aggravated felony for immigration purposes, made detention mandatory for many who were in removal proceedings, reduced the discretion that had enabled immigration judges to weigh positive factors (such as length of residence, work history, or ties to US citizens) during removal proceedings, stiffened border enforcement, and made legalization much more difficult for individuals living in the United States without legal status.[8]

These changes reinforced territorial borders while also multiplying the internal boundaries that the undocumented face when they attempt to travel to another state on a school field trip, go to college, get a job, apply for a driver's license, or qualify for medical insurance. These internal boundaries have exacerbated the degree to which intensified immigration enforcement and overcriminalization particularly target members of ethnic or racial minority groups.[9] Child arrivals, who grow up in the United States alongside US citizen children, are especially disadvantaged, as they may believe themselves to be citizens only to "awaken to the nightmare" of being undocumented when they turn sixteen and seek employment or a driver's license.[10] As young immigrants move through legal and criminal justice systems or are caught between them, they become part of an immigrant underclass. Yet even as these internal boundaries form a web, trapping individuals, there are also gaps and spaces, which create limited room for maneuvering. Therefore, while structural conditions actively push people into an underclass, members of this class may also challenge these conditions, seeking to improve not only their individual lives but also those of others.

The barriers that have created an immigrant underclass have historical roots, through a globally unequal distribution of resources, well-being, and security.[11] The US drug market, the exportation of US security measures, zero tolerance policing, and corruption have weakened state institutions in Mexico, El Salvador, Honduras, and Guatemala, while fueling the rise of criminal cartels, gangs, and narcotrafficking. Factors that compel migration form the basis for an underclass in migrants' countries of origin. For example, Herminia immigrated to the United States from Mexico in 1989 at the age of thirteen. Her mother was a domestic violence victim, and her father, who was in the military, prevented Herminia and her siblings from working and studying but did not provide for them sufficiently. One by one, her siblings left for the United States until, finally, Herminia came too. Likewise, Manuel immigrated to the United States as a child, but from El Salvador, in 1986 at the age of nine. His mother had fled El Salvador in 1982, during the Salvadoran civil war (1980–1992), because she participated in a rebel group and was warned that she was on a death list. Manuel remained behind with his father and an aunt. He described his life in El Salvador: "We were poor, very poor. To be honest, we ate beans three times a day. I remember that's when I started finding out that my mom was sending money. And sometimes we would get cornflakes. That was a treat. On Fridays. And coffee. Things that I take for granted now." Although Manuel did not feel that he was directly impacted, the war shaped his childhood environment. He related, "Once when I went to a garbage dump that was near where we used to live, I found a hand of a guy sticking out. I didn't make a big deal out of that." Manuel's mother eventually sent for him, in hopes that he would have a better life in the United States. However, Manuel's father stayed behind, and at the time of our 2008 interview, Manuel had been unable to see his father since leaving El Salvador.

Immigration laws, which restrict child migrants' movement across national boundaries, reinforce these global inequalities. In countries such as Mexico and El Salvador, visas to enter the United States legally are available only to those with economic resources, qualifying relatives, employment, or study opportunities. Moreover, border enforcement has stiffened in recent years. Deploying Border Patrol agents and surveillance technology along key sections of the border has forced would-be crossers into inhospitable terrain, where many suffer from thirst, are exposed to animals and heat, and are at risk of being robbed or assaulted.[12] Anthropologist Jason De León reports that "between 2000 and September 2014, the bodies of 2,771 people were found in southern Arizona, enough corpses to fill the seats on fifty-four Greyhound buses. These grim figures represent only known migrant fatalities" (for more on the risks of border crossings, see De León's chapter in this volume).[13] Fortunately for them, Herminia and Manuel immigrated to the United States before this latest intensification. Herminia recalled traveling to the United States by bus, and although she did not have a visa, she said that she did not encounter any problems. Manuel flew to Guadalajara with his father, who then told him, "You're going to see your mom, but I'm going to stay behind." Manuel traveled the rest of the way with an alien-smuggler, which, he said, was hard "because I wasn't with my dad, and the guy that my dad handed me over to had to go somewhere, so he handed me over to another guy. And that guy used to get drunk. He was always drinking. Once we went to the beach, and I was crying for my father, because I didn't know this guy."

After arriving in the United States, child migrants encounter another set of legal barriers that can keep them in an underclass. While they are entitled legally to attend US public schools and, therefore, may in many ways be indistinguishable from other children,[14] child migrants are in other ways set apart. In this volume and throughout her work, sociologist Joanna Dreby has documented the degree to which "children in Mexican immigrant households describe fear about their family stability and confusion over the impact legality has on their lives."[15] Even children who are born in the United States may fear the deportation of a parent or other relative. When they become adolescents, child migrants who are undocumented face challenges obtaining driver's licenses, working legally, and qualifying for the financial aid and in-state tuition that would make college feasible. If they complete college degrees but still lack work authorization, they may be unable to pursue careers. Many, such as Lorenzo, who thought that he had become a US citizen when his father naturalized, do not understand immigration law and are dependent on adults to submit applications on their behalf.[16] After they turn eighteen, child migrants who remain undocumented begin to accrue "unlawful presence." Those who accrue six months of unlawful presence face a three-year bar on reentering the United States if they leave the country, while those who accrue twelve months face a ten-year bar.[17]

At the federal level, the termination of DACA will have wide-ranging effects. When recipients' authorization expires, they will no longer be able to work legally and may be targeted for deportation. They face restrictions on international travel, have no pathway to citizenship, and confront heightened vulnerabilities. Moreover, not all child migrants even qualified for DACA. For example, although Herminia immigrated to the United States when she was thirteen, she was over the age limit of thirty-one in 2012. At the time of our interview, she had almost completed a university degree in biology, but due to the pressure of trying to attend school while working at low-paying jobs and without eligibility for federal financial aid, she had stopped going to college. Deeply frustrated at the limitations created by her immigration status, she commented, "It makes me sad that I went to school so many years, and, if I can find a job cleaning, I'll be lucky." Like many, Herminia found herself trapped in an immigrant underclass.

Being Trapped

The 1996 immigration reforms, coupled with subsequent legislation and policies, have created a series of barriers designed to deter unlawful entry, prevent legalization, and encourage what is sometimes referred to as "self-deportation," namely, leaving the country. Child migrants have been particularly impacted by these developments. New arrivals must endure traumatizing border crossings, while longtime residents find both their social mobility and their ability to move about restricted.

Those who are undocumented cannot work legally, face challenges pursuing higher education, may or may not be eligible for driver's licenses, and cannot travel internationally. Under administrative advisories that began in 2017, undocumented youth run a heightened risk of apprehension and deportation; most at risk are noncitizen youth who have been convicted of crimes. Federal programs such as the "priority enforcement program" promote collaboration between US Immigration and Customs Enforcement and state and local law enforcement agencies so that noncitizens who have been convicted of crimes will be removed from the country once their sentences have been completed. These programs have been criticized for including individuals with minor, nonviolent convictions. One study concluded that the policies directed at "criminal aliens" have "removed the pettiest of violators."[18] Because many aspects of youth culture (such as drug use, which is what Lorenzo experienced) have been criminalized and because communities of color are more heavily policed, child migrants are particularly at risk of arrest, prosecution, and deportation.

Roberto had these experiences. He immigrated to the United States from El Salvador legally, at the age of seven, along with his father, through a family visa petition. In El Salvador, his father had been a teacher, but in the United States, he worked long hours collecting trash. Roberto related that when he was in elementary school he misbehaved, and once, when he bruised his knee climbing over a fence, his teacher assumed his father had abused him and sent a social worker to his home. Worried about his behavior, Roberto's father sent him back to El Salvador to live with his grandmother. Under his grandmother's care, Roberto straightened out, always returning regularly to the United States to maintain his lawful residency, and he moved back to the United States to live when he was twelve years old. In the United States, though, he felt like an outsider. He recalled, "I wasn't fitting into the crowd, Mexicans who didn't speak English, Central American people, a little bit of English but still not getting along with Mexicans. And there were the people born and raised over there [in the United States] who spoke English and everything was cool for them. Neither one would accept another one in their social circle or friendship circle." So, Roberto joined a gang. He explained, "They would loan me *cholo* clothes. And I started to get into it, listening to the rap music, and all that stuff. And I got to a point where the question popped, 'So, what? Are you in or you out? Are you gonna be with us or what?' And so I joined the M-S [Mara Salvatrucha or MS-13] gang, representing El Salvador according to me, back at that time."

Although, as a teenager, he dropped out of school and was in and out of juvenile hall, Roberto did not realize he was at risk of deportation. He recalled:

> I was feeling free, I was confident. I felt like an American, because I had the same rights. If something wrong was being done to me, I had the right to speak up for it. I had no issues going places, like to TJ [Tijuana, Mexico] or to a bank. I wasn't going to be treated like less, you know, like I've seen how immigrants have been treated. I didn't feel none of that. I was feeling very good. Having papers over there is a whole big deal.

Eventually, Roberto got into a fight and was arrested for assault. Then, he was picked up for riding in a stolen car. These two offenses led to his deportation. He told me:

> They put me an INS hold [i.e., a detainer to be transferred from a local jail into federal immigration custody]. And people [in prison], they call them "jail lawyers," they told me that if I did more than a year, I qualified for deportation. I told them, "No, man, I've got papers." They said it didn't matter, that if you've got a criminal record, you've got felonies—I told them I do got felonies—they said, "OK, that's it." I told them I had a strike. They said, "That's it! You're going back!" I couldn't believe I was going back.

After being deported to El Salvador, Roberto lived in fear. Because of his tattoos, he was arrested and investigated by the Salvadoran police. When he went out in public, other gang members approached him, trying to recruit him. Eventually, Roberto had his most visible tattoos, the ones on his face, removed, and he realized his fluent English skills could serve him well in El Salvador. He worked at a coffee processing plant, then at an assembly plant translating specifications on how to make clothes, and later at a call center. Though his life had improved, Roberto continued to miss his relatives in the United States and hoped that his father would eventually be able to obtain a pardon, so that he could return.

Roberto's account demonstrates the ways that, as a child migrant, he became trapped in an immigrant underclass. His father had experienced downward social mobility immigrating to the United States and, due to working long hours, was unable to supervise his young son carefully. At school, Roberto did not find the support structures that could have helped him to integrate into his new country. Instead, he joined a gang, thus assimilating, but to a sector of society that was criminalized and marginalized.[19] By his own account, Roberto's offenses were relatively minor and were part of the youth lifestyle that he had joined. Yet, Roberto found himself criminalized, stripped of his residency, and unable to challenge his removal. In El Salvador, he was harassed both by police and by gang members and was at risk of being killed. But rather than being destroyed by these experiences, Roberto was able to create a new life for himself, exhibiting a resilience that is common to migrant youth.

Movement

Child migrants who are in a transnational immigrant underclass face truncated futures. Many experience limited work and educational opportunities as well as criminalization and deportation. And yet youth also exhibit agency in challenging these conditions and attempting to exit this underclass. Many who are deported return to the United States, as Lorenzo did twice. Those who are in the United States seek to better their lives, despite the barriers they face. At the time of our interview, Manuel had obtained Temporary Protected Status (TPS), which was awarded to Salvadorans following the devastating earthquakes that rocked El Salvador in 2001, and was working in airport security. Despite being undocumented, Herminia had almost completed a college degree in biology; at the time of our interview, she was planning to apply for an expanded version of DACA that President Obama announced in 2014, but that was subsequently enjoined due to a lawsuit by Texas and twenty-five other states.[20] And, despite living in El Salvador, Roberto attempted to re-create something of his life in the United States. He told me:

> At the house, it's totally 100 percent English. My sister-in-law, she was raised in Kentucky too. Her husband, he was raised in LA. So her family and me, when we get together, we speak nothing but English. The baby?

We don't talk to him nothing but English. I mean, he'll learn Spanish from his grandma. So, I try to make it as much as I can. At work, that's why I love being at work. Then my dad, when we talk on the phone, it's English. I just talk Spanish with my grandma. And sometimes, I don't know if you remember, there's a lot of helicopters at night. Tch-tch-tch-tch. [Sound of helicopter.] So right here, sometimes when one passes by, I just close my eyes and I feel the breeze at night. I could picture I'm [there]. I miss the whole thing a lot.

Child migrants have also been at the forefront of the immigrant rights movement in the United States, and it was due to their pressure that the DACA program was created.[21] Young people have argued that society at large is harmed by the policies that prevent them from realizing their potential. If they were authorized to work, vote, study, and travel, they contend, they could establish businesses, contribute to the economy, make scientific advances, and help to solve social problems. Adopting the slogan "unapologetic and unafraid," undocumented child arrivals have defied legal barriers to speak out about their status as well as the conditions that led their families to immigrate to the United States.[22] Young people have highlighted the social impacts of policies that divide families and communities, restrict opportunities, and fail to protect current arrivals. Through protests, hunger strikes, marches, lobbying, and social media campaigns, child arrivals have insisted on leaving spaces of nonexistence, becoming visible, and dismantling barriers. The outcome of the 2016 US presidential election posed new challenges to immigrant youth and young adults, exacerbating the uncertainty in their lives. The Trump administration's efforts to ramp up border and interior enforcement also increased young people's anxiety about the fates of their family members. Despite this volatile political context, young people will continue to navigate the legal and extralegal institutions and pathways through which they move. I will conclude with the words of Carmina, a child migrant and youth leader. In an interview, she reflected on how her own thinking about borders has evolved:

I realized that borders are a bit arbitrary. That is, that my friends can go to Cancun or Paris on a vacation, without difficulty, they can go there and live there the rest of their lives, even though they don't have much money. But

I, simply because I was born in the Third World, in Peru, I can't do these things. It is as though these borders exist for me and not for them. That is, not for everyone in this country does a border exist. For me, it does. So I realized that the system is much, much bigger than I had thought. Before, I thought, "Reform it, give us citizenship, give us more visas." And I thought afterward, "Reform the bureaucracy so that we all can have visas." And now . . . I am thinking, "Why do we need visas? Why do we need borders? Who is served by them? These [are] tools to divide us."

5

Youth on Their Own

NINA RABIN AND CECILIA MENJÍVAR

The plight of unaccompanied minors in the immigration court system profiled in the following chapters and essays presents starkly the vulnerability of youth moving through the legal system. Yet there is another group of youth, arguably even less visible, who are also navigating the legal system on their own. Both US citizen and undocumented youth in immigrant families face complex legal decisions and processes when their parents are deported or leave them on their own in this country. They must make major life decisions that are deeply intertwined with the law—decisions about where to live, what types of immigration relief to seek, and, most important, what steps to take to reunify with their family. They confront the laws and policies described throughout this volume both directly—in navigating their own pathways to legal and geographic stability—and indirectly, through the upheaval they experience as a result of family members' encounters with harsh immigration enforcement policies. In this sense, these young people, both immigrants themselves and US citizen children of immigrants, move through the legal system in extremely consequential ways even if they themselves never set foot in the immigration courtroom.

Consider the case of Carlos. When he was three years old, his parents brought him and his six-year-old sister to this country from Mexico. The parents went on to have two more children, who are US citizens. Carlos remembers a time, when he was in middle school, that he came home from football practice and found his mother crying. She explained to him that his father had been "picked up." He recalls, "From what they told me, they told me that my dad was working and on his way back home, that the police got him . . . but they weren't looking for him. They were looking for someone else that had his name. Then they find out

89

that he was an immigrant." When asked if his father had any criminal history, Carlos responded that he did not think so.

After a few months, his father returned home. The family then spent the next three years (unsuccessfully) fighting his deportation in the court system. They paid for an attorney, but as Carlos explained, "From what I heard, the lawyer is the reason we lost the case." So when Carlos was fifteen years old, his father was deported. At first, Carlos's mom stayed with the four children, hoping there might be some way to still make things right with their papers, but "after six months . . . she had depression because of it." His little brother and sister were struggling, and they "started doing bad in school." So his mother and younger siblings joined his father in Mexico. When his mom and younger siblings left, his family "gave me a choice, they said, 'You could come, or you could stay here, and finish school, and do whatever you want.'" For Carlos, the choice was not hard. He wanted to stay, "to see if I could fix their papers and bring them back." He also "just wanted to finish high school and see what opportunities could happen."

At the time of his interview, Carlos was living with his aunt and uncle. He had received a temporary reprieve from deportation through the Deferred Action for Childhood Arrivals (DACA) program, which President Obama created in 2012 to provide temporary protection from deportation to certain undocumented immigrant youth.[1] But DACA recipients could not leave the country—except for particular reasons and only with a form of government permission called Advance Parole—so Carlos could not easily visit his family. He spoke with them on the phone every week, and sometimes they would communicate using FaceTime. The law's role in disrupting Carlos's family through his father's deportation is plain to see. But there is another, more subtle way in which the legal system is shaping Carlos's life: through the decisions he and his family must make about how they might reunite in the face of the harsh, complex current immigration legal system.

In this chapter, we examine how youth navigate such legal decisions and processes, based on data gathered during the Obama administration. This context is important to bear in mind because the Trump administration implemented sweeping increases in immigration enforcement that are significantly altering the landscape we portray here. Although it is too soon to measure the impact of the Trump administration's aggressive enforcement policies, it seems inevitable they will only amplify the significance of our findings.

We draw on thirty-seven interviews of young people we conducted over the course of nine months in 2014–2015 in Pima County, the most populated border county in Arizona. These young people had two factors in common: they were living on their own—without either biological parent—at least in part because of immigration policy, and they all described themselves as Mexican or Mexican American.[2] Of the thirty-seven participants, twelve were male and twenty-five were female. They ranged in age from twelve to twenty-one, with the majority in the fifteen- to eighteen-year-old range. Nearly all described themselves as bilingual. In terms of legal status, twenty-two were US citizens, two were legal permanent residents, ten were undocumented, and three had received DACA. With regard to living arrangements, twenty-seven were currently living with family members (nine with aunts/uncles, four with cousins, seven with grandparents, seven with siblings), and ten had other living arrangements (with a boyfriend/girlfriend or friend, on their own, or in foster care).

All the participants shared the fact that they were not living with either biological parent. However, not all had experienced parental deportation. Twenty of the participants reported that one or more of their parents had been deported (twelve had fathers deported, five had mothers deported, three had both parents deported). Of the remainder, five had parents who had always lived in Mexico, three had both parents still living in the United States but not as an intact family, and nine had one or both parents return to Mexico voluntarily without any parental deportation. In spite of these dissimilar paths and forms of legal status, the young people we interviewed were all in the same position: poor youth with ties to Mexico—either as Mexican nationals themselves or through Mexican family members—whose life prospects depended on their successful navigation of the legal system on their own.

Consistent with other research on immigrants' experiences with the US immigration legal system,[3] our interviews highlight a concerning lack of reliable legal information available to our study participants and their families. Given the momentous decisions immigrant families must make about how to spread risk and opportunity among family members, it is disturbing that they often do so based on erroneous or ambiguous legal information. Some of these decisions involve complex legal analysis, such as whether a discretionary waiver may be successful or whether a humanitarian visa may be granted. Others involve facts as simple as the age at which someone can sponsor a relative or the number of years a visa will take to process. Without a trustworthy and accessible source to provide accurate legal information, immigrant youth and their families often make decisions about the legal process based on guesswork or outright misconceptions.

Here, we highlight two particular types of legal processes that the young people in our study encountered: the family-based petition process and the DACA program. Both these legal remedies are meant to enable immigrant youth to reside in this country lawfully. Yet, the experiences of the young people we describe reveal a fundamental disconnect between the legal processes these young people must navigate and the circumstances of their lives.

We begin with the sociolegal context, describing how the youth we interviewed fit into the larger national picture of immigrants navigating the legal system in the United States today. Then we discuss each of the two forms of legal relief—family-based petitions and DACA—presenting first the relevant legal framework and then the struggles we heard described by youth. We conclude with some brief reflections on the policy implications of our findings.

Sociolegal Context

Studies of immigrants navigating the legal process focus predominantly on the dearth of legal services available to immigrants in removal proceedings.[4] Although fighting against deportation presents particularly starkly the predicament faced by immigrants unable to obtain a lawyer, some scholars have also noted the critical role of legal information about other types of immigration matters, including family-based petitions and humanitarian visas.[5] Accurate legal information can shift the course of immigrants' applications and affect their lives and those of their families in a multiplicity of ways.[6] An attorney can help to elicit information about a client's past that can resonate with the law, or can provide advice that clients take to alter their own lives so as to better fit legal categories.[7] In the process, lawyers educate their clients about the legal process and about how the law can work to their benefit.[8]

However, when lawyers are not available, information about the legal system can come from friends, neighbors, or coworkers, in which case it can easily become "misinformation."[9] Just as often, immigrants consult *notarios* and other entrepreneurs who are not qualified to dispense legal advice but who nonetheless make money off of immigrants' desperate need to regularize their status.[10] Sadly, the immigration bar is also plagued by attorneys who provide immigrants with substandard counsel and representation, like the one who Carlos said may have lost his father's case.[11] We found that the youth we interviewed had obtained inaccurate or incomplete information about the law through both informal social networks and more formal sources that purported to provide legal advice.

It would be misleading, however, to characterize the relationship between immigrants and the legal system as a simple story of immigrant victims of a complex and inaccessible system. On the contrary, researchers have documented the ways in which immigrant adults are both shaped by and actively shaping the legal processes they navigate.[12] Similarly, we found the young people in our study were active participants in the legal system, rather than being passively impacted by it. As Joanna Dreby observes in her chapter in this volume, children of immigrants and immigrant children are often noted for taking an expanded role and gaining increased responsibilities in their families because, as they go through the school system, they attain linguistic skills and learn to decipher the cultural codes of their new home more quickly than their parents do.[13] Children learn to deal with the educational and health care systems, often serving as "brokers" between their families and societal institutions.[14] We build on this literature to examine the experiences of youth who must navigate the legal system on their own, often feeling responsible for the future of their families.

The Legal Framework of Family-Based Petitions

Immigration law allows certain family members to petition for visas for their relatives. There is no limit on the number of visas available to immediate relatives of US citizens, which includes spouses, unmarried minor children, and parents of citizens who are at least twenty-one years old.[15] However, "less favored" family relationships—such as between adult citizens and their siblings, or between legal permanent resident parents and children—face numerical limits that result in long backlogs.[16] The concern is particularly severe for Mexicans, who receive the same annual per country cap as immigrants from all other countries, despite the country's deep geographic, historic, and social ties to the United States.[17] For example, an adult Mexican national who wants to petition for his Mexican national sister will face a nearly twenty-year delay because of the limited numbers of visas available to siblings of US citizens.[18]

Youth Navigating Family-Based Petitions

Plans involving family-based petitions figured prominently in ten of the interviews we conducted. Of these, seven of the young people were planning to petition for a family member, and three were planning to be the recipient of a petition themselves. It is not surprising that family-based petitions emerged as a striking theme in our interviews. All the young people we interviewed were exceptionally motivated and forward-thinking. A nonprofit organization that identified potential participants for our research project requires all homeless youth in their program to demonstrate consistent school attendance and passing grades. Thus, we selected for youth who are beating the odds. These students described childhoods filled with trauma and hardship, and yet they were on track to graduate from high school. In this context, the fact that many of the students in our study described a strong sense of responsibility for their parents and/or siblings may help explain their perseverance.

Yet, while inspiring, the students' plans were also concerning. In several cases, they evidenced a striking lack of knowledge about the actual requirements of the law. For example, Carlos, profiled at the outset of this chapter, explained that he chose to stay on his own in the United States in part to get papers for his parents. Yet Carlos is not a US citizen or permanent resident, and therefore he cannot petition for his family. DACA did not permit children to petition for their parents at any age. Even after Carlos turns twenty-one, so long as he does not have some other form of legal status, he will have no means of seeing his family if he remains in the United States, let alone petitioning for their residency.

Another example from our interviews is Santiago, a sixteen-year-old US citizen, who told us he plans to sponsor his mother and sister when he turns eighteen. They all lived together in Tucson until Santiago was six. Then his mother decided to return to Mexico with Santiago, where she later had his younger sister. When Santiago was fourteen, he decided to return to the United States because his private school in Mexico was too expensive. Santiago plans to sponsor both his mother and sister when turns he eighteen, in part so that his mother "won't be alone over there struggling." He described being especially motivated by his plans to sponsor his little sister, who is seven. He explains, "I don't want her to [go] through what I went through, I want her to be someone better." But Santiago's plans do not square with the current law. In fact, as mentioned in the previous section, the law permits US citizens to petition for their parents only after they reach the age of twenty-one. Even more important, there is a huge backlog of sibling petitions. Santiago's sister will face a wait of nearly twenty years before she can receive a visa through a sibling.

Similarly, twelve-year-old Mateo is the only member of his family who is a US citizen and the only one living in the United States. He has two younger brothers who live with their parents in Mexico; none of them has legal status. Mateo told us that, based on information from his father, he plans to petition for his brothers to join him once he turns eighteen. In fact, for the same reason as in Santiago's case, he will have to wait until he is twenty-one, and barring a major change in the law, it will be another twenty years until they can actually come.

Other youth described more complicated provisions of the law that led to confusion or misconceptions. For example, two eighteen-year-old US citizens, Isabel and Natalia, both separately described their plans to petition for their mothers, who were deported when the daughters were younger. Both knew they will have to wait until they are twenty-one, but they were unfamiliar with the law that would make it illegal to try to petition for their mothers to reenter the country before ten years had passed since their deportations.[19] This law, called the "ten-year bar," states that once individuals have lived in the United States without legal status for more than one year, if they leave—whether due to deportation or voluntarily—they cannot reenter, even with an approved visa, for ten years.

In Isabel's case, the ten-year bar could be longer, and potentially permanent, because of her mother's minor criminal history. Isabel explained, "[My mom's] just waiting for me to turn twenty-one, . . . that's when I can start helping her out to try to get her over here legally. But . . . I'm not sure, because she's also got arrested for domestic violence, for hitting her boyfriend, so I don't know if that would not let us get her to come over here legally." Isabel rightly intuited that this situation will require a relatively complex analysis of her mother's criminal history. The law regarding which crimes of domestic violence create a bar to family-based petitions is complex, and even if a bar exists, there may be a waiver available in certain circumstances that would require additional analysis of the equities of the case.[20] It would be extremely difficult for Isabel to successfully navigate the process to petition for her mother without advice and counseling from an experienced immigration attorney.

In addition to these plans by young people to sponsor their relatives, we spoke with students who were making decisions and plans based on being potential beneficiaries of family-based petitions. For example, eighteen-year-old Olivia came to the United States at age fourteen to move in with her older sister after her mother in Mexico started mistreating her. She explained that she and her US citizen boyfriend are talking about getting married, "because he is from here, and since [for] this Obama thing you need five years and I have four, so the best would be, if God favors it, that I get married to him and he fixes my status. Then I can work and be here."[21] Olivia did not appear to be familiar with the fact that petitioning for a spouse is complicated when the beneficiary is already residing in the country without lawful immigration status. In these instances, the beneficiary can immediately obtain lawful permanent residency only in limited circumstances. In most cases, the beneficiary must leave the country and then face the ten-year bar to reentry. Again, there are waivers available in certain circumstances, but it would involve a complex analysis of Olivia's immigration history to determine if she is eligible for such a waiver.

The Legal Framework of DACA

Immigrant youth like Carlos, whose profile opened the chapter, are often referred to as "Dreamers," young undocumented people whose parents brought them to this country when they were young and who have received all or most of their education in the United States.[22] This population has been one of the key foci of debate over immigration policy in recent years. Although Congress repeatedly has been unable to pass legislation to address their plight, in 2012 President Obama created DACA, which provided limited temporary relief from deportation for undocumented immigrant youth with the opportunity to renew in two-year increments while the program remained in effect.[23] The announcement that DACA would end left recipients in an extreme state of uncertainty about their legal futures.[24] The unsettled conditions surrounding possible passage of a Dream Act only amplify this population's vulnerability.

DACA eligibility was based on age, length of residence in the United States, educational background, and criminal history.[25] Of these eligibility requirements, age and educational background were straightforward. Length of residence could involve somewhat complicated legal determinations about whether certain brief departures over the years were sufficiently frequent or lengthy to disrupt the requirement of "continuous presence." The criminal history bars were the most complex, involving legal determinations about which crimes qualify as "significant" and providing certain waivers upon a showing of "exceptional circumstances."[26]

The agency charged with implementing the DACA program, US Citizenship and Immigration Services, strove to create a transparent and relatively simple application process. It issued pro se materials and created a user-friendly website. After the announcement of the program, the nonprofit community mobilized in impressive ways to ensure that there were numerous opportunities for students and families to access legal assistance in order to apply for DACA.[27]

Youth Navigating DACA

Of the thirteen youth in our study who did not have lawful status, only three successfully applied for DACA. This is significantly lower than the overall application rate. Researchers estimate based on government data that 63 percent of immediately eligible DACA youth had applied for the program as of March 2016.[28] Studies have documented even higher application rates in Arizona, where this study was conducted, and among Mexican-origin youth, who constituted our study pool.[29]

What, then, accounts for the fact that many of the youth in our study did not successfully navigate DACA's legal process? By definition, these young people met the educational requirements for DACA, since they were all enrolled in school. However, several other factors appear to have played a role in participants' delay or failure to apply. One factor was the $465 fee that must accompany the application. Other research on DACA's implementation and impact has also documented this as one consistent reason some eligible immigrants do not apply.[30] The population of young people we interviewed may have faced even more serious financial constraints than the general immigrant population, given their disrupted circumstances and isolated living arrangements. As a result, the application fee was particularly burdensome for them, and several mentioned it as a reason they had not applied or had been unable to do so until recently.

Julieta, an undocumented seventeen-year-old, exemplifies the extreme impoverishment of this population. Currently living with a friend, Julieta was one of the few students interviewed whose parents both reside in the United States. They are no longer living as an intact family because Julieta recently decided to move out due to severe financial stress. She is one of seven siblings, all born in a very small town in the Mexican countryside. With the exception of her oldest sister, Julieta's family moved to Tucson when she was four years old. Her father fixes washing machines and resells them; her mother has heart problems and is "always sick." Julieta has worked at the Tucson swap meet since she was thirteen. It's the one place she can work because "they don't ask for Social Security." When interviewed, she explained that she had not applied for DACA because "we don't have the money . . . it's like $400 and something." Her older sister had put together funds to apply for DACA, and they planned to then save up money for Julieta's application.

In addition to the fee, another recurring obstacle for then DACA-eligible youth we interviewed was the lack of access to legal assistance. This may be surprising in light of the impressive mobilization of community organizations throughout the country after DACA was created, groups that worked arduously to ensure that the eligible population had access to needed resources to apply for the program.[31] The youth we interviewed highlight the ways in which immigrant youth with particularly complex circumstances can fall through the cracks of these broad-based efforts.

Several youth noted that their tumultuous life histories had made it difficult to pull together the documents required for the application. These students might have submitted an application if they had been able to receive more robust support and guidance with the process than the volunteer workshops generally available to DACA-eligible youth. For example, Maria, who has lived here since she was a baby and has no criminal record, would have seemed a poster child for the DACA program. However, three years into the program, she had not applied because she did not have all the papers to show where her family lived over the years. A volunteer who was helping other students apply told her that her case was complicated and she should hire a lawyer to help her. Unable to afford this option, Maria was ultimately unable to submit an application.

As another example, one of our interviewees, Sara, went to an event to learn about DACA, and someone shared potentially incorrect information: "I think she was a lawyer, I don't know what she was, but she told me I couldn't do it because of the two times that I went out [of the country]." In fact, Sara's departures might have qualified as "brief, casual and innocent" and would not have rendered her ineligible, particularly in light of the fact that the departures occurred in the context of extremely challenging life circumstances. But Sara lacked the resources or connections to obtain clear legal advice about her prospects.[32]

Similarly, a twenty-one-year-old man, Marco, did not apply because he had thousands of dollars in unpaid restitution fees due to a graffiti-related conviction when he was nineteen or twenty. The only outright bars to DACA based on criminal history were convictions for felonies, significant misdemeanors, or three or more nonsignificant misdemeanors. However, the entire program was discretionary, and any kind of conviction could have led to a denial based on the adjudicator's discretion. In Marco's case, his conviction may not have qualified as a felony or significant misdemeanor. But a volunteer attorney advised him to pay off the fees before applying, likely thinking this would increase his chances of receiving a discretionary grant. Because the fees were prohibitively high, Marco had not applied for DACA and had no immediate plans to do so at the time we interviewed him. DACA did provide for a waiver of criminal bars upon a showing of "exceptional circumstances" that would have suited Marco's situation well. However, without a lawyer, Marco was ill-equipped to make this case for himself in his application.

Conclusion

The ways the US immigration legal system is failing the young people in our study are a less brazen failure than the charade of young children representing themselves in an adversarial immigration court hearing. Yet the consequences of these quiet failures could be just as severe. Families like Carlos's may make decisions that result in years of separation that might have been avoided. Teenagers like Olivia may marry prematurely. Siblings like many profiled in the foregoing pages may face the shock of learning that decades rather than days must pass before they can live together. High school graduates like Marco and Sara may be confined to the low-wage underground economy whereas they might have had far more opportunities had they received DACA.

Without a doubt, these failures are not simply the result of a dearth of legal advice and services. The fact that these young people face such dire choices in the first place is the product of harsh immigration laws, which often separate families rather than promote their unity. The lonely circumstances of these thirty-seven young people put into stark relief the consequences of the substantive laws and policies that impacted them. The scope of this problem is sure to grow in magnitude as immigration enforcement grows ever more pervasive and aggressive under the policies set in place by the Trump administration.

In this context, the lack of legal services and accurate legal information available to youth in immigrant families is one dimension of the harsh enforcement landscape worthy of attention. With or without comprehensive immigration reform, immigration law is bound to be complex and confounding for immigrant families to navigate for years to come. This is perhaps particularly the case for families with ties to Mexico, who often have long transnational histories that exacerbate the complexity. Given this reality, it is essential that immigrant families have the tools necessary to make use of the laws intended to keep them together and to give young people opportunities to flourish.

We believe our findings speak to the urgent need for schools, social service agencies, legal aid offices, and community-based organizations to create more opportunities for youth in immigrant families—whether US citizens or undocumented immigrants themselves—to receive low-cost, high-quality legal advice and counseling. This may acquire a greater level of urgency in the context of new enforcement policies. Such an effort will require both financial backing and institutional commitments to recognizing and addressing the legal needs of this population. Given the demographic realities of our nation's population, with estimates that nearly half of all undocumented immigrants, or 4.7 million people, are parents of minor children,[33] we have no doubt that there are many young people, like the thirty-seven we interviewed, struggling to navigate a legal process with potentially life-changing consequences for themselves and their families. They should not be forced to do so on their own.

6

Immigration Courts

SUSAN J. TERRIO

In 2014, an unprecedented number of unaccompanied children and youth from Central America and Mexico fleeing violence in their home country—68,500 in all—were apprehended at the US-Mexico border. In contrast to earlier waves of migrants who tried to cross the border undetected, many of these young people ran to, not away from, immigration authorities in the hope of finding protection in the United States. After their apprehension, those who were deemed "unaccompanied"— without lawful status, under eighteen years of age, and lacking a parent or guardian to provide care—were forced *into* and moved *through* an immigration court and juvenile detention system marked by structural dysfunction, conflicting mandates, and wildly different outcomes. Quickly overwhelmed by what the Obama administration called an "urgent humanitarian crisis," federal agencies were directed to reverse the tide of desperate migrants and did so by implementing enhanced deterrence and enforcement policies.[1]

A central component in both the Obama administration's and the Trump administration's attempts to curb the influx of unauthorized migrants has involved regulations governing the adjudication of juvenile cases in federal immigration courts. In 2014, the government made the cases of "unaccompanied children" a top priority for fast-track review by immigration judges. Soon after the 2017 inauguration, the Trump administration began to implement policies that are based on a virulently nativist vision of the nation under serious threat from all immigration—both authorized and unauthorized. The Executive Office for Immigration Review (EOIR), the federal agency operating the immigration courts, issued a new directive for fast-track cases, expanding this category to include all detained individuals and targeting, in particular, unaccompanied children in federal custody who had no US sponsor to whom they could be released.[2] At the same time, those who are released to family sponsors are being systematically recategorized in initial immigration court hearings as "accompanied" and potentially stripped of the legal protections previously afforded to "unaccompanied" children. The result is a catch-22 system designed to contain and control the movement of unauthorized migrant children into the United States. It compromises fair hearings, curbs already limited due process protections, and prioritizes enforcement goals as children are propelled *through* the immigration court system at an accelerated pace.

Since 2014, immigration court policies and practices reveal both continuity and change. In interviews conducted from 2009 through 2016, overburdened judges described courtrooms that were adversely affected by staff shortages, inadequate resources, massive backlogs, heavy caseloads, and antiquated recording devices. They depicted the accumulated stress and ethical dilemmas that have resulted from the fast-tracking of juvenile cases. They shared views on the power imbalances that favor the government and commented specifically on the challenges of adjudicating the cases of unrepresented juveniles and the limitations imposed by US immigration law. The debates over the prosecution of unauthorized children raise questions that are central to American democracy: the constitutional right to due process and equal protection regardless of legal status; the state's responsibility for the welfare of the child; and the right to appear before independent, impartial adjudicators in proceedings that are fair, accessible, efficient and free from unreasonable delays.

A Case in Point

On November 18, 2015, a fourteen-year-old Salvadoran named Jessica appeared on a PBS national broadcast to describe her flight the year before from her hometown of Zacatecoluca. With a population of only 75,000, the town was rife with gang violence, and the number of weekly homicides reached twenty-nine.[3] When her uncle, a local police officer, refused to hand over guns to members of a drug gang terrorizing residents, they began to threaten Jessica, her two sisters, and her young aunt. After gang members physically attacked them, they fled the country. Jessica hoped to rejoin her parents, who had left her with relatives a decade earlier to find work in California. After surviving a perilous journey through Mexico, Jessica, her sisters, and their aunt crossed the southern border and were immediately apprehended by US immigration authorities. Jessica was separated from her female relatives, designated an "unaccompanied alien child," and detained in a closed federal facility for juveniles in Texas. When she learned that the government had begun deportation proceedings against her in an American immigration court, she was extremely frightened. As she recalled: "I didn't know what I would do. What if they ask me something? How would I respond? I felt so scared to go in front of a judge."

When Jessica fled her home country in early 2014, she did not realize that she was part of what media would call a "surge" of unaccompanied children and youth to the United States. Their apprehension by US immigration authorities ensnared them within two parallel but separate federal systems: mandatory detention in facilities for juveniles managed by the Office of Refugee Resettlement (ORR), within the Department of Health and Human Services, and placement in deportation proceedings in immigration courts. Like Jessica, the vast majority of those in in federal custody—88 percent—come from Guatemala, Honduras, and El Salvador to escape domestic abuse, political violence, criminal gangs, and drug cartels.[4] Mexican children and youth are underrepresented in immigration custody because 95 percent are returned to Mexico within seventy-two hours.[5] Traveling though Mexico, many Central American migrants faced an intensely violent economic enterprise that generates enormous profits from kidnapping, human smuggling, drug trafficking, extortion, and killings.[6] Studies based on interviews with unauthorized child migrants who fled to the United States after 2011 concluded that a majority of them were forcibly displaced from their home countries and had potentially valid claims to asylum or other humanitarian protections.[7]

Jessica spent a month in federal custody before being released to her grandmother in Southern California and reestablishing contact with her father. She became one of 27,000 unaccompanied minors who were released to relatives in the United States in 2014, while their deportation cases were pending in immigration court. Her fears were justified because unauthorized minors do not have the right to government-appointed counsel or child advocates. Because most of them are indigent, they must find pro bono attorneys to take their cases (see Young and McKenna, this volume). Working from a list of pro bono lawyers provided by ORR, Jessica and her father tried and failed for months to secure legal representation. All the pro bono lawyers they contacted were too busy to help, and the fees charged by private attorneys were prohibitive.

During the same period that Jessica was struggling to find a pro bono attorney, the issue of the due process rights of unauthorized children in deportation proceedings came to public attention. Legal service organizations, NGO advocates, and professional groups challenged US government policies on two fronts: the failure to provide government-funded attorneys for this population and the use of strong-arm tactics to ensure their rapid removal from the United States. To manage the glut of new cases swamping the immigration courts, the Executive Office for Immigration Review instituted accelerated hearings of juvenile cases.[8] In fast-track hearings, or "rocket dockets," most juvenile respondents faced government prosecutors without attorneys in courtroom proceedings that were chaotic, overcrowded, and rushed. Young migrants paid a heavy price for the lack of legal representation. Between August 2014 and August 2015, immigration judges issued nearly 2,800 deportation orders for unrepresented children after only a single hearing. In at least 40 percent of these cases, the defendant was sixteen or younger.[9]

In this charged context, Ahilan Arulanantham, deputy legal director at the American Civil Liberties Union of Southern California, agreed to take Jessica's case. In 2014, his organization and other groups challenged the government's failure to provide legal representation to minors.[10] Jessica was one of eight unauthorized Central American migrants, aged ten through seventeen, who became plaintiffs in the lawsuit. The suit charged that immigration court hearings are fundamentally unfair because foreign children who have "no knowledge of English or the law" must appear without attorneys in complex, adversarial proceedings where they are forced to represent themselves while facing government prosecutors who are tasked with their removal.[11] Competent legal counsel plays a determinative role in the outcome of deportation hearings (see Young and McKenna, this volume).[12]

In April 2015, a federal court granted class action status to the lawsuit and allowed it to go forward. In October 2015, Jack Weil, a chief assistant immigration judge who oversees the adjudications of vulnerable populations in deportation proceedings, testified as an expert government witness in the lawsuit. During questioning by attorney Ahilan Arulanantham, Judge Weil declared that legal representation was unnecessary for child respondents, claiming, "I've taught immigration law literally to three-year-olds and four-year-olds. It takes a lot of time. It takes a lot of patience. They get it. It's not the most efficient, but it can be done."[13]

A New "Surge"

Judge Weil's sworn testimony unleashed a storm of controversy when it became the focus of articles in the *Washington Post* and the *New York Times*.[14] The controversy erupted in the context of a new "surge" of unaccompanied, unauthorized minors to the United States.

The agencies responsible for border security and immigration violations responded to the new arrivals by implementing enforcement policies intended to deter them from entering or remaining in the United States: by outsourcing militarized interdiction efforts to Mexico and by accelerating the deportation of "recent border entrants."[15] On January 23, 2016, Secretary Jeh Johnson of the US Department of Homeland Security launched Operation Border Guardian, which targeted children who entered the United States without authorization, were over eighteen, and have been ordered deported.[16] As a result, 336 individuals under the age of twenty-one, many of whom had no legal representation, were apprehended during raids conducted at home, at bus stops, or on school grounds and were detained pending their deportation. They risked the same fate as the 83 deportees to Central America who were murdered between January 2014 and October 2015.[17]

US Immigration Law

Unauthorized minors face enormous obstacles in obtaining legal relief under US immigration law. Although children can independently seek legal relief, they are held to the same substantive standards, evidentiary requirements, and burden of proof standard as adults. The status of children as individual bearers of rights is discounted, their right to asylum is compromised, and their citizenship as a basis for family residency is denied.[18] In fact, the one form of relief available specifically for children,

Special Immigrant Juvenile Status, applies only to children who must become wards of a US family or circuit court because of abuse, abandonment, or neglect in the home country.[19]

Immigration law differs from domestic and international approaches to underaged children in juvenile or family court proceedings. Those approaches mandate protective measures by evaluating mitigating circumstances, demanding less accountability for offending, and tempering punishment with rehabilitative measures. In contrast, immigration law makes no allowance for developmental immaturity, cultural incapacity, or the psychological trauma of minors. The only accommodation that exists for minors in deportation hearings is a set of voluntary guidelines that call for a child-friendly atmosphere in the courtroom (see Marks, this volume).[20]

A Rigged System?

The recourse to accelerated deportation hearings for unaccompanied children casts a harsh spotlight on the arcane rules and organizational structure of the federal immigration courts, as well as on the complexity of US immigration law. Recently, senior judges described that body of law as an "ever changing labyrinth of idiosyncratic terminology and seemingly conflicting provisions."[21] In 2014, as the crisis was building, Dana Leigh Marks (this volume) and Denise Noonan Slavin, respectively, president and vice president of the immigration judges' union, denounced the fast-track proceedings on substantive grounds. Both judges emphasized that "the court's role should be as neutral arbitrators" separate from the enforcement priorities of the US Department of Homeland Security.[22] The immigration courts are part of the executive branch and are located within the Department of Justice, an agency whose primary mission is law enforcement. Congress repeatedly increases resources for additional government prosecutors without augmenting funding for immigration judges.

Housed within the US Department of Homeland Security since 2003, the immigration court structure creates a basic conflict of interest. Immigration judges are expected to exercise independent judgment despite the fact that, like government prosecutors, they are employees of the Department of Justice and must rule on cases brought by that department.[23] Government prosecutors have virtually unfettered discretion to initiate removal proceedings, to make release determinations, and to control the information central to the case. However, they are protected from sanctions imposed by immigration judges for unprofessional conduct. These power imbalances mean that government prosecutors largely establish the facts of the case in court.

Immigration Judges Speak Out

To understand immigration courts from the perspective of judges, I observed more than 120 hours of immigration court proceedings and interviewed thirty-nine sitting and retired judges who heard juvenile cases both before and since 2014. I was interested in understanding their views on the court's role as an impartial arbitrator in ensuring both due process and a fair hearing. Did they see their role as compromised by a lack of judicial autonomy and by the enforcement mandates of the government? How did they view the options for legal relief under US immigration law? What professional and procedural challenges did they face in managing the increasing number of children who appeared in juvenile dockets without attorneys? Did the crisis exacerbate what they understood were long-standing problems within the immigration court system?

"You Can't Do Justice without Reading the Law"

When I asked judges about the challenges of hearing juvenile cases in a system where the best interest of the child had no legal standing, a number of judges described their twin roles as adjudicators: a pedagogical role intended to make the legal process more transparent and an investigative function required to establish the facts within the confines of the law. One judge explained the legal procedures even when hearing the cases of unrepresented children who had been charged with offenses that automatically barred them from obtaining legal relief:

> In my courtroom the kids have a voice, they have that right. I am quick to explain the law to them. But my job is to determine removability. We have an obligation to get at the truth. But we are not a criminal court. These are civil proceedings. My job is to focus on the time, manner, and the place of

entry for removal purposes. The information about that has to be elicited. We need to ask the necessary questions. What comes out on the record, comes out. We are starting with the record. If it's the truth, it has to come out. . . . I say that we can use that information within the confines of the law and our authority.[24]

Accepting that "immigration law was not designed for kids," many judges emphasized the importance of upholding the law until or if Congress amends the existing statutes. One adjudicator explained: "The best interests of the child cannot override the law. As an immigration judge, I owe service to young people, but I cannot be their benefactor or advocate."[25] Judge John Gossart, a retired judge who handled the first juvenile docket in Baltimore, concurred:

> I always endeavored to do what was in the kid's best interest consistent with the law. Sometimes the law does not produce the result you want. I am under oath to follow it. For example, a young person is brought in with the mom and dad and the kid is out of status. The parents say, "Please don't deport my child." Now the child is too old to qualify for legal relief in the US and has no one back home. Unless DHS decides to do nothing, the child has to leave. It is very difficult.[26]

Many judges sought to minimize the lack of substantive rights under the law by creating a child-friendly courtroom atmosphere. They described the importance of avoiding legalese, actively listening for indicators of abuse or trauma, putting children at ease—in short, seeing the children first as developing and full human beings, not "aliens." Some judges did this by removing their black robes or providing toys to lessen the children's fears. A majority noted how critical it is not to rush juvenile proceedings, particularly in the detained docket. As one judge said, "There is no trust between judges and kids in detention. We can't just start asking questions in the first hearing and expect them to be honest!"[27]

They Need Attorneys

Many judges saw the voluntary guidelines governing courtroom procedure as a poor substitute for granting the child substantive rights, particularly government-appointed counsel. All of those I interviewed supported legal representation for juveniles. One retired judge insisted: "If we are not to perpetuate injustice, we need appointed counsel for respondents. The pro bono system is hit or miss. Kids should all have attorneys and a child advocate."[28] Some judges insisted that no child's case should go forward in an adversarial proceeding without an attorney and that those under fourteen should be excused completely from appearances in an adversarial proceeding.[29] Aside from the legal ethics, many judges insisted that funding legal representation would make court proceedings more humane, efficient, and cost-effective.

One Size Fits All?

Many judges questioned what difference removing the black robe and using plain language would make in court given the lack of attorneys and the inflexible rules that disqualify most vulnerable petitioners. They described their limited discretion in asylum hearings, noting that there is not one word in the statutes on fear of persecution for juveniles. A retired judge, Bruce Solow, addressed gang-based asylum claims: "Look, I gave them every benefit that the law allows. The wrinkle is that we are dealing with Central America countries with corrupt political systems, an explosion of narcotrafficking, gangs, and macho civilizations where women matter less than chattel. The problem is that the laws haven't caught up. The claim of membership in a social group—the only ground that could apply to kids threatened by gangs—doesn't work, the law has said no."[30]

And, Judge Paul Schmidt, who retired after thirty-three years of practice, argues: "There is little understanding or sympathy for the child asylee, and the rulings on gang persecution are skewed. The standard requires evidence that members of a social group share an immutable trait and have social visibility. But if a kid opposes gang recruitment, it becomes a characteristic that is fundamental to his identity and is particularized. He will be known and recognized in the community as a result."[31] Judges felt both frustrated and stymied by the limitations imposed by punitive immigration laws that foreclosed second chances or rehabilitative interventions when young people appeared in juvenile or criminal court proceedings before their transfer to the immigration court system. One judge, a self-described conservative who granted very few asylum cases, spoke of a case that "broke her heart." It involved an eleven-year-old boy who had fled violence in his native Haiti and come to the United States. Against all odds, he overcame parental abandonment and abuse in a group home in the United States to become a scholar-athlete in college. He happened to be with his older brother, a drug dealer, during a police bust, and both were convicted of selling illegal substances. Although he had no prior record and was a stellar student, his conviction for an aggravated felony was a deportable offense. "He had a good immigration attorney," the judge recalled, "but there was nothing I could do."

In the Midst of the Surge

Judge Carole King, now retired, presided over a nondetained juvenile docket in 2014 and described the experience:

> In the first wave, we had twenty-five unaccompanied kids in each hearing. It was mayhem in the courtroom. When we began to hear their stories, there were no questions about credibility. It can be easy to hide behind the usual rationales, that 50 percent of the stories told are false. But I set that aside with the kids. We believed them. There was no exaggeration, no made-up stories. The country conditions were so powerful. For eons, the primary self-image of the judiciary is impartiality and neutrality. We couldn't obviously set them aside emotionally.

Once again the issues revolved around the limits imposed by the law:

> A lot of cases didn't fit into available forms of relief. In almost all of the asylum petitions I saw, the fear derived from crime. Crime can be a form of persecution, but not all crime is persecution. It has to do with the motivation of persecutors. The difference was a respondent with an attorney who provided evidence versus one who didn't. The response in my court was exemplary. The young UACs [unaccompanied alien children] all went to the asylum office [in an affirmative proceeding]. I know that in some areas of the country the grant rates for asylum were down, but in this immigration court 98 percent of the asylum petitions heard in the full court [in 2014] were granted.

By contrast, in a different immigration court, Judge Eliza Klein, said her disillusionment with the fast-track procedures was one of the factors that led her to retire:

> The major problem is the administration's location in the Department of Justice, the executive branch. The DHS [prosecutors] file the charging documents, and the agency rarely kicks back cases because of legal insufficiency. They move all cases forward. The result in 2014 was the creation of rocket dockets, where we were swamped with pro se kids and a huge volume of cases. We were ordered to resolve those cases quickly, and they didn't want continuances. The kids did not have time to find attorneys or prepare a viable case. With this onslaught of cases, immigration judges felt like whiplash victims. There was inherent immorality in the creation of accelerated proceedings.

Many judges disagreed with the government's treatment of Central American and Mexican migrants since 2014. What should have been the response? Some immigration judges like V. Stuart Crouch in Charlotte, North Carolina, did not hesitate to issue in absentia deportation orders and viewed asylum and other forms of relief as a narrow opportunity to grant sparingly.[32] In contrast, Judge Paul Schmidt was outraged by the government response. He told me:

> By granting recent [child] arrivals due process hearings on the regular (nonexpedited) immigration court dockets, releasing them to qualified individuals or groups in the community, and working with NGOs and other pro bono groups to provide representation, the government could have achieved about a 95 percent "appearance rate" in court while complying with due process and likely avoiding costly and unnecessary litigation and massive detention costs. It also would have been the "right thing" to do.[33]

Conclusion

By 2017, the backlog of cases involving unaccompanied alien children reached an all-time high of 88,069, and there were still 16,693 children's cases that had been opened during the 2014 fiscal year that awaited decisions.[34] Of the nearly 100,000 children and families who appeared in court between 2014 and 2017, judges issued rulings in 35,500 cases, the majority—70 percent—ending with deportation orders in absentia. In absentia rulings have increased dramatically because of the chaotic reception migrant youth received and the dearth of pro bono attorneys to make them aware of their legal obligations. Many did not understand the process for pursuing asylum claims or other forms of relief. Others stayed away from court hearings or Immigration and Customs Enforcement (ICE) check-ins at federal buildings, fearing that they could be deported directly from courthouses,[35] a fear actualized under the Trump administration. Following Attorney General Jeff Sessions's directive to increase the enforcement of US immigration laws, ICE has moved aggressively to arrest undocumented persons in courthouses.[36]

A January 9, 2017, *Washington Post* editorial described the immigrant court system "as a diorama of dysfunction" and courtrooms as places of "Dickensian impenetrability operating under comically antiquated conditions."[37] The editorial declared due process and fair hearings "a pipe dream" when it came to the tens of thousands of children appearing annually before immigration judges.[38] Given the Ninth Circuit Court's 2016 rejection of the advocates' bid for legal representation for all unaccompanied minors in removal proceedings,[39] the reality is that a large percentage of young migrants will continue to face government prosecutors without attorneys.

Legal systems that respect the rule of law require accountability by government officials; statutes that protect basic rights; legal processes that are accessible, fair, and efficient; and judicial proceedings handled by independent adjudicators.[40] As unauthorized children move into and through the immigration system, they encounter legal frameworks that systematically disadvantage them and enhanced enforcement regimes that put them in an expanding category of people who are seen not only as lacking status but as "illegals." Under the Obama and Trump administrations the government response to a humanitarian crisis involving migrants has been punitive. The outcomes in removal proceedings suggest that, despite the best intentions of some adjudicators, immigration courts do more to undermine the rule of law than to uphold it.

REFLECTIONS

Representing Unaccompanied Children

WENDY YOUNG AND MEGAN MCKENNA

It was kind of like my dream was becoming true and I finally had a lawyer because I always dreamed of that.
   —Jeannette, seventeen years old[1]

The idea that anyone can do this without a lawyer is absolute nonsense. I found it very confusing even though I'm a lawyer, so it's inconceivable to me that a nonlawyer—especially a child—could navigate their way through this process alone.
   —Charles F. Rysavy, partner, K&L Gates LLC, KIND
      pro bono attorney

The lack of due process for unaccompanied children has been a long-standing protection gap in the United States' treatment of these uniquely vulnerable children. They face enormous challenges in gaining fair access to US protection and immigration relief available to them under US law. The system was created for adults, and children are forced to move through it like adults despite their unique needs and challenges. It does not ensure that unaccompanied children are provided attorneys in their deportation proceedings, regardless of their age. Without an attorney, a child must navigate the complex US immigration system and counter a US government attorney who is arguing for the child's deportation. It is virtually impossible for children to represent themselves in immigration court.[2] As a result, a child without an attorney does not have meaningful access to the US immigration system or the protection it offers. These children are within the immigration system but outside of it in terms of ensured due process.

The numbers are clear: an attorney makes an enormous difference in a child's ability to access US protection. Consider the experiences of Nellie, a seventeen-year-old who was matched with an attorney in California by our organization, KIND-Kids in Need of Defense. As Nellie described: "I didn't know how I was going to tell my story to the judge. I didn't know how to say it. I have a hard time telling it. But, I am here today because I finally was able to tell my story to the judge. . . . I was able to explain to the judge why I was so afraid to go back to my home country. . . . My wonderful lawyers . . . worked very, very hard for me. I will always be thankful to them and keep them close in my heart." According to Syracuse University's TRAC Immigration database, 73 percent of unaccompanied children's cases are successful if the child has an attorney, while children without attorneys have a 15 percent success rate.[3] In addition, children with attorneys are more likely to appear in immigration court. In 2015, children who were represented by counsel had an appearance rate of more than 94 percent.[4]

The Homeland Security Act of 2002 charged the Office of Refugee Resettlement (ORR) within the US Department of Health and Human Services (HHS) with the custody, care, and placement of unaccompanied children,[5] as well as facilitating access to counsel.[6] Over the years, HHS has provided modest funding for the promotion of legal services for unaccompanied children out of its overall funding for shelter care and processing children for release to sponsors. Yet, from 2005 through 2011, when the number of unaccompanied children coming to the United States averaged 7,000 to 8,000 a year,[7] about half did not have attorneys in their immigration proceedings.[8] The result was that thousands of children went through removal proceedings each year without legal representation, risking removal orders and returning to situations in which they faced serious harm or even death.

Legal services provided to unaccompanied children and youth in ORR custody have evolved over time and currently include Know Your Rights (KYR) presentations, screenings to determine eligibility for immigration relief, and free assistance in securing direct legal representation by NGOs or with pro bono attorneys.[9] By and large, the only children and youth who have obtained legal representation are those detained throughout their immigration proceedings as most federal funding has been directed toward those in ORR custody.[10] The balance of funding started to change after 2012 when large numbers of unaccompanied children began arriving in the United States. The system of legal assistance was not designed to deal with the nearly 14,000 children who were referred to ORR in 2012, about double the previous year; most were from Honduras, El Salvador, and Guatemala and were fleeing increasing gang and narcotrafficker violence. In 2013, the number rose again, to 25,000. The number peaked in 2014, when about 68,500 children came alone.[11]

Thousands of children arrived at the border in the spring of 2014, many turning themselves in to immigration authorities after fleeing violence in their home countries. As one high school student from Maryland explained:

> Do you know what it is to live with the fear of leaving home and not knowing if you are coming back alive? You know what it is like to travel by yourself, without your parents or any friend, with the knowledge that you can die at any time? Well, I do because I had to make a trip like that to come to America. However, I am glad to be in this country because I am safe from gangs and poverty.

The high numbers of migrant children who arrived in 2014 profoundly impacted the ability of unaccompanied children to access representation. The legal services program was overwhelmed and, as a result, many children fell through the cracks. According to TRAC Immigration, only 32 percent of unaccompanied children in deportation proceedings as of October 31, 2014, had an attorney.[12]

Factors Affecting Rates of Legal Representation

The Flores Settlement Agreement (1997),[13] the Homeland Security Act of 2002,[14] and the Trafficking Victims Protection Reauthorization Act of 2008[15] have greatly improved the due process protections and standards of care and release for unaccompanied children in ORR custody.[16] However, the system established in 2002 through the Homeland Security Act was by no means perfect. Some children in custody faced overly long stays that led some to decide to return home, even if they had a strong case, because they could not tolerate detention. ORR facilities often had punitive rules and at times overzealous discipline that made life difficult for some children.[17] Lists of legal assistance organizations posted in federal facilities were often out of date and incomplete, leaving many detained children with little or no way to find an attorney.

From 2005 to 2012, approximately 65 percent of unaccompanied children were released from ORR custody to a sponsor in an average of seventy-five days.[18] This provided ample time for a child to receive a KYR training, legal screening, and a referral to an attorney or information about where to find one. However, when the number of children arriving alone increased significantly in 2014, ORR changed its screening of sponsors to speed up release and to free up bed space for the many thousands backed up at the border and being held for days and weeks by US Customs and Border Protection in inappropriate facilities that put their safety and welfare at risk. ORR released some children within days of their transfer to ORR custody, with the majority being released in less than ten days.

The accelerated release of these children resulted in a number of concerning consequences. One was that a number of children—it is not known how many—did not receive KYR presentations, were not screened for immigration relief, and were not referred for legal representation or provided information on where to get legal assistance. Therefore, they did not know their rights and responsibilities within the US immigration system or whether they were potentially eligible for US protection. They were not referred to an NGO for legal assistance or given a list of legal service providers. Without this assistance, it would be very difficult for these children to know what to do or how to find an attorney.

Compounding the crisis in legal representation, in July 2014, the Department of Justice (DOJ) created so-called rocket dockets at the immigration courts to expedite the removal proceedings of recent arrivals, namely, the thousands of unaccompanied children and families who had crossed into the United States.[19] These dockets prioritized the removal proceedings of unaccompanied children and adults with children over other cases and directed that unaccompanied children be scheduled for their first master calendar hearing within twenty-one days after their referral to the immigration court (see Marks, this volume).[20]

The prioritization of children's cases and the fast-track hearings meant that children had even less time to find an attorney. Securing legal representation was already enormously difficult with the unprecedented numbers of unaccompanied children placed in immigration proceedings, given the lack of pro bono or volunteer attorneys to represent them (see Terrio, this volume). In some instances, children and their families, desperate to have an attorney in time for their master calendar hearing, unwittingly hired *notarios*,[21] or unlicensed legal representatives, so children would have someone by their side during their hearings. Another consequence of the expedited court dates was that a number of children did not receive notices of their master calendar hearings due to clerical errors; for example, at times notices were sent to incorrect addresses. A number of children did not appear in court because they had not received notification of the hearing date; as a result, thousands of children were ordered removed in absentia.[22]

Expedited cases posed another challenge to fair adjudication. Most of the unaccompanied children fled very difficult situations (see Guevara Martínez, this volume). They needed time to develop a relationship with their attorney and to build trust before they would share—frequently for the first time—often deeply traumatic experiences. At the same time, many immigration judges were decreasing the time they allowed for continuances, which postpone any action until a later court date. Continuances are often used by judges in cases of unaccompanied children without attorneys to allow them more time to find legal representation (see Marks, this volume). Researchers at Stanford University found a significant drop in the median time allowed for continuances for unaccompanied children and families, from ninety-four days in 2013 to seventy-eight days between August 1, 2014, and January 1, 2015.[23] The additional time can have an important impact on a child's ability to find representation and prepare a thorough case.[24]

On February 8, 2016, the federal agency that operates the immigration courts, the Executive Office for Immigration Review (EOIR), relaxed the time limitations for the initial hearing for unaccompanied children.[25] A year later, on January 31, 2017, the Justice Department issued an order outlining new docketing priorities for immigration courts. Currently, priority hearings target all those in immigration detention but, significantly, exclude unaccompanied children who are released to identified sponsors and recent border crossers who were initially detained but then subsequently released from custody.[26] The new priority hearings include unaccompanied children in ORR custody who are without an identified sponsor.

The shift away from accelerated hearings for all unaccompanied children will relieve a great deal of pressure on them to find attorneys and prepare their cases in very limited periods of time. However, the prioritization of unaccompanied children in ORR custody without sponsors could be problematic for some children, even as the government says that they are receiving representation.

US Government Responses

The Obama administration made limited efforts to increase the resources available through HHS and DOJ to support direct representation through funding for permanent attorneys. It also launched time-limited attorney fellowship programs and increased support for the facilitation of private pro bono counsel for unaccompanied children in their immigration proceedings. While increased support for the representation of unaccompanied children was desperately needed, the programs and funding were relatively small and not on the scale required to ensure that the majority of unaccompanied children had attorneys in their proceedings.

Congress directed EOIR "to better serve vulnerable populations such as children [and to] improve court efficiency through pilot efforts aimed at improving legal representation."[27] However, the program relies on the direct representation model exclusively and prohibits the use of government funds through the private sector. Private sector pro bono representation is an effective and efficient way to use limited government resources to represent large numbers of children and could have leveraged these resources to reach more children. Providing legal counsel saves resources by lessening the need for continuances and leads to higher appearance rates in court. In 2014, EOIR responded to the crisis in legal representation with new pilot programs to fund direct legal representation and related services, notably at the Baltimore immigration court. Although these programs are a step in the right direction, they all have significant limitations and should in no way be seen as a replacement for full legal protection within the United States or at the nation's borders.

As the number of unaccompanied children coming to the United States has increased, so has the funding for legal services through the US Department of Health and Human Services, which operates the unaccompanied children's legal services program. Within overall funding, more has been allocated to facilitate private pro bono representation for children released from ORR custody. This is a complement to the direct services model, effectively leveraging some private sector resources to represent increased numbers of children.[28]

A number of proposed bills in 2015 would have significantly reduced the protections for unaccompanied children by restricting the definition of an "unaccompanied alien child," limiting effective screening of unaccompanied children at the border, and introducing more obstacles for these children to access asylum and other immigration relief.[29] Advocates pushed back on these bills, particularly when proposed legislation would have deeply eroded protections for unaccompanied children.[30] Some of the same bills were reintroduced in 2017 without success.[31] Protections would have been supported by the Fair Day in Court for Kids Act of 2016 (S. 2540), which mandated legal counsel for all unaccompanied children in removal proceedings, and by the Secure the Northern Triangle Act (S. 3106) bill of 2016. It was designed to create a coordinated regional response to better protect refugees and asylum seekers from Honduras, El Salvador, and Guatemala.[32] In the 115th Congress (2017–2018), the Fair Day in Court for Kids Act was reintroduced (H.R. 2043/S. 2468) by Representative Zoe Lofgren (D-CA) and Senator Mazie Hirono (D-HI) to ensure that no child will have to face court alone by providing attorneys to all unaccompanied children for the duration of their immigration proceedings.

The Trump administration is working to undermine basic protections for unaccompanied children. On September 19, 2017, EOIR issued an internal legal opinion that says immigration judges may independently determine whether a child meets the definition of unaccompanied children during the course of removal proceedings, and that statutory protections for unaccompanied children may not apply to children who cease to meet that definition.[33] Thousands of unaccompanied children could lose vital protections as a result. As of the fall of 2017, EOIR and US Citizenship and Immigration Services had not publicly released guidance or announcements on the legal opinion. However, some immigration judges reportedly have referred to principles discussed in the legal opinion during court hearings after the memo's issuance.

On October 8, 2017, the Trump administration issued immigration "principles" that, if enacted, would decimate protections for immigrants and refugees, including unaccompanied children.[34] The principles include terminating the Flores Settlement Agreement, which mandates that unaccompanied children be held in the least restrictive setting possible for the shortest period of time possible; removing all unaccompanied children without a hearing at the border if they do not present a fear of return; stripping protections from children who already have a parent present in the United States; eliminating one-parent Special Immigrant Juvenile Status and eviscerating a needed avenue of protection for children fleeing abuse and trafficking; and eliminating the requirement that unaccompanied children's asylum claims first be considered in a nonadversarial interview before an asylum officer rather than in a defensive proceeding before an immigration judge.

Conclusion

Without an attorney, unaccompanied children cannot meaningfully access due process and US protection. They have little to no chance of presenting a successful case and are at great risk of deportation, which could have devastating consequences for children, such as grave harm or even death. Attorneys also provide unaccompanied children protection by having a unique view into children's lives and can be someone children can turn to in difficult situations in which they feel unsafe. By allowing tens of thousands of unaccompanied children to stand in immigration court without an attorney, we are abandoning this country's bedrock principles of child protection and due process.

While the number of unaccompanied children coming to the United States has dropped in recent years, the numbers are still significant, and the root causes of their flight remain unaddressed. El Salvador, Honduras, and Guatemala, from which most of the children flee, remain among the most murderous nations globally. From a historic high in 2014, when 68,500 children crossed the US border, their number dropped to 39,970 in 2015 and then rose to nearly 60,000 in 2016.[35] As of August 2017, 38,495 children had come to the United States that year.[36] The drop in numbers does not signify fewer children are seeking safety in the United States. In fact, large numbers of children and families are still fleeing these countries but are not making it across the US border. Guatemala's National Safe Spaces Network says that in June 2017, the number of children in transit traveling with their families or unaccompanied increased 745 percent in comparison with the previous year. Of all children in transit, 54 percent traveled unaccompanied.[37] Although Congress appropriated $750 million in 2016 to help address the root causes of unaccompanied children's flight, little has changed.

The representation rate has improved since the low point of 2014 thanks to increased federal funding and programs for legal services. Yet, it is deeply concerning that representation rates started to drop again in 2016.[38] Once again, near-record child arrivals that year strained NGOs' capacity to provide legal services at existing funding levels. Currently, half of children in deportation proceedings do not have an attorney.[39] Modest but important gains have been made in the representation of unaccompanied children since 2014, which has led to the protection of more unaccompanied children, but significant problems remain.

The challenges children faced in the past and continue to face—in custody and after release—mirror the challenges in an overall system that prioritizes immigration enforcement over child protection. Tens of thousands of children do not have attorneys and are likely to face immigration court alone. Attorneys for these children are needed now more than ever as numerous policies under consideration and bills winding their way through Congress would decimate key protections and children's access to fundamental fairness. Ensuring representation for unaccompanied children with a robust mix of government-appointed attorneys and pro bono representation is a commonsense solution that benefits all involved. It is also basic child protection, a value on which this country was built. To abandon this core virtue is a repudiation of who we are as a nation and sends a dangerous signal to the rest of the world.

REFLECTIONS

Judging Children

DANA LEIGH MARKS

For me, it is just another workday.[1] I walk down the crowded financial district street to the modern, high-rise building that houses my court. As I reach the elevators, I see a dazed young woman, probably in her late teens. Stuck to her jacket I see the paper badge that our building issues authorizing her to go to the court floor, so I motion to her to come with me. I push the button, and as the elevator gently slides into motion, her eyes widen suddenly and she swiftly grabs both my arms. My knees almost buckle from the adrenaline surge, but then I realize it is just the normal elevator motion—the unnatural movement that gives you the feeling that your stomach is being left behind. It occurs to me that this woman has likely never been in an elevator before, but even worse, she is heading to court, a place that fills her with uncertainty and fear. She is still shaking as we reach the correct floor. I am relieved when I see a lawyer walking toward her in greeting. Although she is clearly already terrified, I know that her tribulations in this building have just begun.

On a daily basis, I see anxious children and adults embark upon their journey through our complicated immigration court system, not know-ing what they can expect, nor what is expected of them. After almost thirty years on the bench, I am very comfortable in my courtroom, but I remind myself daily that this is not the experience of most who appear before me. It is my job to help them overcome their discomfort with the environment and protocol so they can communicate effectively, allowing me to make a more accurate ruling in their case.

As a judge in an immigration trial court, I interact with people from around the globe. Nationwide in 2015, approximately 250 judges heard more than 260,000 matters in more than 258 languages; only 11 percent

123

of the cases were conducted in English.[2] A large number of asylum seekers, primarily Central American women and children, has caused our local dockets to be overwhelmed and has dramatically lowered the average age of those who are summoned to our courts. Many people we see come from remote rural communities, some without electricity, running water, or public institutions like schools or police. The fortunate ones are blessed with family or friends here who help guide them through the difficult transition to life in a new country, not the least of which is navigating the byzantine system of our immigration laws.

The challenges a respondent—the legal term for those in immigration court proceedings—faces in our courts are many and diverse. The workings of an immigration court are so unique that they surprise seasoned lawyers. Imagine how puzzling this process is to people who do not speak English, may not be literate in any language, or have no familiarity with our government or legal system. Many come fleeing repressive or corrupt government regimes, where police and judicial authorities are part of the problem rather than a safe haven where one can seek protection.

Because immigration proceedings are technically classified as civil matters, there is no right to appointed counsel. Respondents can pay for their own attorney, or perhaps find one who will work pro bono or gratis, but if they are unable to find an attorney, they are required to proceed on their own and represent themselves. This is true whether an adult or a child is appearing alone in court. The challenge this presents cannot be overstated (see Young and McKenna, this volume).

Federal appeals courts repeatedly describe immigration law as being second in complexity to tax law. I believe our immigration law is even more complex, and to make matters worse, it changes rapidly due to frequent decisions interpreting the law issued by federal courts and the US Supreme Court. The cases we routinely see more closely resemble death penalty cases than civil matters because when immigrants who fear for their life are forced to leave the United States, the decision to "remove"—the legal term used for deportation—is a penalty that can result in their death. Even more difficult is the reality that even if an immigration judge is persuaded that such a tragic outcome is likely, there may be no option within existing law other than to issue an order of removal. The gravity of these situations and potential for tragedy are not lost on immigration judges, nor are the special challenges faced by children in these proceedings (see Terrio, this volume).

One of the important but little-known aspects of our immigration law is the fact that children and youth are treated the same as adults, with only two exceptions. A child under age fourteen cannot legally be served official notice of the initiation of proceedings, thereby requiring an adult or guardian to be involved in the process at the outset. Equally important, judges may not accept statements admitting removability made by minors under age eighteen unless they are represented by an attorney, legal representative, adult relative, or legal guardian. By practice and regulations, additional guidelines have been adopted, such as separate juvenile dockets, child-sensitive questioning, and even encouragement for judges to forgo the normally required use of a judicial robe when in court.[3] The sole purpose of these adjustments in protocol is to make the hearing environment age-appropriate to enable children to tell their story. The best interests of the child cannot provide a basis for relief that does not otherwise exist under the immigration laws. Additionally surprising is the fact that children can be held responsible for the acts of others that are beyond their control. For example, a child can be ordered removed for failing to appear at a hearing, even though grade school–age children have no control over their attendance. Another harsh reality is that in the crucial aspects of the proceedings, the law treats children like adults, with no relaxation of qualifying criteria or burden of proof.

A respondent's first experience with our courts occurs at a "master calendar" hearing, an arraignment-type proceeding at which twenty-five to fifty cases are scheduled. These are brief hearings that focus on assuring that respondents know their legal rights and any potential remedies under the immigration law; if cases are ready, a final hearing is scheduled. During most of this calendar, the press of cases means that words fly so fast and furiously between the lawyers that even a native English speaker or adult would find the jargon confusing. It is difficult to imagine how children who may not speak English must feel. For example, how can children be made to understand that they may qualify for what is erroneously referred to as "political" asylum if they have been the victim of domestic violence in a country where police will not protect them? From my vantage place on the dais, I sometimes see individuals looking disengaged, appearing not to follow the conversation, or seeming to be mentally absent from the room. Many are particularly vulnerable due to their age and exposure to trauma either in their home countries or during their journey to the United States. Those without legal representation are clearly more overwhelmed. Throughout the hearing process, but especially at these initial hearings, our training as immigration judges teaches us to be vigilant for signs of sex or labor trafficking or exploitation by smugglers, unethical *notarios* (notaries public) or attorneys. When signs of these abuses appear, judges must report their suspicions to administrative officials charged with referring cases to investigation, and proceed only with great caution.

Judges advise respondents without attorneys of their legal rights and responsibilities, explaining that they have the right to find an attorney at their own expense and providing a list of attorneys who offer pro bono or low-cost services. Most judges readily concur that the involvement of competent attorneys makes the proceedings go more efficiently and quickly, especially in cases involving children (see Terrio, this volume). Judges also explain the consequences should a respondent fail to appear at a future hearing: failure to appear typically results in removal because immigration laws generally require a judge to enter a decision even if the respondent is not present. Judges struggle to put into plain English the different requirements for many forms of potential relief.

After a reasonable period of time to find an attorney has elapsed, respondents go forward, and the judge decides whether or not they are subject to removal (see Young and McKenna, this volume). Most of the time spent in immigration court cases focuses on determining whether the respondent is eligible for some form of relief from removal or benefit in the immigration law. When the case involves criminal convictions, the question of whether or not someone should be removed often becomes complex and contested. The misalignment of immigration law with state criminal law frequently requires complicated legal analysis and sometimes results in inconsistent outcomes for similar behavior occurring in different states. Another large source of disconnect comes from the fact that the definition of aggravated felony under immigration law includes some state convictions that are nonviolent misdemeanor offenses. The immigration law rules regarding juvenile offenders are intricate and distinct from state law provisions, so any matter involving a juvenile with a record necessitates careful scrutiny and legal analysis.

Federal immigration law sometimes differs starkly from state family law on issues as basic as who is considered to be a child: Is the age of majority eighteen or twenty-one years? To be recognized as an adopted child under immigration law, the adoption must occur when the child is under age sixteen (among other requirements). So, for example, children who are older than seventeen and legally adopted by extended family in the United States do not qualify as adopted children for immigration purposes. A harsh reality is that state orders regarding custody and best interests of the child may not have an effect in the immigration law context because immigration detention of parents can inadvertently impact parental rights adversely or even result in involuntary termination of those rights. When children are found by a state court to be eligible for Special Immigrant Juvenile Status, they cannot sponsor parents in the future, not even a parent who was innocent of any abuse, abandonment, or neglect.

The challenges increase in an individual hearing, which is the respondent's "day in court," a one-on-one hearing with the Department of Homeland Security attorney and immigration judge. For example, at this hearing, if the respondent's case is the only one on the calendar, being fifteen minutes late can result in an order of deportation. Because it is individuals' responsibility to gather evidence to prove themselves worthy of the legal remedy, even respondents who are children must show that they qualify—no easy task for asylum seekers suffering from past trauma or for juveniles who may need to show that they have been abused, abandoned, or neglected.

Immigration judges make their decisions under the pressures of tremendous caseloads. On average, they have active dockets of more than 2,000 cases, and the assistance of only half of an attorney law clerk's time. This heavy docket generally keeps judges in court, on the bench, an average of thirty-six hours a week, leaving little time to study the impact of new court decisions and review the documentary records and pretrial submissions of upcoming cases. The system is geared toward oral decisions delivered immediately at the end of testimony, which skews against judges choosing to prepare written decisions, even when cases are factually or legally complex.

During courtroom proceedings, judges are expected to monitor the digital audio recording that becomes the official record; maintain notes of testimony; mark exhibits; operate the video-teleconferencing equipment if used; monitor the performance of the foreign language interpreter; observe the testimony of witnesses to assess credibility; and determine the evidentiary weight to be accorded testimony. Judges also rule on objections raised by the parties and, at the end of several hours, orally render a cogent legal decision that must include a clear statement of the legal standards being applied and an analysis of how the evidence presented in the case—testimonial and documentary—supports or undermines the determination arrived upon. This is what is required if all goes smoothly. It rarely does.

Sometimes interpreters omit testimony or do not have the proper vocabulary and must be disqualified. Not infrequently, respondents or witnesses are overwhelmed and incoherent when attempting to recall traumatic events, requiring time to compose themselves and creating confusing judicial records. At times, attorneys lose their composure in their passion to convey legal arguments. With no bailiffs present in court during most proceedings, the judge must serve as security officer. Then, in the midst of emotionally wrought testimony or legal argument, the televideo feed can drop off or the digital audio recorder might send an error message, and the proceedings must be stopped until these technological glitches are rectified. Painful emotional testimony may need to be repeated, and it can be extremely difficult to convey it a second time with equal detail and emotional content.

However, this courtroom scenario skims over the surface of one of the most difficult aspects of hearings: the crucial credibility determination that must be made in every case. Unlike cases in which the judge must decide between versions of an event told by multiple witnesses, the cases that come before the immigration courts often hinge on the testimony of one person, the respondent. The child respondent may not have the maturity to comprehend the dynamics of crucial events as they unfold, nor the ability to put them into context. Traumatic events impair memory at any age, but especially for children. Most respondents must deliver their testimony through the filter of an interpreter, making the task of assessing credibility exponentially more complicated for judges.

Immigration judges are constantly confronted with situations that require them to reassess their assumptions. Some cultures find it disrespectful to look an authority figure in the eye, yet the hallmark of veracity in our culture is to look directly at someone while telling a story. Many of the young people appearing in courts come from cultures where chronological time has different meanings, so the timing of even traumatic events may be difficult for them to relay. In a courtroom setting, this might raise doubt about whether or not the story is truthful. In addition, a common reaction found in people who suffer from post-traumatic stress is that they speak of the unspeakable with a detachment and flat affect that may undermine veracity. Yet, it is equally common for someone suffering from post-traumatic stress to become overly emotional, sometimes to the point that speaking at all is impossible. After devastating trauma, how can a judge hope to put a child sufficiently at ease to share excruciatingly painful, sometimes shameful memories? These are all factors that a judge must consider when trying to assess the veracity and proper weight of testimony.

These are not the only complications that hearings present. For example, many respondents testify about events of which the judge has little knowledge, and that may seem unbelievable without a deep familiarity with the cultural history and context where they occurred. Determining whether or not corroborating documentation is available or safe to procure must also be ruled upon by the judge; this, too, is problematic without a clear understanding of conditions in the place where the events occurred. To draw appropriate conclusions in such cases, a judge must scour legal precedent for similar fact patterns and push litigants to provide materials that educate the court on country conditions and customs. When these materials are not presented, respondents may fail to prevail in the case merely because they cannot meet the burden of proof. Thus, the consequences of limited access to counsel, lack of fluency in English, youth, and lack of ability to obtain corroboration can result in a devastating denial of any relief from removal.

Experts agree that all of us, including judges, are affected by assumptions formed throughout our lives that affect how we perceive information, respond to events, and make decisions. This phenomenon is called "implicit bias."[4] Implicit biases are those automatic attitudes or stereotypes that affect our understanding, actions, or decisions in an unconscious manner. There are many techniques for recognizing and adjusting for one's implicit bias, but there is no miracle or onetime cure-all. One must remain conscious of the influences that are at work, rather than allowing opinions to be based on these unconscious attitudes. A recurring theme in suggestions to judges on how to address implicit bias is to take time off the bench to reflect and defuse its harmful effects.[5]

From the comfort of my dais, I realize that I can never truly understand the tribulations experienced by any respondent who appears before me in court. How can I hope to know how it must feel to them to be in court, with so much hanging in the balance—even if I have a glimpse of the anxiety evoked by a morning elevator ride or the fear of young adults who cannot remember their homeland but whose DACA status has expired or been revoked? What I can do—indeed what I must do—is to educate myself about diverse cultures and countries, to remain patient, and to always be vigilant against my own assumptions and implicit bias. I try to remember all these subtle influences as well as the overt ones that create the dynamics of any given day in court. Every day in court, I strive to keep foremost in my mind that each hearing, each person's story, has its own unique blend of unseen influences and complexities: the interplay of the laws, culture, age, personality, language, trauma, resilience, and the presence or absence of legal or familial support. Many days I feel the pull of diverse and sometimes competing currents—cultural, political, social, legal, psychological, and perhaps others I cannot readily identify. It can feel difficult to navigate and sometimes seems almost impossible to control these factors. As I struggle to do my part to assure that justice is served, always present are the challenges and weighty consequences that could result if I fall short during the trials I conduct.

PART III

Out

Responding to "Illegality"

In this final part of the volume, contributors focus on young people on the margins—or outside—of legal systems, communities, and the nation. Children and youth may be *out* in various ways as they exit the courts with different outcomes, are deported from the United States, or are excluded from national membership. Some young people are forced to reconstruct lives after deportation, others were able to qualify for Deferred Action for Childhood Arrivals (DACA) and stay in the United States, while still others have come out of the shadows to actively challenge US immigration laws and high rates of deportation. Even if children and youth have limited or compromised rights, they also survive, get by, and/or engage with new forms of resistance in response to state control. In a time of increasing immigration enforcement, young people respond to the injustices of US immigration policy and remain outside of state structures, as they challenge government actions and collectively work toward possible alternatives to the current immigration system in the United States.

As the contributors explore in Part III, youth can be physically out of the nation, expelled through deportation (Heidbrink). In addition to being forced outside the nation because of "removal," some young people have elected to temporarily travel outside of the United States through a process called Advance Parole (Boehm). Children, youth, and young adults also come out of the shadows through activism and other actions that contribute to public dialogue about the specific effects of US immigration laws on young people (Valdivia). Finally, young immigrants (Salas-Crespo) and their allies (Núñez and Gittinger) are actively engaged in work that seeks to identify a path out of the circumstances that surround the migration of young people in the current moment. In

131

each of these situations, the condition of being out may limit or open up possibilities for the future trajectories of children and youth.

In chapter 7, Lauren Heidbrink chronicles how young people experience deportation from the United States to Guatemala, examining the policies and institutional practices that govern the removal of unaccompanied children and tracing the ways young people and their families understand and navigate these policies and practices. She shows how the forced repatriation of children—as well as the migration to Guatemala of the children of deported adults—not only exacerbates the conditions that spurred migration but also introduces new interrelated uncertainties and risks for young people after deportation. As youth are physically expelled from the United States through deportation, they technically move out of US legal systems. However, the effects of a halted migration to the United States and a forced return to a nation of origin produce new challenges and dangers such that, in many ways, young people continue to be in and moving through regimes of illegality. Demonstrating the long-term and geographically distant effects of the US government's deportations, Heidbrink outlines the confining character of being *out* of a system, especially if once in it.

In chapter 8, Carolina Valdivia explores how "illegality" and immigration status exclude undocumented youth from participating in formal political acts, such as voting and running for office, and may prevent them from legally driving and traveling. Undocumented youth also live under the constant threat and fear of deportation. At the same time, undocumented youth experience their immigration status in a way that gives them strength to become political participants within their communities. Valdivia describes how undocumented young adults perceive—and also challenge—the boundaries of restrictive immigration laws through their organizing efforts. She discusses the ways that undocumented young adults are building and sustaining critical spaces of belonging and resistance within a nation that legally excludes them. By "coming out of the shadows" and advocating for immigrant rights, migrant youth show how being outside of political structures—and *out* as undocumented migrants—can also create spaces within them.

Deborah A. Boehm's chapter describes the undeniably transnational lives of undocumented migrant youth. Yet, despite transnational ties, youth may find themselves trapped in the United States, unable to leave the country while also ensuring secure return passage. This landscape changed to some extent with DACA, which created the possibility for young people to travel outside of the country and return through Advance Parole. However, even if the possibility of approval to travel exists, leaving the United States through Advance Parole can result in young people being denied reentry by US officials and thus being permanently *out* of and excluded from the country. Focusing on a group of DACA recipients who were invited by the Mexican government to visit "their homeland," Boehm considers such border crossings in a time of increasingly blocked movement for the majority of undocumented migrant youth. The experiences of DACA recipients who traveled to Mexico underscore the precarious status of "Dreamers," but also the ways their transnational citizenship gives them irrefutable claims to two nations.

In their piece, Abel Núñez and Rachel Gittinger outline how local civil society actors at each stage can play a key role in protecting immigrant children, underscoring how the divide between those understood to be within or outside of communities is typically a false one. Even as they are excluded from communities in the United States, migrant youth have a crucial part in ensuring a secure future—for migrants but also for US civil society more broadly. The authors propose ways that migrant youth might take the lead on articulating their visions for a better world. They discuss how civil society and government might build effective networks and implement policies to provide immediate protection, direct service coordination, and longer-term advocacy. As more vulnerable populations cross militarized borders, there is a need to ensure that their human rights are respected. Policies that address only the migratory flow into the United States will not resolve issues of violence, poverty, and political exclusion in countries of origin that force people to flee. Migrant youth and their advocates are well positioned to lead the nation *out* of the current crisis it faces.

Finally, Margarita Salas-Crespo's reflections describe her experiences as an immigrant to, and member of, the United States. She explains how she came to the United States as an undocumented immigrant at the age of ten. Despite language barriers and without access to US citizenship, Salas-Crespo excelled in every way. Living without authorized status throughout her childhood, she later qualified for DACA and was able to pursue an education and career working in and with Latino/a communities. Salas-Crespo describes her migration to the United States, the challenges she faced as a young undocumented migrant, and the process through which she qualified for DACA. As she writes, undocumented immigrant youth have been shut *out* of certain aspects of national membership and yet are also positioned as citizens in many ways. From this vantage point, Salas-Crespo speculates about what the future may hold for her and other immigrants in the United States.

7

Youth Negotiate Deportation

LAUREN HEIDBRINK

In 2014, the media and scholars alike turned their attention to the spike in child migration to the United States. Though this spike is frequently attributed to an increase in gang violence, child abuse, and deepening poverty in Honduras, El Salvador, and Guatemala, the experiences of migrant children are nevertheless largely unknown. Viewed among advocates as a "black hole where unaccompanied children easily fall through the cracks,"[1] the deportation of children is an increasingly pressing yet underexamined social issue.[2] Scholars have thoughtfully examined the uncertainty and insecurity that removal generates in communities of return; yet to date there have been few studies on the everyday experiences and long-term trajectories of young migrants who themselves are subject to detention and deportation.[3]

Through multisited, mixed-methods research in the United States, Mexico, and Guatemala, this chapter chronicles some of the intimate and interrelated ways youth experience and embody removal[4]—both their own and that of their family members.[5] For clarity of prose, this chapter focuses on two broadly conceived profiles of removal—US citizen children who accompany their parents following deportation and young migrants who are deported as "unaccompanied minors."[6] It is important to note that these profiles derive from juridical constructions rooted in the legal status of oneself or one's family member. I likewise recognize that the lived experiences of removal are far more diverse and multifaceted than these profiles suggest. Thus, rather than reify young people's experiences, I look across their experiences of removal and ask: How do young people experience deportation? How does removal affect their integration and reintegration into families, peer groups, and communities? What are the reverberating risks related to young people's experiences of forced or de facto deportation?[7] And how do young people navigate these risks?

This chapter acknowledges that young people are actors in the construction of local and transnational social fields and are agents of migration, not merely "luggage" sent for by patriarchs or agentless victims of geopolitical processes.[8] While recognizing young people as social actors routinely clashes with public discourses and institutional policies that depict them as vulnerable victims,[9] I argue that considering the perspectives and contributions of young people is essential to uncover the transnational effects of deportation. In so doing, I trace the wide-ranging experiences and perspectives of young people who arrive in their parents' country of origin following parental deportation and of youth who themselves are deported as *retornados* (returnees) to Guatemala.

Research with youth and their families in Guatemala indicates that deportation is not a synchronic event; rather, it has sustained impacts on youth, their families, and broader communities. The acts of apprehension and removal may thwart efforts to seek and maintain family reunification, disrupt future employment or educational plans, and limit one's ability to support family, escape poverty, and ensure safety—critical impacts that are often overlooked by both policy makers and scholars. Deportation not only exacerbates the conditions that spur migration but also introduces interrelated uncertainties and related risks for young deportees. At the same time, and as this chapter discusses, young people learn to navigate these uncertainties and risks, most notably as they socialize with peers, care for their families, pursue employment, and, at times, re-migrate.

Llegadas/Arrivals

The estimates of US citizen children who accompany their parents following deportation from the United States are staggering—nearly half a million children in Mexico alone.[10] This is a near doubling over a three-year period (2013–2015). Emerging scholarship reveals the complex landscapes that US citizen children must navigate as they adapt to life in a new country, including the challenges of securing identity documents, enrolling in school, and learning a new language.[11] While this literature predominantly centers on the experiences of youth in Mexico, US citizen children confront many analogous obstacles in Central America. Carla, Sonia, Antonio, and Julian, young US citizens who were de facto deported to Guatemala following their parent's or parents' removal from the United States, share how they navigate new institutions, family formations, and peer groups, along with the impacts of these realities on their identities, relationships, and sense of belonging. Schools are sites of pronounced tension as US citizens must present a series of legal and institutional documents to school administrations that are ill-equipped to verify documents and ascertain equivalencies.

Carla and Sonia

Carla and her younger sister Sonia were eager to speak of their lives in the United States when we knocked on their door as part of a community survey. For two years, their mother struggled to independently support Carla and Sonia in Nebraska following their father's deportation to Guatemala. Unable to pay rent, a financial challenge compounded by their father's third failed attempt to re-migrate, the girls and their mother decided to join their father. Upon arrival in Guatemala, Sonia recounted crying often, initially afraid to leave the house, and fighting often with her parents. Carla described their first months in Guatemala:

> It was really tough. My parents fought all the time. My mom didn't like it. It is so different. People treated her poorly because she's Mexican, and we're not from here. For me, it's been an adjustment . . . even little things like not having a refrigerator for our food or to kiss adults' hands after I finish a meal . . . or going to the store. When there isn't enough money to buy something for everyone, we can't go.

In addition to differing material realities and social practices, Carla and Sonia also confronted interrelated institutional obstacles, including securing identity documents, health care, and school enrollment. "The school said we need a *cédula* [identity document], and RENAP [national registry][12] kept saying we don't have the right documents to get a *cédula*. We spent so long trying to get my dad the right documents [in the United States], and now we're the ones without papers." Without copies of their US birth certificates or the requisite consular documents, Carla and Sonia were unable to secure a Guatemalan national identification document necessary to enroll in public school. Only after their father bribed a RENAP official six months later were they able to obtain the requisite documents to begin school in Guatemala.

When asked to share their impressions of school, Sonia chimed in: "The other kids would make fun of us when we'd speak English. But some kids were curious about us and asked us lots of questions. For me, the biggest shock was that there is no water in the school, no library . . . even the English teacher couldn't speak English."

Overtaxed and underfunded, Guatemalan state schools often lack the most basic resources such as textbooks, bathrooms, blackboards, and qualified teachers. Families are asked to purchase desks, writing materials, and uniforms for their children, making the nation's "free and compulsory" school attendance a financial impossibility for many. While the rates of primary school attendance have risen in recent years, the poor quality of education persists. The Guatemalan Ministry of Education indicates that in 2010 only 45 percent of the nation's students reached national mathematics standards, and 30 percent reached national reading standards by the sixth grade.[13] Guatemala's 1996 Peace Accords called for the incorporation of a multilingual educational model, but public schools remain ill-equipped to support Spanish-language learners, including English speakers such as Carla and Sonia. As such, many families prioritize the use of remittances to enroll their children, particularly those raised in the United States, in a growing number of urban private schools that purport to offer a higher quality of instructors and accommodations.

In spite of her school's stark conditions, so different from those she encountered in Nebraska, Carla's parents encouraged her to focus on her studies. She explained, "I want to continue studying so that I can teach, I can travel, go new places, but I'll always have a job." She described how her father pressured her to pursue a career as an educator rather than a musician, as she had hoped. Albeit reluctantly, she grew to appreciate the career choice and the opportunities and security it might bring. Carla's desire for a consistent income stands in marked contrast to the employment realities of her parents. Her mother's income fluctuates as she sells produce at the local market. Her father works collecting iron to recycle.

Carla and Sonia shared how they have grown closer as a result of their precarious economic situation and struggles to adapt to a new home. Describing Carla, Sonia explained, "My sister really helped me.

Everything was new, but Carla was always supporting me and encouraging me. She understands best how I'm feeling when no one else does. I couldn't survive without her. Our parents have their worries—they are working hard to support us and to make this work—but they don't always get ours. How could they?" Sonia described how, with her sister's support, she gained more confidence—emerging from their home, attending classes, and eventually befriending her English teacher. Recognizing their precarious living conditions and their parents' ongoing efforts to eke out a living, Carla and Sonia adjusted their expectations for their parents and instead relied primarily on each other for emotional support. Together, they negotiated school and peer relationships in a new country with a different language, customs, and economic realities.

Antonio

I met seventeen-year-old Antonio at a local Internet café in Xela in the Department of Quetzaltenango. Overhearing me speak in English to my daughter, he asked: "I'm from New York, you?" He traveled to Guatemala to reunify with his mother, who had been deported from Arizona following a workplace raid three years prior. Antonio's relationship had grown tense with his father, who, still in the United States, began dating another woman. Laughing, Antonio would later explain, "My mom always told me about Guatemala—the land of eternal spring—and how beautiful it is. I always had the illusion that I'd come here to visit. But only to visit."

When I met with Antonio a year later, he had found a job at a local call center, a coveted position for many English speakers where he earned US$500 per month, well above the national monthly minimum wage of US$350. Praised by his mother for being "a good son who avoids trouble and works hard," Antonio was earning enough to buy a used motorcycle and to support his mother with monthly rent. Feeling most comfortable with the English-speaking tourists who frequent the highland city of Xela, he began dating a white woman from Wisconsin, much to his mother's delight. In spite of appearances, Antonio wondered aloud: "What the hell am I supposed to do *here*?" Though he was able to avoid many of the institutional challenges that confronted Carla and Sonia, Antonio struggled to belong in his adopted country. Even with his relative material success and a growing peer group, Antonio felt out of place and without purpose. Struggling with social isolation, he planned to return to the United States but could not bring himself to share his decision with his mother.

Julian

Born in Colorado, eighteen-year-old Julian described his experience living in a small border community near Tacaná in the Department of San Marcos following his father's deportation the previous year. Before joining his father, he had spent several weeks reading about Guatemala's violent history of colonialism and genocide and ongoing structural violence, conditions that spurred his father's migration in the 1990s. Following his arrival, Julian desired to (re)discover his indigenous heritage. "I didn't work in the US but here I am learning how to work the fields. It hasn't been easy, but I'm learning about the land, my culture, and what it means to be indigenous. I even speak a few words of Mam. . . . I'm learning that although we have little, we have something."

In the absence of friends and the attractions of urban life, Julian focused his attention on "discovering myself and my identity." He described an awakening as he came of age in a new country. "But it isn't always pretty," he added. Battling both the tedium of small-town life and the discrimination he encountered as simultaneously indigenous and foreign, he shared, "I don't feel like I really belong anywhere."

Young people who are de facto deported share in the challenges of adapting to a new life following parental deportation. Carla, Sonia, Antonio, and Julian describe learning to navigate new material realities, social contexts, peer groups, and family dynamics. They also confront institutions that may impede their access to public good, such as education and health care, and to secure citizenship documents in their parents' home countries. In the process, young people recount the vital support provided by siblings, parents, teachers, and mentors, as well as by learning about their histories and cultural identity—all critical to forging a sense of purpose and belonging over time.

Retornados/Returnees

Scarce data are available on the numbers of children who are deported. Guatemala's Dirección General de Migración (Department of Migration) indicates 14,349 unaccompanied Guatemalan children were deported from Mexico and 149 were deported from the United States in 2015. According to the Guatemalan Secretaría de Bienestar Social (Secretariat of Social Welfare), 95 percent of returned minors aged 0 through 18 are indigenous—primarily Mam and K'iche' youth from rural communities in the Departments of Quetzaltenango, San Marcos, Huehuetenango, and Totonicapán (personal communication, May 29, 2015). By 2015, with an average age of 14.5 years, 66 percent of deported children are boys and nearly 34 percent are girls, a notable shift in gender composition from two years prior, when 18 percent of children were female. The Secretaría de Bienestar Social reports that more than 86 percent of deported children indicate that poverty and the search for employment are the primary reasons for unaccompanied migration, while an additional 12 percent seek family reunification in the United States, and 2 percent pursue travel or work in Mexico.[14] However, poverty rates and the pursuit of employment mask far more complex understandings of the root causes of migration.[15] These statistics further fail to consider the number of children who migrate accompanied by an adult, who pass undetected into Mexico and the United States, who are removed outside of official channels, and who attempt to migrate multiple times.

The deportation of young Guatemalans is a critical area of focus in particular because Guatemalan children are consistently the largest group of unaccompanied minors entering the United States.[16] They are also disproportionately deported from the United States and Mexico compared with their Honduran and Salvadoran counterparts.[17] Although Guatemala was once touted as a leader in attending to the short-term needs of returned children and deterring remigration, Guatemalan authorities now struggle to keep pace with the reception of young deportees such as Camila, Julio, and Sebastian, as discussed later, while they are simultaneously pressured to thwart the through-migration of neighboring Salvadorans and Hondurans, among others, en route to the United States.

Camila

Criminalized by government bureaucrats and often ostracized by their communities or even families, unaccompanied youth return to a complex landscape of government surveillance, limited support services, and considerable stigma associated with deportation. Camila, a sixteen-year-old who was deported from Houston, described her Justice Prisoner and Alien Transfer Systems flight to Guatemala City's air force base, where she was then shuttled to a processing center for returned unaccompanied children. "I was scared. I've never been on a plane and behind me were these men with handcuffs. We arrived and the guards signed some papers, pushed us off the plane, and then slammed the door. They didn't even get off the plane, like they'd get sick if they stepped foot in Guatemala." Quickly shuttled to a processing facility for unaccompanied children run by the Secretaría de Bienestar Social, Camila described undergoing a series of humiliating experiences—from the absence of food to the way professionals ridiculed her and her family for being indigenous[18]—all while waiting for her parents to arrive at the facility.

Many young people describe the return to their home communities in Guatemala following deportation as fraught. Surrounded by rumors of delinquency, failure, and, for girls, allegations of prostitution and promiscuity, deported youth may be assumed by their community to have committed a legal transgression or to have succumbed to a moral weakness of drinking or taking drugs, thereby warranting their detention. The comments of several young people from the Guatemalan departments of Quetzaltenango, San Marcos, and Totonicapán illustrate this situation:

So many rumors. So much whispering and jokes. People can be cruel.

My brother told me that people were asking how many people I slept with to get to *el norte* because migration isn't free.

People looked at me differently after I returned. They were afraid of me. They wanted to know who I robbed or if I joined a gang . . . what I did wrong to be put in jail [in the United States].

In spite of rising numbers of deportees to Central America, there is little distinction between youth who enter immigration detention due to unlawful presence and youth who are charged with committing a delinquent or criminal act in the United States. In many ways, this reflects US social and legal discourses that also conflate illegality with criminality.

In Guatemala, migrant youth and their families recognize that migration is highly susceptible to failure and is undertaken at great cost. Many youth and their families—including Camila—discuss the decision to migrate collectively, weighing, for example, the age and earning potential of youth over older family members; the Spanish language ability of the child—a skill necessary to negotiate migration through Mexico and to navigate everyday life upon arrival in the United States; the child's character amid the temptations of alcohol, drugs, sex, and consumerism associated with the United States; and the child's gender, given the stark realities of sexual abuse and rape that place female migrants at increased risk. Camila identified the decision to migrate as a collective investment in her family's future, a gesture that her parents' trusted her to provide for the family. Thus, for Camila, deportation generated feelings of failure, shame, and guilt for not arriving, and remaining, in the United States. Upon removal, Camila hid in her home for four weeks, embarrassed by what she viewed as a personal failure.

Julio

Deported from Mexico to Guatemala after two failed attempts to migrate to the United States, Julio stated, "I am ashamed they caught me. We mortgaged our land. My family depended on me to work hard and to support our family, but now this. I'm a failure. I don't know what to do." Because crossing through Mexico has become increasingly violent—and arrival in the United States progressively unlikely—smugglers offer prospective migrants three attempts to reach the United States from Guatemala in exchange for US$7,500 to $10,000. With his third and final attempt, Julio grappled with the decision to try again. The family's mortgaged land had been his inheritance—it was the land where he might build his home and start a family. Now, with the land in peril, he weighed the risks. It is important to note that Julio never envisioned his migration as a rejection of "home"; instead, it signified an investment in his and his family's well-being. His forced returns powerfully complicate this sense of place and future.

In some instances, home communities associate young people's experiences in the United States as a contamination, one that results in a suspicious "loss of culture" upon their return home. Such was the case with Julio, who returned to Guatemala with an iPod Shuffle and camera and who grew resentful of his parents' inability to provide even for his basic nutritional needs. His mother explained to me, "He is not the same as before. He looks different. He speaks different. I see him but he is not *here.*" To his mother and others, the fact that Julio wore his pants slightly lower, purchased hair gel from the town store, and offered little enthusiasm for subsistence farming marked the corruption of his indigenous identity in the United States.

What is perceived as a "loss" by home communities is, however, a set of behaviors and social values reinforced in the United States. In detention facilities for unaccompanied children, for example, behavioral modification programs incentivize "good" (nondelinquent) behaviors, such as obedience to daily hygiene regimens, cleaning one's room thoroughly, learning English, eating a full plate of food, drinking milk, making eye contact, and shaking hands firmly. A three-page list of rules in English and Spanish posted on bulletin boards throughout an Illinois facility for unaccompanied children where I conducted research delineates acceptable versus unacceptable behaviors. Incentivized by daily earnings of two dollars and regular shopping trips that allow children to purchase iPods, MP3 players, watches, jewelry, and hair products, detained youth are socialized as would-be consumers. Little consideration is given to the impact that such behavioral modification programs, institutional values, and consumption practices have on children after they rejoin their families following deportation. These social values are reinforced not exclusively by detention facilities but also by schools, places of employment, and peer groups.

When I saw Julio a year later, he mumbled, "I am worse now. I can't make enough here to survive. I mean, I want to help my family and to work but earning fifty *quetzales* a day selling empanadas or growing maize or even selling in the market . . . it doesn't make a difference. I failed. I know I failed. I will make it right. I swear." In three months' time, Julio would begin another journey on top of La Bestia (the Beast), the freight train running from Chiapas to the US-Mexico border.

Sebastian

With no institutional services for young people after deportation to Guatemala, the conditions that spur their migration are often compounded by the financial debt enlisted to migrate irregularly. The emotional ramifications of financial insecurity on the lives of young migrants and their families cannot be discounted. Sebastian's father described how his son's deportation at age seventeen placed considerable financial strain on their family. "We mortgaged our land and our home to the bank to support Sebastian. It was a difficult decision. My wife was sick, my knees and back are no good anymore. I cannot work like before. I didn't think we had another choice."

Sebastian's failed migration and subsequent deportation from Mexico to Guatemala signified not only an inability to provide for his family and his newborn son but also the family's default on their bank loan. Following Sebastian's two additional failed attempts and with a quickly mounting debt, the bank foreclosed on their home and evicted them from their ancestral lands in Malacatán. Ashamed at what he viewed as a personal failure, Sebastian spiraled into depression and alcoholism over the next two years. His father explained, "We lost our home, our land, our livelihood, and our son." Sebastian died of alcohol poisoning at the age of twenty.

Conclusion

As this chapter illustrates, young people differently experience removal from the United States and Mexico, yet across these experiences are critical commonalities. For one, the material changes wrought by deportation profoundly impact young people's everyday lives, including access to food, shelter, or health care; pursuit of education or employment; and migration decisions. Through deportation, youth also experience consequential—however spatially distinct—realities of institutionalized violence. By examining young people's negotiations of legal processes and institutional actors, we see how policies and practices may compound violence that youth and their families experience following removal. Finally, as Camila, Julio, and Sebastian pointedly attest, there are also sustained social and emotional consequences of deportation.

These are nuanced and intimate consequences, altering young people's personal relationships as well as their sentiments of self-worth and belonging.

As demonstrated here, deportation powerfully constrains young people's lives over time and across considerable geographic distances. Nevertheless, many young Guatemalans negotiate these constraints, even if at times with only modest success. Consider, for instance, how youth learn to navigate new and complex institutional, material, and emotional terrains. They nurture relationships with parents, deepen bonds with siblings, meet extended family, and build rapport with new peer groups and mentors. For those returned to Guatemala after living many years or entirely in the United States, some youth discover—or rediscover—indigenous identities, learn ancestral cultural practices, and develop linguistic knowledge. That these creative and even resilient experiences exist alongside, and often in spite of, the constraints of deportation deserves more scholarly and political attention. Such research likewise has particular potential for the development of more humane migration policies. Indeed, only by sustaining our attention to the everyday struggles *and* triumphs of young people might we begin to recognize their lives and contributions on a global scale.

8

Youth Activism

CAROLINA VALDIVIA

Norma was born in Mexico and immigrated to the United States with her mother and younger siblings at the age of sixteen. In 2010, she joined an undocumented youth–led organization at her university, marking the beginning of her political participation. Since then, she has actively engaged in fund-raisers, rallies, and even civil disobedience actions. And while her political participation is commendable for various reasons, her political engagement comes with risks. As an undocumented immigrant, Norma has worried about the potential threat of deportation for more than ten years. Norma's mother shares this fear. This became evident when Norma spoke with me about her experiences: "So people constantly will be telling [me], 'Oh, why are you part of that?' Even my mom she's like, 'Don't be part of all that 'cause you could get hurt or you could get deported in a protest . . . you shouldn't be a part of that. I know you want the change, but you can be deported right now and you would not be able to do anything, and your friends won't help you.'" Norma's experience reveals the extent to which immigration policies shape undocumented young adults' ideas and experiences in political organizing. The threat of deportation, in particular, has forced those around Norma to warn her that she may be deported if she engages in public acts of resistance. Although she remains active in the immigrant rights movement, Norma constantly has to consider the risks and limitations that come with being politically engaged as an undocumented immigrant—a reality all the more pressing in light of the Trump administration's focus on enhanced enforcement.

Like Norma, fellow undocumented young adults who participate politically are constantly navigating spaces of inclusion and exclusion in the United States. Illegality creates a set of social relations by which clear and distinct boundaries shape the kind of activities undocumented youth can engage in or must avoid, as well as the places they can travel to when organizing. For example, the condition of illegality excludes undocumented youth from participating in formal political acts, such as voting. It also prevents them from legally driving and traveling abroad (see the discussion in Boehm's chapter about Advance Parole under DACA). Moreover, undocumented youth live in constant fear of deportation. DACA temporarily blurred the lines between "legality" and "illegality" by providing eligible undocumented young adults with temporary work authorization and relief from deportation. Nevertheless, the Trump administration's decision to terminate the program reveals how conditional such relief is.

This chapter examines the ways in which undocumented youth make meaning of—and challenge—the boundaries of illegality through their political participation, drawing on in-depth interviews with undocumented organizers from across the country. The majority of research participants were eligible for DACA; half of them had DACA status at the time of the interview, while others had submitted their applications but were waiting for a final decision. The remaining research participants represented different immigration statuses, including undocumented (and not eligible for DACA), a pending U visa application, and a pending I-485 adjustment of status application. All but one of the participants were born in Mexico.

At the margins of US society, undocumented youth are experiencing their immigration status in a way that gives them strength to become political participants within their communities. They are motivated to become politically active as they learn that they are not alone, and that there are undocumented young adults across the United States with shared experiences. In turn, their involvement in undocumented youth–led networks fosters a sense of belonging and collective identity.[1] By contesting immigration policy through organizing efforts, undocumented youth are finding that they have a voice, a responsibility to give back to their communities, and the opportunity to make a difference.

Despite organizers' ability to create spaces of belonging, their lack of legal immigration status prevents them from fully collaborating with other organizations, traveling to meetings and events, and networking with fellow organizers. Given these limitations, undocumented organizers must develop strategies to circumvent legal boundaries. To overcome the sociopolitical boundaries created by their immigration status, undocumented organizers have extended their offline organizing efforts into the online world. They are able to transcend certain aspects of the legal barriers they face through the use of online tools. For example, through social media they have been able to connect with undocumented organizers across the country. Notably, the use of online tools allows undocumented youth to build and sustain critical spaces of belonging within a nation that legally excludes them.

Undocumented Youth Navigating Spaces of Exclusion

An in-depth look at undocumented students' educational experiences reveals how their first encounters with contradictory messages of inclusion and exclusion occur within the educational system. For many undocumented children and youth, the school becomes one of the first sites of inclusion and protection. Under the US Supreme Court decision in *Plyer v. Doe* (1982), undocumented youth have the right to a free public K-12 education.[2] In K-12 schooling, undocumented students often feel no different than their documented peers. They are taking similar classes, being encouraged to go on to college, and pledging allegiance to the US flag.

For many undocumented young adults, however, their senior year of high school marks a time of uncertainty and exclusion as they realize that they do not have a legal immigration status and thus face significant barriers.[3] For example, undocumented youth come to learn that, unlike their documented peers, they do not qualify for federal financial aid. Under Title IV of the Higher Education Act (1965), federal financial aid is limited to US citizens and legal permanent residents only.[4] Moreover, as of 2016, only nineteen states allowed eligible undocumented youth to pay in-state tuition rates in college.[5] Thus, undocumented young adults who do not qualify for in-state tuition benefits—because they either do not meet the requirements or do not live in a state that grants such opportunity—often have to postpone their plans and dreams.[6] This limitation also applies to undocumented youth who do qualify for in-state tuition because they often lack access to college loans and grants.

The marginality of undocumented youth becomes increasingly acute during the transitional period between high school and college. This period marks the time when their general sense of belonging during their K-12 educational journey is violently ruptured as they realize they are largely excluded from working, receiving financial aid, and traveling. Having arrived in the United States as children and youth—ranging from infants to teenagers—all the undocumented young adults with whom I spoke shared this experience. Erica, for example, arrived in the United States when she was sixteen years old. Transitioning to a new culture, educational system, and learning a new language was very challenging for Erica, especially because she is the oldest sibling in her family and had no fellow undocumented students to reach out to for support. Nevertheless, driven by her personal determination to go to college, her teachers' guidance, and her parents' emotional support, Erica learned English, grew accustomed to American cultural codes, and graduated from high school.

However, Erica also became acutely aware of the ways in which she was excluded as an undocumented student with limited opportunities to pursue a college education: "I remember when they did these workshops at school for the people who are about to graduate when they have to fill out the FAFSA [Free Application for Federal Student Aid] and stuff. . . . I asked [about applying] and they said, 'Oh, you can't because you need a social security and you don't have a social security so you can't apply.' So I knew I couldn't apply for that, so it was for me, like [I was] set apart from the group." At the time of our interview, Erica was twenty-eight, struggling to finish her education at the local community college. As an undocumented student, she had difficulty finding sources of financial aid and employment opportunities that would pay more than the minimum wage. When we spoke, she had hopes of one day transferring to a four-year university and studying to become a nurse. However, as an undocumented immigrant ineligible for legal relief, Erica often wondered how long she would have to wait before she would have the opportunity to legally work and receive financial aid.

Navigating the college application process, often as the only undocumented student in a class and with minimal resources, a young person is likely to find that transitioning to adult life can be quite challenging. The feeling of exclusion is exacerbated when undocumented youth learn that even though they have grown up alongside their documented peers, their immigration status prevents them from accessing the same opportunities. As Erica described it, this was the moment she discovered she was "set apart from the group." The psychological shock of exclusion is a common experience among undocumented youth, and it largely shapes their decisions after high school graduation.[7]

While all the participants in my study were able to enroll in college, they continued to face a series of challenges related to their status. For example, recall the experience of Norma, who became involved in immigrant rights organizing. As the oldest of three children, she has to worry about paying for her college tuition while also making financial contributions to the family. This has led her to take breaks from her studies to save enough money to continue paying for tuition. At twenty-nine years old, she had been in college for more than eight years and was still dreaming of being the first one in her family to obtain a college degree. However, that dream seemed further out of reach than ever as her financial responsibilities increased and her resources diminished.

Not only do undocumented young adults face significant barriers when trying to pursue a higher education, but their status as unauthorized immigrants also prevents them from legally working. Thus, even after high school and/or college graduation, many undocumented students enter labor markets similar to those of their undocumented peers without a college education.[8] Undocumented immigration status also limits physical movement; for undocumented immigrants, common activities such as driving to and from the grocery store or school can be filled with anxiety, stress, fear, and uncertainty.[9] If caught driving without a license, undocumented immigrants not only may have their cars confiscated but also may even face detention and deportation.

Undocumented immigrants also have to worry about the presence of immigration checkpoints in their communities. For example, they often described San Diego, a community within the US-Mexico borderlands, as distinctly bounded from the rest of the United States by its southern and northern immigration checkpoints.[10] There is the geographic international border with Mexico south of San Diego. Heading north from San Diego, there are two immigration checkpoints intended to stop and detain undocumented immigrants who are seeking opportunities beyond San Diego—at San Clemente (in the west) and Temecula (in the east). These boundaries, along with raids in local stores, routine police checkpoints, and the inability to legally drive, are all reminders of the limitations faced by undocumented immigrants living in San Diego. Driving through these checkpoints could result in being apprehended, detained, and deported. On July 13, 2013, Deysi Merino and her family were directly affected by the federal immigration checkpoint in Temecula.[11] Deysi's father, Teodulfo Merino, was driving along the 15-North freeway when federal immigration officers near the Temecula checkpoint stopped him. Teodulfo, an undocumented parent of five children, was on his way to work the morning he was apprehended. Deysi, who was a student at California State University of San Marcos at the time, was tirelessly organizing to stop her father's deportation when we talked.

The undocumented young adults with whom I spoke often referenced the legal and geographic boundaries that limited their opportunities, including their political participation. For Cecilia, a twenty-six-year-old undocumented woman, the physical boundaries found in border communities were constant reminders of her immigration status. She has been living within this policed geographic space since she was just two years old. She explained: "There's two checkpoints that separate us from both Clark Heights and Jackson, and the atmosphere in Santos [a border community] is hard because people are very suspicious and they're very cautious themselves and so it makes it hard to build a movement because everybody there is so . . . kind of like watching their backs, making sure that they're OK."

Much like the ineligibility for federal financial aid, the existence of federal immigration checkpoints has reached into the lives of undocumented organizers and limited their mobility. These boundaries affect not only the extent to which undocumented organizers like Cecilia can perform their everyday activities but also their efforts to motivate others to do so as well. Marcos, who had been organizing as an undocumented immigrant in California for more than three years, also expressed that "sometimes it's hard with our movement, with undocumented people it's hard to have them come out because of fear of getting caught or forms of mobility, transportation." As undocumented youth grow up, immigration policies limit their opportunities for both social and physical movement. Nonetheless, undocumented immigrants employ various organizing tools to create their own spaces of belonging.

Finding a Sense of Belonging through Organizing

For the last decade, undocumented young adults have been at the fore-front of immigrant rights organizing. Before a form of the Dream Act failed to pass through Congress in 2010, undocumented youth largely organized through national networks that were led by individuals who had legal status.[12] Between 2001 and 2010, Dream Act legislation was repeatedly introduced in Congress but failed to secure enough votes to become law. Despite those frustrating failures, undocumented youth began to assert their political voice and move to the forefront of immigrant rights organizing. Many undocumented youth felt empowered to continue organizing, but only a subset of these organizers continued to fight for comprehensive immigration reform, while another subset began to engage in antideportation campaigns.[13] Oscar, for example, initially became involved in organizing after the defeat of the Dream Act in 2010 because it both "devastated" him and motivated him "to contribute to the Dream Act movement." Undocumented youth such as Oscar have mobilized to build a strong infrastructure and message. To do so, they have created community- and school-based organizations across the United States. It is in these spaces that undocumented youth most often find a sense of belonging through shared ideologies and identities.[14]

United We Dream (UWD) is the largest undocumented youth–led network in the United States to date. As of 2016, the network was made up of more than fifty affiliate organizations that are located in different cities across the country. Known for advocating and working with immigrant communities, the network provided assistance to youth applying for DACA, organizes to stop deportations, and develops a number of educational resources for undocumented students.[15] At the state level, California is home to one of the largest numbers of undocumented youth–led organizations, with many of them located on college campuses.

Many of the undocumented young adults with whom I spoke first became politically active offline through organizations that are affiliated with UWD, while others began to organize online instead. Both groups were largely motivated to take civic and political action because they realized that they were not alone. Rocio, for example, first became an organizer in 2010 when she met fellow undocumented youth at a hunger strike. Rocio learned what it meant to be undocumented during high school when her peers began to ask her why she did not have a driver's license. She expressed that in many ways her high school experience happened in a "bubble" because her peers were predominantly white, of higher socioeconomic backgrounds, and documented. In all, she felt protected to some degree.

It was not until Rocio came across undocumented organizers staging a hunger strike in support of the Dream Act that she decided it was time for her to also become politically active. Rocio elaborated on the impact this event had on her:

> It was an amazing moment to get involved. It was a hunger strike, which was a very drastic form of organizing, very aggressive. And I met wonderful organizers who inspired me to continue to be involved. It was very empowering. I was like, "This is it. I'm at home" because I've always been involved, always volunteered, I've always been a leader, but it was very . . . I don't want to say superficial because it did mean a lot to me, but it wasn't like real-life stuff. It was more like résumé building, or it was more like competing against your own, other members in that same organization, or it was for the school, it was for an institution, it was to represent a system. Until I got to Dreamers, until I got to that hunger strike, I was like, "This is real. This is so real." Everyone is on the same page, for the same purpose, without getting anything in return.

Undocumented youth find offline actions to be particularly empowering. From hunger strikes to "coming out of the shadows" rallies, these events provide youth with a sense of empowerment and community. Organizing offers a way to experience belonging. Through these efforts, they are able to better address the issues that are affecting the broader undocumented community. In unity and solidarity, undocumented youth are coming together offline and organizing workshops, press conferences, rallies, and more. Offline organizers are able to reach fellow undocumented immigrants and motivate them to take action while providing information and resources in person.

And yet, as mentioned previously, undocumented organizers must take into consideration the ways in which their lack of legal status shapes the extent to which they can participate politically and encourage others to do the same. Esmeralda was confronted by this reality when she was helping organize the first "coming out of the shadows" rally in her city in 2010. She shared her experience and some of the challenges that came up: "Someone had e-mailed me saying, 'Why are you asking people to come out?' Was that even safe? Was I trying to get people arrested?" It is during this moment that Esmeralda decided to make use of online tools to reach a wider audience. She responded to that e-mail:

> I answered that question publicly on the [organization] website because I thought, "Well, there must be other people thinking the same thing, right?" Or asking the same question. So then I thought, "OK, well, this is probably something a lot of people are thinking about." So when I was asked that I said, "Then we should have an advice column." The person I had been checking with asked me my first question just to get it off the ground. He asked me, what was I pushing for? And so I responded to his question, and all of a sudden it just took off and I received questions from all over the place—from youth trying to go to college, to older people that want to have kids, folks that have never been involved, folks that are citizens and want to get married with someone who is undocumented.

Undocumented youth, like Esmeralda, find that it is difficult to organize and motivate others to do so as well when the threat of deportation is present. How have undocumented youth made strategic use of online tools to circumvent these challenges?

Undocumented Organizers' Use of Online Tools

The use of information and communication technology, such as group websites, online petitions, and e-mail addresses, came to the forefront of social movements during the mid-1990s.[16] Some of the largest undocumented-led networks to date were created by undocumented youth who first connected with each other over the Internet.[17] The more I spoke with youth who first started their organizing online, the more I became aware that forms of inclusion and belonging are also being created over the Internet. Moreover, it is in these spaces that undocumented youth can temporarily reach beyond some of the limits of their status.

Cesar, for example, first became politically active through a Facebook group of undocumented young adults. Marcos has never met some of his fellow organizers in person, but over the years, they have developed a level of mutual trust and closeness. Marcos described the online community he has been a part of for over five years:

> There are a lot of people that have had their entire families deported and they're the only person that's staying here. One of the administrators of the [group], he is a full-time activist. Sometimes he works and sometimes he doesn't. Sometimes he has to ask us for help for rent or food, and there's different venues that we use online so we can chip in and help for food or rent, but we know he's working really hard to help the movement so we help him. I like that we're able to connect with people like that. It's like a family, we call each other a family. I feel like I really know them. A lot of them I really know them, but I've never met them.

Like Cesar, other undocumented young adults are using online tools to create and build upon online communities where they can support one another. The youth I spoke with primarily used Facebook, Twitter, Skype, and e-mail to stay in touch. For these immigrants, civic and political involvement consists of sharing their undocumented status to raise awareness, fighting deportations, declaring oneself "unafraid" and "unashamed," and fighting against anti-immigrant legislation.[18]

In addition to making it possible for undocumented youth from across the country to connect with each other, online tools have also been helpful for organizers to partially transcend national borders. As undocumented immigrants, it would be very difficult for youth to travel outside of the United States and legally return. For organizers like Cecilia, online tools have allowed them to make connections beyond national borders. Cecilia shared the following about her friendship with a formerly undocumented young adult who was deported to Mexico in 2011: "I've also chatted with him and we talked about, like, his experience in Mexico and it's, like, I've never met this guy . . . never, but we both heard about each other because we're both undocumented, we're both part of this movement and so . . . there's already, like, a connection . . . something that connects us."

In addition to finding a sense of community using both offline and online tools, undocumented youth are resisting anti-immigrant policies in solidarity with fellow activists across the United States. Marcos, for example, first became involved online in 2012. His online activism includes managing the social media accounts for an offline undocumented youth–led nationwide campaign. After becoming an online activist, Marcos also began to organize offline as a member of an undocumented youth–led organization. As an offline activist, Marcos was fortunate to attend a legislative visit in Sacramento, the state capital, with fellow activists. Consequently, he was able to connect with others beyond the online audience and with those outside of his offline organization. When I asked him to tell me about events that have impacted him the most, he thought back to the time he traveled outside of San Diego to the state capital. As he described: "There's so much energy, so much happening, and it does empower you. It does help you understand you do have a voice even if you're undocumented." Marcos also spoke about using Facebook to stand in solidarity with fellow activists: "Here in Victorville [Marcos's city of residence] at least we're in contact with, like, the DREAMS or UNITED [undocumented youth–led organizations] further up north in California. Having Facebook does help communicate."

Undocumented organizers are increasingly using online tools to connect with youth beyond their local communities. In doing so, they are able to share information, meet, plan events, network, sign petitions, and more. Online organizers use their voices to reach larger audiences and to contribute to changing the representations of what it means to be undocumented. Online tools not only facilitate the dissemination of information but also can be used to foster feelings and spaces of inclusion among undocumented organizers. Those who are unable to organize offline, due to their immigration status, can find online spaces that provide support to undocumented immigrants and offer opportunities to become politically active. For example, in online settings, undocumented youth share and sign petitions to fight deportations. To be sure, organizers are finding that online tools are enhancing their offline activism rather than replacing it. Both forms of organizing allow for a group that is legally, socially, and culturally marginalized to find a voice in their power to fight back, but also to create a space of belonging with fellow undocumented youth who share their experiences and goals.

Conclusion: Organizing in the Present Time

The executive order creating DACA allowed beneficiaries the opportunity to become somewhat more socially and physically mobile. With a work permit and a Social Security number in hand, youth with DACA were able to apply to higher-paying jobs, obtain a driver's license, and return to school.[19] Maribel, an undocumented young adult in California who did not qualify for DACA, was hopeful that such a federal program might ultimately strengthen the immigrant rights movement more broadly. She recognized what it means to be undocumented, including the precarious state of "deportability" and the other limitations and challenges undocumented immigration status entails. In her view: "We still have a lot to do and hopefully the deferred action makes the movement stronger because then I know more people are going to be more free, they're going to move freely, not thinking about checkpoints, thinking about being deported, and so these people if they are still committed to the cause, I know for sure that the movement is going to become stronger."

DACA opened up possibilities for individual immigrants as well as created spaces for a number of undocumented youth–led actions. There have been efforts to move away from the Dreamer narrative by helping stop the deportations of undocumented immigrants whether or not they are students.[20] Undocumented organizers have also been raising awareness about the ways in which their different identities intersect and shape their experiences. For example, the UndocuBlack Network first convened in 2016 in the state of Florida as an effort to advocate for the undocumented and Black community.

In all, undocumented young adults have been increasingly motivated to act from the understanding of a shared experience. They have been seeking not only to address the barriers associated with being undocumented but also to challenge its root causes and suggest alternatives. As they engaged in organizing, they were both coping with and resisting a climate of exclusion. By creating and sustaining undocumented-led networks, youth made a space to support each other and use their agency to create change. With the use of both online and offline tools, undocumented youth created a space of inclusion, one where they could be resilient and collectively fight for political, social, and cultural transformation.

9

Dreaming across Borders

DEBORAH A. BOEHM

In the fall of 2014, forty-two *sonadores*, or "Dreamers"—undocumented immigrant youth and young adults—traveled from the United States to Mexico to visit their nation of origin. Selected to participate as leaders in their communities, they went as guests of the Mexican government through a program coordinated by Mexico's Secretaría de Relaciones Exteriores (Ministry of Foreign Affairs). Because those in the group had come to the United States without authorization, most had not had the opportunity to travel to Mexico since first migrating as young children; many had left Mexico as infants or toddlers and had no memories of their nation of origin. Traveling with an Advance Parole issued by US Citizenship and Immigration Services (USCIS),[1] the young people spent five days in Mexico City, visiting museums and archaeological sites, attending educational and cultural sessions, and participating in press conferences and other media events.

At one of the early panels, participants spoke of their individual and collective *sueños*, or "dreams," describing what they hoped the future might bring: opportunities in higher education, successful careers, families reunified after years apart. Several participants also spoke of the "dreams" that had motivated their parents'—and thus their own—migration to the United States decades earlier. One participant also mentioned what he called "another dream," the chance to return to Mexico after so many years, adding that, through the Mexican government's program, his "dream had become a reality." Finally, someone mentioned that many of the young people in the room lived "un sueño partido [a dream divided]." For everyone there, their lives, families, and futures were indeed split down the middle, divided by one of the world's most militarized international borders.

* * *

Dreamers, or undocumented migrant youth,[2] are undeniably transnational: they were born in one country yet are living in another; their families have ties to two places; and two nations may, in fact, be home for them. Still, young people without authorization may find themselves trapped in the United States in a sense, unable to leave the country while also ensuring secure return passage at some point in the future. In part, this landscape changed after DACA, which provided eligible immigrant youth with work authorization, a temporary deferral of deportation, and the possibility of international travel through Advance Parole. Everyone at the first gathering of Dreamers traveled on Advance Parole and, although reentry was not guaranteed, hoped to return to the United States with government approval after several days in Mexico.

Based on ethnographic research with this group of DACA recipients—or "DACAmented" immigrants—who were invited by the Mexican government to visit "their homeland," I consider the particular border crossing of these forty-two immigrants, but also border crossings more generally, in a time of increasingly blocked movement for unauthorized migrants living in the United States.[3] Although all participants on this trip requested and were granted permission to travel to Mexico through Advance Parole, their "returns"—first to Mexico and then to the United States—demonstrate how DACA created a curious status of being both *in* certain legal categories and part of two countries, and also *outside* of the United States in a sense, on the margins of legal membership and without direct access to US citizenship.

The group trip also illustrated how "dreams" for family, self, and future can circulate transnationally—at times with relative ease, but often blocked by US policies that, without comprehensive immigration reform, provide limited opportunities for changing one's status and starting on a path toward citizenship. The experiences of the Dreamers who traveled to Mexico underscore the ways they are transnational subjects with family on both sides of the border and irrefutable claims to two nations, but their trip also reveals the precarity of undocumented migrant youth who were born elsewhere and raised in the United States, those who rightfully view the country as their home but do not have the legal rights of citizenship that they deserve.

Between Two Nations

When Ceci arrived at Mexico City's airport for the gathering, she did not know what to expect: as she later recounted, after living throughout her childhood, adolescence, and early adulthood in the United States, it was a challenge to imagine how she would feel "back" in Mexico, a place she had migrated from as a young child. Ceci described the strange feeling she had as she walked off the plane and made her way toward Mexican immigration officials. When she discovered there were two lines to choose from—"nationals" and "foreigners"—she felt uncertain. She paused, wondering which category best fit her status; as she later said to fellow Dreamers, "I wasn't sure where to go." After reflection, she decided it was most fitting to enter the country as a "national," especially since she was traveling with a Mexican passport. Still, she was also traveling with documents acquired through DACA, including the paperwork for Advance Parole that she would use the following week to return to the United States. In that strange moment in the airport, Ceci was at an actual and symbolic crossroads, one that captured what she and other undocumented young adults experience on a daily basis.

Thus, liminality—or the experience of being "in between"—is often familiar to, if not a way of life for, Dreamers, DACAmented immigrants, and migrant youth whose de facto membership in the United States may not be formally recognized as such. Part of two nations, though also excluded at times from either or both, undocumented immigrant children, youth, and young adults may find themselves between two places. Those who migrated to the United States without documents as children are undeniably in the nation—members of the country and part of communities just as US citizen children and youth are. And, yet, because they do not have access to formal membership or an easy path to citizenship, youth and young adults without documents are also outside of the nation, legally excluded from the country that is in every other way their home.

These are indeed "lives in limbo,"[4] an uncertain status that is familiar to young people living in the United States with transnational ties to other countries. Both "here" and "not here" in a sense, young immigrants have lives rooted in two places, even as they might be on the margins of both.[5] Scholars working with transnational immigrants in diverse circumstances in the United States have identified similarly contradictory positionalities, calling them "spaces of nonexistence,"[6] "vulnerable stability,"[7] or "liminal legality"[8] that blurs categorization of documented and undocumented migrants. Such forms of "legal limbo"[9] also describe the DACA recipients who traveled together to Mexico in 2014, a group of immigrants whose "heritage trip" underscored the complexities of belonging and exclusion for so many in the United States.

Transnational Ties

Nearly everyone traveling with the group had family in Mexico and hoped that the trip would provide an opportunity to reconnect with loved ones, to visit relatives the Dreamers had not seen for years, or to make a first contact with others they had never met. One delegate, Teo, described tracking down several family members, despite the challenge of finding them without a phone number or street address. Years earlier, Teo had migrated to the United States with his parents and siblings. Teo's father had lost contact with his family after their phone number suddenly stopped working; because Teo's father was undocumented in the United States, he could not easily return to Mexico, and so after the phone line was disconnected the family had no easy way to reach each other. Although it seemed like "finding a needle in a haystack," Teo's father made a small map to guide Teo to the family home. Teo closely followed his father's directions for taking the metro, walking along particular streets, looking for a specific gate. He was surprised—and thrilled—when a cousin he had never met opened the door.

Another participant, Daniela, had a chance to visit with her father and brother the night before the formal gathering began; the men had traveled by bus from the coast to visit with Daniela in Mexico City. Deportation had split the family years earlier. Because of Daniela's undocumented status, she had not been able to travel to visit with her father and brother since their return to Mexico. Although Daniela was disappointed that their time together was so brief, she was happy to see her father and brother and reconnect after years apart. Without DACA and the possibility of Advance Parole, Daniela, Teo, and others on the trip would not have had the chance to spend time with family, and they were grateful to have had the opportunity.

So DACA provided increased flexibility and possibility to the travelers, even if they were not able to spend extended time with family or, as was the case for most participants, did not have enough time to travel to visit with family members living in other parts of Mexico. Recognized by the US state—though with a status of being "partially authorized"—DACAmented immigrants were granted certain privileges. With an approved application, DACA recipients could seek employment, pursue an education, and, as I focus on here, potentially travel internationally with Advance Parole. In this way, the partial status of DACA translated into an opportunity to physically move transnationally and to enact or fulfill the de facto transnationality that shapes the lives of DACA recipients. All the young people on the trip were there because of DACA and specifically because of the openings that Advance Parole provided. Thus, the chance for individuals to visit their home country and for families to reunite—even if fleeting—illustrates the transnational connections that DACA supported. Many of those in Mexico City wondered if they would ever again see family members in Mexico; for those who did, the trip, facilitated by Advance Parole, provided what was quite literally the chance of a lifetime.

"A Dream Divided"

Although several travelers were able to connect with family while in Mexico City, the trip also underscored the limitations of DACA and the uncertainty of transnational movement and one's ability to connect with family across borders for those with a temporary status. While DACA was designed to permit residence and work authorization in the United States, it did not allow the kind of "freedom of movement"[10] that reflects the Dreamers' actual lives and family networks. And, in the case of this trip, because the participants had family members from states throughout Mexico, not everyone had the same opportunity to reconnect with loved ones. Even as the event moved forward with a forum to explore "hopes and dreams," the realities of living in two nation-states—but without citizenship and full rights in one's nation of residence—was also present.

During one of the sessions in Mexico City, officials from the Ministry of Foreign Affairs provided a presentation titled "Important Information for Your Return Trip." Representatives of the Mexican government described what to expect. All participants would enter the United States through one of two ports of entry: Houston, Texas, or Atlanta, Georgia. The plan was to closely monitor the border crossing for everyone on the trip—officials from both the Mexican Consulate and the US Department of State would be available to ensure that the process went smoothly or to intervene in the event that it did not. As the representatives from the Mexican government spoke, the Dreamers were reminded of their tenuous status. One speaker asked the travelers to keep Mexican officials informed about their whereabouts, saying, "If you are staying in Mexico to visit family and not returning with the group, please let us know right away." They provided contact information for the Mexican Consulates in Houston and Atlanta and reminded participants that, although they anticipated that all would be able to reenter the United States without problems, they wanted everyone to be prepared should there be any unexpected developments.

The session about travel with Mexican officials underscored the more general precarity of DACA status and the tenuous character of Advance Parole in particular. Even if approved, leaving the United States with Advance Parole can result in being denied reentry by US officials, putting individuals at risk of being permanently out of and excluded from the country. And, despite the travel that was made possible because of Advance Parole, this trip and the transnational movement that it facilitated were, in many ways, exceptional. Advance Parole relies on the approval of USCIS in the first place, and, given the requirements of an application for Advance Parole—it is granted only in certain cases, such as family emergencies or organized educational programs like the trip for the Dreamers—it was never an option for the majority of DACA recipients.

And, as the young people discussed throughout the trip, travel authorized by the US government is not possible for the millions of undocumented children and youth living in the United States who never qualified for or received DACA or for undocumented migrants who entered the United States as adults; for most, there is no Advance Parole. The Dreamers frequently reminded the group that their family members had never been given the opportunity to return to Mexico for a visit, just as they did not have access to a temporary deferral of removal such as DACA. Again and again, the Dreamers spoke of their family members,

DREAMING ACROSS BORDERS | 165

and especially their parents, who were unable to travel to Mexico, those who were "left out" and not included in possibilities for administrative relief. The young people spoke of "the civil rights that families have" and asked why their parents were often blamed in public discourse for bringing their children to the United States in search of a better life. Throughout the sessions, the travelers challenged the demonizing narrative that blames parents for migrating with children to the United States without papers. As one participant asked, "Who is actually at fault?"

In, Out, and In Between

Throughout the week's events, conversations revealed shifting identities as participants candidly described the liminality that was commonplace for them. The sessions' titles captured the transnationality of the participants and their families, including "*Diálogo transnacional y agendas compartidas*" (Transnational Dialogue and Shared Agendas) and "*La visión de los Dreamers sobre sí mismos y temas de la agenda nacional de EUA y bilateral con México*" (The Dreamers' Vision of Themselves and Topics from the US National Agenda and Bilateral Agenda with Mexico). Events during the visit focused on transnational connections as well as the many contradictions that came out of the experiences of young people who are indeed from two countries.

Especially during the discussion periods following each panel, the participants described the paradoxical feelings the trip highlighted, emotions that they had long experienced but that came into relief during their travels to Mexico. In many ways, the young people felt like tourists, but the trip was also a meaningful homecoming. Throughout the week, there was frequent code-switching, and one organizer told me the trip was an opportunity for the Dreamers to "practice their native language," adding that perhaps they had *two* native languages. Mexican officials embraced the delegation as "our future," calling the young people "our ambassadors in the United States," even though the delegates were in fact representatives of the United States in Mexico as much as they were Mexican "diplomats" living abroad.

Both organizers and participants understood the Dreamers to be from two places. Throughout the week, the young people spoke of their shifting national identities. "Now I feel as though I am from both *here* and *there*," said one immigrant; another declared that, regardless of one's place of birth or upbringing, "we are *all* Dreamers." Many mentioned that they were undeniably "Mexican" and very pleased to visit the country where they were born. As one delegate said: "The United States adopted me, but I will always be Mexican." And at an event with Mexican university students, a participant called himself "Latino, American, Mexican, Mexican American, *and* Hispanic." And, in fact, a multifaceted identity such as this was what most attendees claimed as their own.

Regardless of, despite, and/or because of a particular form of state-defined national membership, the Dreamers described their status within the United States—and to some degree within Mexico—as partial and uncertain, but also as multiple, fluid, and something more than membership in only one nation. At one session, as participants talked with each other about possible ways to foster formal transnational ties, they expressed both pride and frustration when they reflected on each nation's role in shaping their own trajectories. At times, they described anger toward their two countries, asking, What steps is the Mexican government taking to strengthen its economy, actions that might prevent migration in the first place? Doesn't the United States have a responsibility to provide formal membership to the young people raised there? At times, the fact that the participants did not have US citizenship was described as resulting in a form of exclusion, but at other times, they refuted such marginalization by claiming membership within both Mexico and the United States.

Members of this delegation arguably do have citizenship in two places: in this case, formal or legal Mexican citizenship and de facto US citizenship. Throughout the events, Mexican officials addressed the young people as their *paisanos*, or fellow nationals, and of course they are Mexican citizens. However, the participants also spoke of the ways in which they may not identify (or at least not exclusively) with Mexico. For many, the trip was to a country they did not remember and a homeland that is, paradoxically, a foreign place. At the same time, the US government does not formally recognize any form of "citizenship" for these travelers despite their undeniable membership within the United States. In this sense, they were, and continue to be, outside of both countries, but also important members of two nations.

DREAMING ACROSS BORDERS | 167

The experiences of the invitees—during their travels in 2014 but also in their everyday lives—demonstrate how those who came to the United States as children live in a liminal space, within but also "in between" two countries. Whether they identify with both places, at times with neither place, and/or as divided by the border, where DACA recipients situate home—as so many participants described—can be "complicated." They expressed ambivalence: nearly everyone who spoke up during the public sessions said they considered the United States to be "home," or at least one of their homes, but they also described how at times they did not feel accepted by "either," highlighted by the phrase that was repeated by so many: "I am from neither here nor there." One participant explained the experience as a kind of conundrum—yes, they are from both places, but they also face "double invisibility" or "double the discrimination."

Still, despite this bind the participants described—the challenge of being "from neither here nor there" or "doubly invisible"—they also spoke of the strength that comes from a liminal status. The participants expressed a range of emotions throughout the visit to Mexico City, including confusion, frustration, and longing, but they also spoke of, and embodied, strength and tenacity. Both organizers and participants described this first cohort as determined, persistent, and committed, those who would continue to work for justice. In one session, an immigrant called the group "fighters," and other speakers highlighted their "human capital." As one member of the delegation commented, "Sometimes I feel that I have been broken" by the complicated, even tricky, situation of being raised in the United States without US citizenship. "Yes," said another, it is a mess in many ways, and I feel "divided," but remember, "Somos guerreros [we are warriors]!"

* * *

Throughout the week, the group would load onto a tour bus, ready for travel to the next event or day trip. The mood on the bus, as it drove through traffic in Mexico City, was upbeat, with people talking, laughing, and getting to know one another. The organizers would make announcements about upcoming events, ranging from a discussion with students from Mexico City's leading public university, Universidad Nacional Autónoma de México, or a trip to the pyramids at Teotihuacán, to a visit to a modern art museum or dinner with city officials. On one bus ride, a group of those sitting near the back starting calling for a game, chanting, "Spirit animal, spirit animal!" The organizers passed the microphone, sending it around the bus, row by row, as each person identified a "spirit animal" and then explained why. One woman described herself as "a kitten because I am cuddly." Another traveler identified with horses "because I am strong." Near the end, one participant said that perhaps a "spirit insect" was most fitting: "Soy cucaracha [I am a cockroach]. I can survive anything!" Loud cheers, applause, and whistles filled the bus.

Returning Home?

Although it was not initially part of the schedule, several delegates had reached out to a group of fellow immigrants and set up a final session with a special panel of invitees—those who identified as "los otros Dreamers."[11] These "other Dreamers" were young adults who, like those on the trip, were born in Mexico but had grown up in the United States. But unlike those with DACA, the other Dreamers had returned to Mexico and were now living there for a variety of reasons: deportation (their own and/or that of a family member), the recession, family hardship, the death of a loved one. As they spoke that final day, just before those with DACA prepared to leave, it became clear that for all the Dreamers, regardless of their trajectories, a series of circumstances outside of their control had resulted in transnational lives and families rooted in both the United States and Mexico. And, like those who were DACAmented, the "other Dreamers" had been raised in and were indisputably members of the United States. But unlike those with DACA, the possibility for administrative relief or deferred deportation had come too late.

It was a sobering end to a whirlwind trip. As many of the panelists described, had they stayed in the United States, they, too, would have likely qualified for DACA. "We feel forgotten," said one panelist. "We, too, are 'Dreamers,' but Dreamers who have returned or been deported." They spoke of dreams fulfilled and dreams shattered, dreams attained and those not actualized. The invited guests described how their lives had changed since returning to Mexico—some were studying, others had started rewarding careers, all said they wished they could again go to the United States, even if only to visit. But, as they had discovered since returning to Mexico, such returns were challenging; for most Mexican nationals, it was difficult to get even a tourist visa. For those who had been deported, it was nearly impossible. The panelists also spoke of "some other Dreamers," those they called "los terceros Dreamers." This "third group" of Dreamers also dreamed across borders: Central American youth who were migrating north, young people who faced grave danger as they made their way through Mexico en route to the United States.

This final session with the "other Dreamers" reminded everyone in the group that, like migration, return can be complicated. Whether north or south, by force or by choice, the returns of those who call themselves "Dreamers" underscore transnational ties, but also illustrate the ways that families and communities are separated across borders. Similarly, the different groups of Dreamers shared a common experience of residing in the liminal spaces of binational identity, of where to place home, of one's own geographies. All in attendance were notably frustrated by state policies that define national membership in a way that privileges political borders and according to divides that do not accurately reflect the lives of so many.

Finally, the participants were reminded that returns can bring the unexpected. This was certainly the case for these participants who traveled to Mexico for the first gathering of Dreamers in 2014. It was also the case as they traveled "back" to the United States, returning once more. After the trip, I learned that the process at airports in Houston and Atlanta had gone smoothly—for the most part. Everyone was admitted to the United States using Advance Parole. Still, some reported that individual US agents had hassled them, asking a series of questions and holding the DACA recipients for much longer periods than others attempting to enter the country. One agent even told a traveler that he disagreed with DACA and thought it was bad policy, underscoring the fragility of Advance Parole as a path to return after traveling outside of the United States.

In the end, the (albeit liminal) status of DACA provided some flexibility, including the chance for these forty-two Dreamers to visit Mexico as guests of the Mexican government. Still, the border crossing after the trip reminded participants that theirs was a temporary status, part of a program that has provided some security but has also created uncertainty for DACA recipients. Underscoring this point, on September 5, 2017, three years after the group of Dreamers returned, US attorney general Jeff Sessions announced the devastating news that President Trump would discontinue DACA in 2018, creating an (even more) uncertain future for the nearly 800,000 DACA recipients who call the United States home and whose national belonging is indisputable even as it is not formally recognized by the US government. DACA came about because of the actions of young people, many of them part of the first group of Dreamers to visit Mexico City. As they gathered in Mexico in 2014, they recognized how fruitful their actions had been; as one participant stated, "DACA was the result of all of us," but "it is only *un paso*, a first step" in the struggle for recognition.

REFLECTIONS

Looking Forward

ABEL NÚÑEZ AND RACHEL GITTINGER

As the last rays of sunlight disappeared over the nation's capital, a crowd fell silent at the steps of Saint John's Church. Typically a place of worship for US presidents and their families, for several months in 2014 the front steps of the church welcomed Monday night vigils with those at the opposite end of the spectrum of social and political power: unaccompanied, undocumented children and their advocates. This night's group was diverse and included university students, professionals young and old, advocates, faith leaders, journalists, and more. That evening, for the first time, the vigil was led entirely by unaccompanied children and youth themselves, and all eyes focused on them as they fidgeted nervously at the foot of the steps.

Erminia, a petite sixteen-year-old Salvadoran, took the microphone. She spoke timidly at first, but her voice gained strength with every word as she responded to the executive action President Obama had announced just four days earlier. She spoke of the expanded DACA protections: "It's good, but it doesn't cover the youth and children who are recent arrivals. If the president and Congress don't help us, many young people will not be able to achieve their goals." As the mic passed from child to child, they shared their stories, the situations that forced their migration, and their hopes for a safe and vibrant future. Then, megaphones and posters in hand, they led the crowd in chants and a slow march through Lafayette Park, stopping directly in front of the White House.

Another young student, Eduardo, took the mic and took a deep breath. His jawline hardened several times before he finally spoke. He cleared his throat and began to rap: "We are a people asking for freedom / To not be afraid that we will be deported / We're crying out to the president that this must stop." Eduardo's voice cracked and faltered, long enough that it was possible to hear anti-immigrant protesters yelling, "Go back to your country! No illegals here." Eduardo continued with new resolve. As he reached the middle of the song, the young people took hands and faced the White House: "All the youth united as brothers and sisters / are here together because we are already tired / We are protesting for our loved ones / We want this message to be heard." Finally, speaking directly to Obama, the crowd joined in the familiar refrain: "Mr. President, we come humbly so you will tell us something. We are right here in front of you." As the vigil, and their first political action, concluded, the youth embraced and leapt in victory. The adrenaline they felt at the crowd's support, and at visibly challenging the status quo just steps from arguably the most powerful house in the world, was undeniable. For the moment, they were filled with hope, all but certain that change would be coming, as if their request was undeniable.

Erminia and Eduardo: A Tale of Two Unaccompanied Minors

Years later, there has been no such change. The group has gained and lost some faces, but nearly all are unrecognizable; physically, voices are deeper and faces more mature, but it is the emotional transformation that is most striking. These young people have lost their naïveté, gained confidence, and learned to negotiate life as undocumented refugee youth in Washington, DC. More than anything, they have come to terms with the reality that nothing in this fight will be quick.

Some are thriving. Erminia has blossomed into a confident young woman, pursuing the many opportunities afforded her through public speaking, advocacy, and leadership programs. These have included a prestigious weeklong Congressional Hispanic Caucus Institute fellowship, testimony at the DC Council, and a high-profile roundtable on immigration with then presidential candidate Bernie Sanders. She still grins when "her friend Bernie" mentions her in speeches as "a young Salvadoran woman I met who traveled here unaccompanied." She is succeeding in school, on track to graduate and attend college, and on a path to legalize her status and pursue citizenship. For Eduardo, the American Dream has proved more elusive. Following a fight with his father and an interaction with the juvenile justice system, he disappeared from DC for some time. Upon his return, he reenrolled in school and was doing well until economic realities forced him to drop out to work full-time, unable to both support himself and continue his studies. His music career is on hold, perhaps forever, and there is no legal relief in sight.

What made the difference in these stories? Both of these young people were doing well in school, with aspirations of higher education, and plenty of resilience and ambition. One might say that of the two, Eduardo had the raw talent and, with a pending record deal, was in a better position to capitalize on those skills to ease his integration. So what went wrong? This is a haunting question for those of us who are service providers. Why did we fail to help break down Eduardo's barriers in the same way that we did Erminia's? These are the questions that local communities across our nation are struggling to address.

Responses: Information, Advocacy, and Coordination

Just as this cycle did not begin with the president's declaration of an "urgent humanitarian situation" in 2014, it cannot be broken without addressing the root causes of migration and the policies that created them. Unequal economic policies, political interventions, and militarized responses to crime will likely increase human rights violations and instability across the Americas, while failing to reduce the migration of Central American youth. To date, the United States has ignored root causes in favor of a strategy of "Prevention Through Deterrence" (see De León, this volume), a program through which the US government denies humanitarian responsibility under national and international law by preventing migrants from reaching the US-Mexico border. US administrations fail to recognize the futility of a deterrence strategy aimed at children whose migration is driven by a simple goal: the will to live. In an increasingly globalized world, the criminalization of human movement should be challenged. Migration is, and will continue to be, a symptom of systemic inequalities and lack of opportunity. A more appropriate response is one in which people throughout the Americas are provided the opportunity to thrive in their country of origin—one in which migration is an option, not a necessity.

The same images that accompanied sensationalized 2014 headlines sent shockwaves through the community of service providers and activists working with Central Americans in the Washington, DC, metropolitan area, Maryland, and Virginia (the DMV). Many had been working locally since the 1980s, when the DMV became home to the second-largest Salvadoran community in the United States. Activists knew it was only a matter of time before the border crisis would become a local one; the children would be here soon. In anticipation of this shift, more than 200 individuals came together to organize a regional response. The group, named the DC-MD-VA Coalition in Support of Children Fleeing Violence, represented diverse sectors, including community-based organizations, communities of faith, legal and medical practitioners, and local government institutions.

The Central American Resource Center (CARECEN) was a founding member of the coalition. CARECEN is a community-based organization established in 1981 as Central Americans fleeing US-funded civil wars settled in Washington, DC. Today, its mission is to foster the comprehensive development of the Latino community in the Washington metropolitan region by providing direct services while also promoting grassroots empowerment, civic engagement, and human rights advocacy. CARECEN, which views migration from a transnational perspective, recognized that worsening conditions in Central America and at the US-Mexico border would soon affect the local DC community and thus concentrated its efforts on the coordination of a local response.

Initial coalition meetings focused on gathering information to determine an appropriate response. The coalition ultimately decided to form three groups to address different aspects of the crisis: (1) coordination to address detention processes at the border, (2) local and federal advocacy efforts and (3) coordination of local service provisions. The coalition held weekly vigils at the White House for more than five months, which were successful in mobilizing support, generating consistent news coverage, and forcing the issue to remain ever-present in the minds of the public and policy makers. The final vigil, described at the opening of this essay, was led by youth from CARECEN's newcomer leadership program, days after President Obama's anticipated executive action failed to address the plight of unaccompanied children.

At the federal level, CARECEN helped organize a meeting with the White House, where the Obama administration's lack of commitment to international protections for unaccompanied minors became evident.

Despite the fact that the Northern Triangle countries of Guatemala, Honduras, and El Salvador have some of the highest homicide rates in the world, the administration refused to recognize Central American children as forced migrants, labeling them instead as "economic migrants" and alleging that false claims asserted by human smugglers had triggered the surge. In lieu of a federal response, the coalition focused efforts at the local level, pushing the DC Council and surrounding county governments to implement proactive policies and coordinate and align crucial services for children arriving to the region. Aiming to ensure that youth receive the support and protection they need—both in countries of origin and in their receiving communities—the coalition turned its focus to filling the gaps locally.

"We're Going to Need a Bigger Room": The Power of Youth Voices

The newest arrivals are best suited to inform our short-term goals: How can we support the immediate needs of incoming children? However, as youth mature and transition from newcomer children to immigrant adults, their perspectives shift away from immediate survival to long-term stability and fulfillment. The question then becomes: What are the support systems and resources necessary to thrive as young adults within a system that continues to exclude them? As youth mature in age and are integrated within their new communities, they are increasingly equipped to provide guidance on this transition. Viewing diverse youth as equal partners with seasoned adult advocates is critical to achieving a measured, effective response grounded in youth feedback while also garnering strategic support from other members of communities.

As students learn about local government systems, they can transition from informing the priorities of adult advocates to directly participating in advocacy efforts themselves. The importance of this shift was evident in February 2016 at the DC Council hearing regarding the UDC Dream Act.[1] Council staff expected minimal public turnout, but minutes before the hearing was scheduled to begin, more than a hundred newcomer students and their teachers filled the room, sitting on the floor, crowding around the podium, and spilling out the doors. Council staff initially tried to limit attendance but finally was forced to announce, "It is clear this is an issue of importance to all of you here today. We're going to need a bigger room."

After the hearing was relocated to the largest room in the DC government building, Alfonso, a Guatemalan and one of the vigil leaders, testified alongside other newcomers. The room was silent as he shared his goal of being a pilot, his desire to attend university, and the barriers preventing him from achieving these goals. Through powerful actions and testimony such as this, newcomer youth call for their presence to be recognized, and challenge the contradictions in communities that both include and exclude them. When youth assert their presence and demand rights, local policy makers take notice. Not long after youth participated in a series of hearings, a DC Council member worked with CARECEN to introduce a resolution in support of unaccompanied children, which stated:

> The District of Columbia is immigrant friendly. . . . The Council of the District of Columbia urges President Obama and the Department of Homeland Security to cease the mass deportation raids of Central American refugees and to make it a priority to establish comprehensive humane immigration policies that preserve the unity and safety of refugees and asylum seekers.[2]

Legislative hearings are but one way to elevate youth voices, but they are not likely to initiate systemic change among a broader public.

Creative outlets such as art, photography, and poetry are tools that can effectively foster empathy and solidarity among the wider community, while providing young immigrants with the opportunity to express themselves, take ownership over their stories, and contribute to a larger narrative about immigrant youth in the United States. For example, CARECEN's youth program collaborated with *Washington Post* photojournalist Oliver Contreras to provide photography and storytelling workshops and to offer a platform for youth to narrate their own immigration stories through an interview and professional portrait. The project was converted into a photography exhibit entitled *Unaccompanied: Youth Seeking Refuge* that was featured in the *Washington Post*, at arts festivals, in conferences, and at universities. After viewing the exhibit, many audience members walk away with the desire to stand in solidarity and take action in support of newcomer children.

Youth leadership and storytelling can be equally effective in coalescing participation among peers. At the Civic Center in Silver Spring, Maryland, in April 2016, adult advocates were ushered out of the room, leaving the seventy unaccompanied youth gathered there to discuss their newcomer experience among peers. This youth summit was nearly a year in the making, as adult advocates guided young people through the process of creating goals and outcomes, developing an agenda, and planning the event. After an afternoon of intense dialogue around a variety of themes, youth provided recommendations regarding actions that would improve their immediate and long-term situations. Community advocates translated these suggestions into policy demands for local actors. The "roadmap forward" created by the DC community following the youth summit and a similar event aimed at service providers included several recommendations and guiding principles.

First, participants identified that legal representation is critical to successfully obtaining relief and must be expanded through creative pro bono partnerships and improved service coordination. Next, the groups shared that mental health services, such as emotional support, counseling, and trauma-informed care, are critical. Participants outlined that medical services should include on-site access to mental health services to help remove stigma and to ensure youth can process their experiences, form positive relationships, and overcome the trauma of their past. Third, youth and service providers described family reunification as a challenging process, as both parent and child will struggle to rebuild the relationship that was severed so long ago, and advocated for support such as reunification classes and family counseling to ease this transition.

Participants also outlined that educational institutions need to provide clear guidance on enrollment practices, be staffed with appropriate language access personnel and resources to ensure effective communication, offer programs that encourage English-language acquisition, cultivate respect through antibullying programs, and celebrate diversity among their student bodies. A fifth recommendation focused on extracurricular activities that provide youth access to a supportive environment to develop leadership skills, cultural understanding, and strong relationships among their peers. And, participants in the dialogues agreed that employment opportunities are essential as economic necessity will drive youth to seek employment.

As providers at CARECEN and members of the coalition have emphasized, local municipalities bear the responsibility of caring for unaccompanied youth and therefore should include youth directly in their efforts to do so. Often, undocumented youth remain acutely aware of their "illegality" despite local efforts, as day-to-day interactions are reminders of limited opportunities. In partnering with youth and supporting their demands with policy and advocacy experience, local communities can promote inclusion and a pathway toward a bright future.

Transnational Approach

A transnational approach to migration is central to viewing migration as part of the human condition and to creating the legal infrastructures in support of immigrants' rights in countries of origin, transit, and reception. What does a transnational dialogue look like in practice? Where can these collaborations begin? One example was a meeting of civil society actors held in San Salvador in July 2016. Attendees included representatives from Central American universities and social service agencies, international advocacy groups, and CARECEN. Using the story of a young Salvadoran pursuing asylum as a case study, participants shared information, clarified misconceptions, and identified several opportunities for collaboration.

One priority focused on supporting immigration legal cases. There were misconceptions about legal relief available in the United States and the processes through which immigrants might obtain such relief. For example, US community-based organizations could work with actors in the country of origin to assist young immigrants in obtaining documents such as birth certificates, school transcripts, or police reports, while local academics might provide expert statements on country conditions to support an asylum claim. The group also identified opportunities to help with the repatriation process if asylum is denied and the child is deported. Access to services and support upon repatriation are critical to the well-being of children and youth.

Participants also suggested actions to ensure safe passage for young people, such as coordinated efforts to document and prosecute crimes against migrants, to provide safe shelter, and to monitor law enforcement human rights abuses and violations of international law. There was also discussion about the importance of developing a unified regional policy agenda that promotes safety and prosperity across the Americas. Traveling delegations, for example, are an effective way to immerse local lawmakers and elected officials in the realities of migration and the necessity of the proposed policy agenda. CARECEN and other organizations participated in one such delegation in 2016. The group visited a detention center in Tapachula, Mexico, where Central Americans apprehended by Mexican immigration police are held prior to deportation. Elected officials were stunned to see so many youth and families desperate to escape violence and extreme poverty. As the guide shared stories of the traumas of gang violence, robbery, and sexual assault, the context of the "humanitarian crisis" became clear. When transnational advocacy is achieved, civil society has the power to promote long-term solutions that defend the human rights of communities and migrants across the Americas.

Moving forward, advocates face an increasingly hostile landscape under the Trump administration. Within days of Trump taking office, the administration's efforts to criminalize immigrants' journeys to and presence within our communities, limit options for legal relief, and narrow interpretations of asylee and refugee eligibility created new obstacles to advocating for humane immigration policies. However, these actions have also reawakened social movements, creating a sense of urgency and prompting massive outpouring of community support. The challenge in the coming months and years will be to effectively combat xenophobic narratives and criminalization while directing the power of new allies toward a transnational policy platform. As our work in the United States and transnationally has shown, strengthening existing relationships, forging new partnerships, and developing strong transnational alliances provide a promising way forward.

Conclusion

In the summer of 2016, Erminia dropped by the CARECEN office, as she frequently does. Sometimes she stops by just to say hello, sometimes for assistance in completing an application, or sometimes to talk through a challenge at home, school, or work. That day, Erminia beamed, pulled out her wallet, and showed me what had come in the mail the day before.

It was her work permit. Grinning from ear to ear, she said, "You'll have to tutor me for that citizenship test soon." I laughed, and we agreed that "after everything else, this is the easy part." That same week, I ran into Eduardo on the street. He was wearing blue coveralls and was about to start a twelve-hour shift. He was late for work, but I reminded him to drop by the office if he wanted to talk. He said that he would like to return to school in the future, but for now, "the money just doesn't add up."

Eduardo's story exposes the work left to do, and the gaps local service providers and policy makers must close. Erminia's story shows what is possible, and why that work is worth the effort. Her trajectory should be the expectation, not the anomaly. Civil society and government can create change. Advocacy and collaboration within local communities foster safe havens where immigrants and communities can flourish. By unifying these efforts and amplifying our voices on a transnational scale, civil society and especially youth themselves can lead the region toward a safer future where human rights are respected and all residents of the Americas can thrive.

REFLECTIONS

Still Dreaming

MARGARITA SALAS-CRESPO

My parents never thought of immigrating to the United States until my seventeen-year-old sister ran away to the United States with her boyfriend—a boyfriend we later found out was physically abusive. Once my parents learned of my sister's situation with her partner, they decided to travel to the United States and began to make arrangements to go north. When they first made the decision to immigrate, they did not plan for it to be a permanent move, but destiny chose otherwise. At first, my parents explored every option for migrating to the United States through legal channels. They processed our Mexican passports and then proceeded to Guadalajara, Jalisco, to request the visas. We made the trip three times, and each time we were denied US tourist visas due to insufficient proof of assets. Officials asked my family to provide proof of property ownership, bank statements, and other evidence of wealth that would ensure that we would not be traveling to the United States to stay.

My father, who had worked the land he inherited from his father, my grandfather, since he was eight years old, had experienced some of the worst years in agriculture. His land had become depleted after many years, and it barely provided any crops. My mother helped by selling candy and other Mexican goods from our porch. Aside from owning the land my father worked on, my parents owned a house in the town they grew up in and an apartment in the city in which we were living at the time. This was not enough for immigration officials, and after exhausting our funds in an attempt to gain legal entry to the United States, my parents decided to enter the country "illegally," or without government authorization. The decision was not an easy one to make, but the welfare of my sister was at stake, and so my parents did what they had to do to protect her. As a child, I had little to no understanding of the ramifications of our actions. I was ten years old at the time, and for me this was more of an adventure. I was so unaware of what was happening that I did not even say good-bye to the many friends I would never see again.

Our journey began as we traveled to Sonora, Mexico, where my father had been put in contact with an indigenous man in the area who, in conjunction with a coyote, would be facilitating our border crossing. We spent a few weeks there. Our guide wanted to make sure that we had the best chance of crossing the border without getting caught, so we had to wait until he thought it would be the best time to do so. The day finally came, and we set off to cross through the desert into the United States. The indigenous man brought us to a point where we met the coyote, who would be in charge for the rest of the journey. Our walk was only about twenty minutes long. As we made our way through the desert, I—a young, adventurous, and unafraid child—walked all the way to the front with the coyote and asked him as many questions as I could think of. The whole scenario was fascinating to me. I felt as though this was some sort of exploration and the coyote was the expert from whom I wanted to know more.

Soon enough we made it to a road and into a car. We were taken to a house where we would stay for a couple of days until they deemed it safe for us to travel to Las Vegas, where we would meet our family. Once in Las Vegas, we were reunited with my sister and other family members who had immigrated to the United States years before. The first few days were great as we bonded once again. Soon after our arrival, I learned that our move was to become permanent. My parents had exhausted our savings and sold all our belongings to cover the expenses of crossing the border without documents. The situation in Mexico had worsened as the Mexican government moved forward with a war on drugs. Jobs were disappearing and the economy was declining as crime and poverty increased. Having lost all our possessions in order to pay for the journey, my parents saw no reason to return, especially now that our family was reunited once again.

As we began settling into our new life, I made a fair attempt to fit in. I was the least happy about our move. I missed my friends, I missed my school, and I missed my freedom. Growing up in a small town where everyone knew each other, I had had the liberty to roam free without any worry. In the United States, my mother was fearful to have me even look out the window. I was not allowed to walk outside without adult supervision, and I was not allowed to speak to anyone except my family. I was told repeatedly not to get in trouble and to keep away from law enforcement. Fear was instilled in me very early on. As I grew older and transitioned to middle school, my mother's fears only grew. Every day she would walk with me to school and be there at the end of the day to walk me home. I was never allowed to spend the night at a friend's house, or to get in the car with anyone other than my parents or other family members. I was still very naive about our situation, and I hated my mother for restricting me so much. Nonetheless, I did as I was told, and by default I spent most of my time either at school or at home. I always had a desire for knowledge, and so I concentrated on that. I excelled academically despite my restricted life due to my undocumented status.

Much changed during my high school years. It was then when I was forced to face the reality I had long ignored. I was in this country without government authorization; I had no documentation to prove I was a citizen because I was not one. While my peers got ready for their driver's test and showed off their new driving permit, I stood quietly and ignored the conversation or changed the topic. The only form of identification I could feel proud of then was my school ID because I had nothing else from this country that acknowledged my existence. As I got closer to high school graduation, college became a topic of importance. Instead of thinking about college and scholarship applications, my worry was how to get hired as an undocumented individual after graduation in order to contribute to my family's income. I had worked small jobs here and there since I was fifteen years old to help my family financially. Aside from that I had other responsibilities, like taking my mother to work every morning before school and picking her up in the evenings. While in high school I suffered academically due to my responsibilities outside of school, yet I managed to graduate with an advanced diploma, as a GEAR UP Scholar, and as a Millennium Scholarship recipient. I graduated with scholarship money that I would not be able to use for college due to my undocumented status. I had become the first in my family to graduate from high school, and although I wished to further my education, the possibility for me to do so seemed impossible at the time.

A year after I graduated, I learned that I did not need a Social Security number to enroll in college. In fact, I had been admitted while in high school after completing a college application at a workshop at a local community college, the College of Southern Nevada. I had assumed I would not be able to attend classes because I had left the section regarding my legal status blank. After I learned I had already been admitted to college, I was hesitant to enroll. During high school I had received little to no counseling regarding college. I had no idea of my options to fund my tuition, especially as an undocumented student—I had never disclosed my status to anyone in high school. I made up my mind to continue working and to defer higher education. I saw no point in attending college because I knew I would not be able to pursue a job and career without the authorization to work. Yet again, I had no formal or legal status in the country that had been my home for half of my life. My mother, who always pushed me to be better, asked me to continue with school even if the future was uncertain. She argued that regardless of my status, as an educated woman I would be better off. She urged me to arm myself with knowledge and insisted that my hard work would pay off someday. My mother agreed to help me pay for my tuition and books for the first few semesters, while I also continued to help with bills at home. Together we made a financial plan at the beginning of each semester.

The first two years of college were challenging. I had to readjust as I had been out of high school for over a year. I also had to budget my time and money to accommodate both school and work. Typically for an average student to earn an associate degree from a junior college it takes about two years; for me, it required five years. There were semesters I could only take one or two classes because of the need to work in order to afford tuition for the following semester. And some semesters I just needed a mental and physical break. At times I had multiple jobs— paying for tuition and books completely out of pocket was not cheap, especially when earning minimum wage. My life during junior college was undefined for a period. Often, I would question why I was working so hard to earn a degree. I really had no end goal: How could I when my whole life was full of uncertainties? Thankfully, after two years I found a counselor who provided me with guidance. I met Mr. Ezeta through a mutual friend who had just enrolled into college. Mr. Ezeta had previously been a counselor at a predominantly Latino high school, and at the time he was the only Spanish-speaking counselor at the College of Southern Nevada. He, unlike the other counselors, had been around students like me for years. He understood my situation, as it was more common than I realized. For once, I had nothing to hide. I disclosed my status to Mr. Ezeta, and he became the mentor I desperately needed. He helped me figure out my academic aspirations, provided the guidance I needed to accomplish my goals, but more than anything he gave me hope.

On June 15, 2012, when the Obama administration announced DACA, I was very hesitant to apply for this relief. Like many others, I was afraid to share information with government agencies that had the ability to remove me from this country. I had lived in the shadows for so long that I had become accustomed to that way of life. In my mind, disclosing my status to immigration officials threatened that peace. Six months later, after much insistence from Mr. Ezeta, my mother, and other DACA-eligible students like myself whom I had befriended, I decided to move forward with the application process. I had never filled out such paperwork, so I turned to an immigration attorney for help to ensure that all my forms were properly completed. My mother helped with the cost of the attorney and the application fee.

Three months later, I received the greatest news: I had been approved for DACA, and my employment authorization card was on its way. Thanks to DACA, I could transition from low-skill, low-wage employment to a job where I could demonstrate my talents and abilities. After receiving DACA, I graduated from the College of Southern Nevada with two associate degrees, and I was hired at a local political consulting firm to work with the Latino community as an educator for the Affordable Care Act. With a new higher-paying job, I could transfer to a university to pursue a bachelor's degree. My transition to a university involved negotiating with my boss for a job transfer, so I could study and support myself at a costly, four-year institution where I was still not eligible for financial aid due to my immigration status. Once the transfer was granted, I set off on a new path to further develop my professional and educational aspirations.

My years at the University of Nevada, Reno, were life-changing. After receiving the benefits of DACA and having the ability to do more for myself and the community, I became part of numerous community outreach efforts. I started helping with community meetings about driver authorization cards, DACA, and citizenship workshops, among other things. I involved myself in the work of nonprofit and student organizations while I attended school and continued to work as an educator for the Affordable Care Act. The opportunities provided through DACA led me to realize that there was much more I could do for those who had gone through—and continued to face—my struggles. Thus, I dedicated my time and efforts to better the lives of Nevada's immigrant and Latino populations. My hard work soon paid off. I was recognized by organizations at the local and national level for my work toward the betterment of the immigrant community.

After about a year of hard work and dedication, I was invited by the Fast for Families national campaign to lobby for immigration reform in Washington, DC, and later that same year I was selected by the Mexican Consulate of Las Vegas and the Mexican Ministry of Foreign Affairs to travel to Mexico City for a weeklong civic engagement, educational, and cultural conference along with forty-one other nationally selected activists and students (see Boehm, this volume). I was able to travel back to my home country through Advance Parole, a benefit made possible because of DACA. I was also recognized for my academic achievements in conjunction with volunteerism. I was awarded the Dr. Juan Andrade Scholarship for Young Hispanic Students in Chicago at the United States Hispanic Leadership Institute's 2015 National Conference, and I received a scholarship from the Committee of the Mexican Consulate and the Mexican Ministry of Foreign Affairs for the 2015–2016 academic year.

In two short years, I had done more than I could have ever imagined. I became one with others in my community—I felt their struggles, I knew their fears, and I helped them gain a voice. And for the first time, like my mother had once told me, my hard work had paid off. It took me a while to realize that much of my involvement came from my loss of fear. I wasn't ashamed to accept that I was a product of migration and the sweat and tears of my hardworking parents who only wanted a better future for their children. I owned the fact that I was an undocumented Latina woman of color who deserved to be acknowledged as a human being. Once I learned to accept my existence as such, I felt an even greater responsibility toward my community. Through my work on issues of immigration, I've learned that helping others become part of and thrive in this nation is among the most rewarding endeavors I can engage in.

While many things have fallen into place in my life over the years, one thing remained uncertain. Regardless of the road I paved for myself and the privileges provided through DACA, I realize that DACA was temporary, and I continue to be an undocumented citizen of the United States. In the current political climate, with the lives of millions of immigrants at stake, the question now is: What comes next for once DACAmented students like myself who have learned to thrive and, in turn, have invested in our own communities? What will become of our undocumented friends and families who came here under similar circumstances and are only looking for a better future? While DACA provided some relief, it is imperative that we not lose sight of the fact that DACA was only temporary. DACA and other temporary statuses will not remedy the fact that our families continue to be criminalized under restrictive immigration policies.

Commentary

The Best Mankind Has to Give?

JACQUELINE BHABHA

In 1924, the first ever international agreement on children's rights, the Geneva Declaration on the Rights of the Child, opened with the following assertion: "Men and women of all nations . . . recogniz[e] . . . that mankind owes to the Child the best that it has to give."[1] This statement reflects a long-established and widely accepted principle about social priorities, priorities derived from ethical conceptions about the inherent value of human life rather than utilitarian calculus about its consequential benefits. Despite their lack of political power or productive capacity, the statement implies, children have a distinctive claim to society's resources, to its protective and nurturing capacities. This normative position reflects the modern conception of childhood as a period of vulnerability, dependence, and distinctive needs justifying special attention and investment.

By contrast with earlier phases of history in which children were largely considered family assets, participants in the productive enterprise of the kinship unit with no distinctive status or separate institutional needs, a dominant contemporary notion, reflected in both international law and domestic policy and practice, places special emphasis on the importance of protecting children and promoting their best interests.[2] This approach is often understood to entail, for children and even for adolescents, a protected space of relative freedom from responsibilities, of opportunity to explore, experiment, develop, and eventually to grow, gradually into the responsibilities of adulthood.[3] The 1989 UN Convention on the Rights of the Child crystallized this emerging view of childhood, establishing as a nearly universally ratified set of international norms both the primacy of the best interests principle and the obligation of nondiscrimination in respect of all children.

A compelling account of the origins of this approach is offered by the sociologist Viviana Zelizer. Focusing on turn-of-the-century America, she describes the dramatic and rapid progression from a conception of children as "useful" laboring parts of the family unit, in need of no particular care or privilege, to the contrasting approach to childhood that, she argues, generates a notion of a "priceless" but "useless" child. This "useless" child is entitled to support and education; the child is the recipient of parental care, nurture, and aspiration, the intended beneficiary of substantial savings (for college education), a family member who is prohibited from working and is not expected to be responsible for parents or indeed for other family members.[4] This portrayal of childhood, somewhat caricatured though it may be, largely corresponds to the reality of the first two decades of life for significant numbers of young people in the global north and for their economically and socially privileged counterparts in the global south. Indeed, in some contexts, it is not just children who occupy this protected and "useless" role—young adults in many families remain in the parental home well into their middle to late twenties as students or unsuccessful job seekers.[5]

The anthropological and normative approach to childhood thus conceived—distinctive vulnerability and uncontested protection entitlement—is in several important aspects consistent with emerging scientific knowledge about the nature of childhood and the impact of environmental factors on human development. Early life experience has a dramatic, even irreversible impact on the future life course. Not only are nurture, physical and psychological care, and protection essential, but, conversely, stressors including physical and emotional deprivation or harm, material suffering, and exposure to violence, abuse, or neglect can lead to trauma and "toxic stress," with grave consequences.

A substantial body of recent neurophysiological evidence confirms that early exposure to traumatic experience alters brain pathways to produce psychological reactions of stress, insecurity, fear, and anxiety that can impede normal developmental processes. Uncertainty, absence of consistent nurture, separation from or loss of caregivers, exposure to violence, insecurity, fear, and deprivation are all experiences with a potential to generate enduring human detriments.[6]

Both ethical and biological factors therefore justify some fundamental human rights principles relevant to children. One is the right to respect for family life, for home, and for one's private life. The importance of enduring family ties, of a predictable and secure home, and of a nurturing, safe, and nonthreatening private life is hard to overstate when it comes to infancy and childhood. Their absence, by contrast, can have searing effects on a person's sense of well-being, self-confidence, and self-efficacy and on the ability to trust others. Another cardinal right is the right to nondiscrimination, a principle that establishes the equal entitlement of all children to the building blocks of a secure childhood, to equal access to health care, schooling, shelter, and social protection.

Nothing is further from these normative principles than the experience of children described in this book. This volume has detailed how, for a sizable minority of children living in the United States today, these well-established international principles translate in practice into precarious access to child protection and basic human rights entitlements such as education, health care, and enjoyment of family life. The precarity and rights denial described in this volume are not the consequence of individual or family failings—of parental neglect, of individual psychological shortcomings, of educational incompetence, of economic failure. Rather, it is the result of historical legacies of colonial domination that have generated gross inequality and dramatic lack of encouraging future opportunities for young people. These historical traces in turn are now mediated and developed by contemporary state policies governing border control, immigration status, citizenship eligibility, and the legal impact of residence.

These legacies and enduring policies undermine the efficacy of a countervailing body of historical legacies and contemporary policies that mandate inclusionary and nondiscriminatory principles. As this volume has so meticulously shown, citizenship does not guarantee continuity of one's family life at home, law-abiding long-term residence does not protect one's future enjoyment of the community ties built up over time, diligent educational achievement or national service does not entail access to the expected rewards for high performance or consistent integrity. Instead, the overdetermining mantle of "illegality" contaminates future prospects of inclusion, vitiates the promise of nondiscrimination, and undermines the protected space that childhood is supposed to afford.

This volume has captured the story of a troubling contemporary reality—the acceptance of long-term, and all too often irreversible, status inequality at the heart of contemporary democracy. This acceptance is concomitant with the willful production of situations that signify social exclusion and a lack of legal identity. Shockingly perhaps, given international norms and contemporary scientific data on the importance of early childhood security, this inequality also affects children, in some cases with the prospect of stretching to the indefinite future. The population affected by some or all of the rights deficits just touched on, from educational exclusion to family separation, from premature adult responsibilities to indelible exposure to toxic stress, includes children from many different backgrounds and living in a range of contexts. It spans many legal statuses, many migration histories, many family arrangements.

Much of the applicable legal apparatus, designed for adults by adults, does not fit well with the particular circumstances or needs of children but continues nonetheless to determine their treatment and the outcome of their claims to protection. This volume has provided rich detail on these multifaceted rights deficits, deficits that face citizen and noncitizen, authorized and nonauthorized, infant and teenage children alike. As we have seen, it has offered careful accounts of the impact of traumatic journeys to join family in early life as much as the effect of dramatic deportation away from family and home later on; it has described the consequences of discovering one's unauthorized status after years of blissful ignorance, as much as the perverse impact of a legal system that can impose irreversible harm on children without legal representation to challenge the legality of the proceedings (as the editors note, proceedings that resemble death penalty cases but are conducted with the procedural trappings of traffic court, see Marks, this volume).

Rights deficits affecting this diverse and changing population of children and young people manifest themselves in many domains, creatively examined in different pieces in this volume. The digital sphere is the most recent and one of the least studied, a domain where the gap between entitlement and reality, between the promise of inclusion and the experience of stigma and marginalization can be explored from a range of perspectives. It is also a potential site of empowerment, a virtual commons where young people who might experience themselves as "disintegrating subjects" can experiment with agency, convening their peers, exploring ideas, crafting empowering identities. Digital performativity thus becomes a way to address unequal communication opportunities, to counter adverse stereotypes and constricting social circumstances through displays of both individual and collective resilience. The volume's lively discussion of digital activism by growing numbers of migration-affected children and young people illuminates the inadequacy of a one-dimensional portrayal that locks this constituency into a stereotypical victimhood or dependency.

The digital commons has a counterpart, also flexible and multifaceted, in the historically antecedent domain of social organizing that takes place on the streets and within communities. Several pieces in the book have explored this more traditional but equally transformational site of contestation, of challenge, of resilience. This is the site visibly occupied by the Dreamers and, most recently, the DACAmented activists, young people who reject, indeed defy, the disempowering imposed identity of "illegal" and replace it with a unifying symbol of resistance and agency. By courageously turning vulnerability to strength, DACAmented activists insist on interrogating the arbitrary boundary between "legal" and "illegal" and subverting the moral judgment embedded in it.

This volume has challenged the facile binary of legal-illegal, just as others have contested the apparent legitimacy of categories such as "deportable," "illegal migrant," or "criminal alien" or the implicitly derogatory connotations of "failed asylum seeker." Beyond highlighting the porous effect of irregular status on those who are contiguous, the book has interrogated the apparently self-evident boundary between "legal" and "illegal" status in other provocative and original ways.

The construction of "illegality" can be a form of contagion that vitiates access to basic security, predictability, and enjoyment of human rights for an expanding group of children, adolescents, and young people. Like infectious diseases, it can radically compromise the health not only of individuals but of whole communities, with spillover effects onto multiple spheres of life and state activity, from school to health care, to peer relations. The contagion of "illegality"—one's own or that of someone close—can swiftly replace confidence, optimism, and a sense of self-worth with depression, anxiety, forebodings of separation, personal disaster, and socioeconomic failure.

Thus it is that well-integrated and highly functioning young children may experience dramatic negative effects as assumed certainties about their status and lives are undermined by unexpected revelations or realizations. Worse still, these forebodings can result in traumatic encounters with the state—arrest, detention, removal, deportation. The sanctions for behavior not linked to personal culpability may be severe, extreme, and devastating. The political failure to address this social and economic threat has consequences no less devastating for individuals, families, and groups than, in other ways, the failure to address the risks of disaster or epidemic. Several contributions in the volume poignantly drive this point home.

The discussion about mixed-status families and the implications for US citizen children (more than 3 million of them) of intimate engagement with the risks of undocumented status within their families highlights the irrationality of foundational assumptions about who does and does not belong, and who deserves the manifold benefits that flow from robust enforcement of human rights.

As the editors noted in the introduction, serious contradictions emerge "when the state serves as both the body enforcing immigration law and the entity ostensibly tasked with providing a humanitarian response to crisis and suffering."[7] When these responsibilities affect something as basic as the security of one's home life, including the continued proximity to one's parents, and the reality in question is that 7 percent of all school-going children in the United States live with the daily prospect of returning home to find parents arrested, removed, or deported, the scale of the harm and the extent of the political abdication of protective responsibility are immense.[8] They betray the promise of nondiscrimination in respect of the citizenry. By seeping into the supposedly safe space of family and home, by corrupting the oft-assumed inviolability and privacy of family life, immigration enforcement not only undermines but vitiates child welfare as protective obligations are obliterated by criminal procedures.

Nowhere is this more evident than in the ongoing incarceration of young children never charged with criminal offenses, including young children who are fleeing circumstances of demonstrated danger and risk. We have been presented with the stubborn paradox that the most serious form of noncapital, criminal sanction—deprivation of liberty—can be applied to noncriminals under the guise of a purely administrative measure. We are forced to ask, from the perspective of children, how it can be that the fiction of immigration detention as a nonpunitive sanction can survive in the face of devastating evidence of its traumatizing and enduring impact.

By exploring from multiple vantage points—legal, anthropological, psychological, and political—the contested and shifting boundary between being considered legal or illegal, this book has challenged some dominant aspects of current mainstream immigration debate. It undermines the association between moral probity and legality: US citizen children and DACAmented adolescents self-evidently lack the mens rea necessary to establish culpability. But so do children recently smuggled into the United States to join undocumented parents.

The issues raised in this volume primarily concern the United States, though historical and political legacies in the countries from which most US migrants originate also feature prominently. However, the underlying problems discussed—the porous boundary between legality and illegality in the immigration context; the protection deficit that undermines children's access to rights in this sphere; and the growing evidence of a radical disjuncture between migration law, policy, and practice and accepted standards applicable to children—are global in scope and increasingly pressing. By casting a clear and multifaceted spotlight on one of the most extensive and complex global child migration situations, this volume has provided an invaluable contribution to scholarship in a newly burgeoning field, that of migrant and refugee children or, as the field is sometimes called, "children on the move."

But the book also comes at a critical time, when the international community is actively engaged in a global discussion about the refugee and migration system as a whole and children's place within it in particular.[9] By providing irrefutable and overwhelming evidence that a large group of children in one of the most prosperous member states of the United Nations is not getting "the best" mankind has to give, to paraphrase the Geneva Declaration quoted at the start of this commentary, this book strengthens the heft and legitimacy of calls for urgent intervention to ensure that safe, legal, and regular migration becomes a reality not just for this but for future generations of migrants, refugees, and their families.

ACKNOWLEDGMENTS

We want to thank the many people who, in different ways, have helped to bring this volume to fruition. Our editor at NYU Press, Jennifer Hammer, was enthusiastic about the project from the beginning, and her feedback and guidance at each stage were so helpful. We especially appreciate her vision and dedication to publishing scholarly work that goes beyond the academy—a commitment that is needed now more than ever. Thank you to Amy Klopfenstein for her assistance throughout the process, and to Susan Ecklund and Alexia Traganas for copyediting and production support. We also appreciate the close reading of the volume by the anonymous reviewers and their thoughtful comments, which provided helpful insight and strengthened the volume overall. Thank you to Diane Evia-Lanevi for reading the full manuscript and providing such detailed feedback.

We are so grateful to each of the contributors for participating in the project, for writing from their diverse perspectives, and especially for their individual and collective work to support immigrants and to advance immigrant rights in the United States and beyond. We also thank Jasmine Hankey for her many contributions, including editing the full manuscript, and Austin Rose for his assistance with research and translation. Special thanks to Gabriela Muñoz for providing the image on the book's cover and for exploring migration through such compelling artwork.

This collection came out of a collaborative research project that we started in 2014. Thank you to the many immigrants, family members, attorneys, researchers, practitioners, social workers, and advisory board members who have made our research possible. We want to especially thank Jacqueline Bhabha, Kim Haynes, Kristen Jackson, Katie Kuennen, Cecilia Menjívar, Kristyn Peck, Jennifer Podkul, David Thronson, Dawnya Underwood, and Marjorie Zatz. We also appreciate the opportunity to work with the amazing advocates who lead and volunteer with the American Immigration Lawyers Association's CARA Family Detention Pro Bono Project in Dilley and Karnes City, Texas, where we volunteered in the summer of 2017. It was a harrowing experience to spend time in our nation's "baby jails," but also heartening to witness how dedicated attorneys and volunteers fight for justice every day in these horrific spaces.

Thank you above all to the young people and their family members who are described throughout this book—those we cannot name here, but whose experiences direct our ongoing research and advocacy. We are grateful to our institutions, Georgetown University and the University of Nevada, Reno, for funding our research through several grants—including a Presidential Reflection Grant from Georgetown University and a Research Enhancement Grant from the University of Nevada, Reno—and for providing the resources to conduct ongoing fieldwork and to complete publications such as this volume. We thank our families for their ongoing support, and, finally, we thank each other for such a rewarding partnership and friendship.

NOTES

INTRODUCTION

1 Orozco 2017.
2 Schmidt and Holley 2017.
3 Nevarez 2017.
4 Faier and Rofel 2014.
5 For example, see Goldstein 2012; Heyman 1999; Nordstrom 2007.
6 For example, see Chavez 2007; Coutin 2000; De Genova 2002; Menjívar and Kanstroom 2014.
7 De Genova 2002:419.
8 "Deportability" is the possibility and risk of being deported by the state. See De Genova 2002.
9 Terrio 2015; Heidbrink 2014; Uehling 2008; Zatz and Rodriguez 2015.
10 For child-centered studies of migration, see, e.g., Bhabha 2014a; Coe et al. 2011; Ensor and Goździak 2010; Hess and Shandy 2008.
11 For example, Boehm 2016; Glenn-Levin Rodriguez 2017; Rabin 2011.
12 Gonzales and Chavez 2012; Gonzales 2016.
13 Terrio 2015.
14 Geary Act of 1892.
15 *Fong Yue Ting v. United States*, 1893.
16 *Wing Wong v. United States*, 1896.
17 De Genova and Peutz 2010; Stumpf 2006; Dowling and Inda 2013.
18 Welch 2012:19–21.
19 Boehm 2012; Dreby 2010.
20 Gonzales 2016.
21 Sigona 2012.
22 Gonzales 2016:xix; Menjívar and Kanstroom 2014:6.
23 Santos, Menjívar, and Godfrey 2013; Súarez-Orozco et al. 2011.
24 Migration Policy Institute 2018.
25 Kandel 2017:2.
26 Young and McKenna 2010:252; Terrio 2015; Women's Refugee Commission 2009, 2012; Women's Refugee Commission, Lutheran Immigration and Refugee Service, and Kids in Need of Defense 2017; Zatz and Rodriguez 2015.
27 Thronson 2006, 2010–2011; Young and McKenna 2010.
28 Gomberg-Muñoz 2017.

200 | NOTES

29 Kids in Need of Defense 2016.

30 Capps, Fox, and Zong 2017.

31 Migration Policy Institute 2016. Lauded as the largest US immigration benefit program ever authorized by the executive branch at one time, at the time of its termination on September 5, 2017, DACA covered nearly 800,000 young immigrants. It extended eligibility only to those who had finished or were enrolled in high school, had no criminal records, and were under thirty-one years of age. It provided a two-year deferral of deportation and work authorization but gave no formal legal status or permanent residency. It required extensive documentation and a costly application fee. It set forth numerous eligibility requirements, but the final decision was made on a case-by-case basis of prosecutorial discretion and could not be appealed. The termination of DACA will disrupt many aspects of immigrants' lives, including introducing the real risk of detention and deportation as well as the loss of health coverage, financial aid for education, and driving privileges.

32 Batalova, Ruiz Soto, and Mittelstadt 2017.

33 Johnson 2016.

34 Barrick 2016; Harlan 2016; Lowenstein 2016; Manning 2015; Women's Refugee Commission, Lutheran Immigration and Refugee Service, and Kids in Need of Defense 2017.

35 For example, American Medical Association 2017; Hoffman 2017.

36 Flores v. Lynch no. 15-56434 (9th Cir. 2016).

37 CARA Family Detention Pro Bono Project 2016.

38 Capps, Fox, and Zong 2016.

39 Ibid.

40 Boehm 2012; Gomberg-Muñoz 2017; Maddali 2016.

41 Dreby 2015.

42 Boehm 2016; Kanstroom 2012; Zayas 2015.

43 Immigrant Legal Resource Center 2017.

44 The White House 2017.

CHAPTER 1. RISKY BORDER CROSSINGS

1 This chapter is from *The Land of Open Graves: Living and Dying on the Migrant Trail* (De León 2015). Reprinted with permission. Felipe and Manny are pseudonyms.

2 These details come from multiple interviews with José's cousins, his girlfriend, parents, and other family and friends who were in sporadic communication with him during the trip. Details of this journey have been condensed to focus on the last few moments in the desert.

3 Dunn 2009:21–22.

4 Dunn 2009:59–60.

5 Dunn 2009:61.

6 Dunn 2009:61.

7 Nevins 2002:90–92.

8   Dunn 2009:61.
9   This has also been referred to as the Southwest Border Strategy (GAO 1997). While the official title has changed over the past two decades, the general strategy that uses the natural environment (along with various deportation practices [De León 2013] and legal proceedings) to impede undocumented migration is often simply known as Prevention Through Deterrence.
10 USBP 1994:6.
11 Ettinger 2009:156–157.
12 In the late nineteenth and early twentieth centuries, many undocumented Chinese and Eastern European migrants who could not pass inspection at Ellis Island or who were banned based on ethnic exclusion laws attempted to cross the Sonoran Desert on foot and died as a result of dehydration, exposure, and murder by bandits (Ettinger 2009: fig. 2; St. John 2011:106). Federal agent's 1926 testimony quoted in Ettinger 2009:157.
13 USBP 1994:2.
14 GAO 1997, 2006, 2012.
15 USBP 1994:7.
16 Heyman 1995:266.
17 Heyman 1995; Singer and Massey 1998.
18 USBP 1994:1.
19 Dunn 1996.
20 García 2006.
21 GAO 2001:24 ("harsh"); Haddal 2010:19 ("inhospitable").
22 See, e.g., GAO 2001.
23 USBP 1994:4.
24 GAO 1997:50.
25 Cornelius 2001; Nevins 2002; Doty 2011; Magaña 2011.
26 Haddal 2010:19.
27 GAO 1997: appendix V, table.
28 Comment by "TYRANNASAURUS, 8/19/2012" in Moreno 2012.
29 See Rubio-Goldsmith et al. 2006.
30 GAO 1997: appendix V.

CHAPTER 2. SOCIAL CITIZENS AND THEIR RIGHT TO BELONG

1   All names are pseudonyms. Some identifying details have been changed to preserve anonymity. This research was supported by the Wenner-Gren Foundation for Anthropological Research; the Social Science Research Council, with funds from the Andrew W. Mellon Foundation; and the University of Oregon's Center for the Study of Women in Society, Center on Diversity and Community, Center for Latina/o and Latin American Studies, and Global Oregon. This chapter is based on unstructured and semistructured interviews and street ethnography, conducted over eighteen months, with fifty-four Mexican national men. Eighteen of the interviews followed a life history format and included longitudinal follow-

up interviews. All study participants migrated to the United States at age twelve or younger and at the time of the interviews ranged in age from twenty-one to sixty-six years. I conducted interviews in English, in Spanish, or by code-switching, following interviewee preferences. I analyzed data by coding field notes and interview notes thematically to identify theme frequency and "rich points" surrounding identity and belonging (Agar 1996:31).

2 For more on noncitizens' legal, economical, spatial, and corporeal removal, see Nathalie Peutz's "ethnography of removal" (2010); see also Deborah A, Boehm's people "out of place" (2016:99–101); Susan Bibler Coutin's "lives in the breach" (2013), and the "immigrant underclass" (this volume) that is "exiled home" (2016); M. Kathleen Dingeman-Cerda and Susan Bibler Coutin's "ruptures of return" (2012); Katie Dingeman-Cerda and Rubén Rumbaut's "unwelcome returns" (2015); Heike Drotbohm's "island *criminosos*—'criminals'" (2011); Daniel Kanstroom's "new American diaspora" (2012); and Elana Zilberg's "geographically disoriented" deportees (2011).

3 See Boehm 2012 for a discussion of the social belonging and political nonrecognition of "alien citizens." See also Ngai 2004 on "citizen aliens." For mixed-status US families, see Dreby 2015; Gomberg-Muñoz 2017; Zatz and Rodriguez 2015.

4 T. H. Marshall coined the term "social citizenship" in 1950, although in the context of welfare rights; see also Del Castillo 2002. For social citizenship as economic integration, see Faist 1995. For mentions of social citizenship that refer to social belonging, as I employ it here, see Brotherton and Barrios 2009:42; Coutin 2011, 2013; Golash-Boza 2014:219; Levitt and Glick Schiller 2004:1025; Park 2005. See also Anderson 1983 on imagined communities and Stephen 2007 for how lives span political, geographic, ethnic, gender, and racial borders.

5 See Coutin 2013 for ways that social belonging results in the "approximation" of citizenship.

6 Dowling and Inda 2013; De Genova and Peutz 2010.

7 See Vigil 2007 for gangs as oppositional institutions; see also Olguín 2010 and Rios 2011. See Gonzales 2016 for more on childhood arrivals who become college attendees or early exiters.

8 Wildes 1976:51.

9 Ibid., 50.

10 Kanstroom 2007:228.

11 White House 2017.

12 Baker and Williams 2017:9.

13 Cantor, Noferi, and Martínez 2015; Ewing, Martínez, and Rumbaut 2015.

14 Boehm 2016:17–18.

CHAPTER 3. ILLEGALITY AND CHILDREN'S POWER IN FAMILIES

1 Boehm 2008, 2012; De Genova 2002; Dreby 2015; Gonzales 2016; Menjívar and Kanstroom 2014; Zayas 2015.

2 Brabeck and Xu 2010; Chavez et al. 2012; Gonzales, Suárez-Orozco, and Dedios-Sanguineti 2013; Henderson and Bailey 2013a, 2013b; Zayas et al. 2015.

3 Dreby 2012, 2015.

4 See Child Trends 2014.

5 Espiritu 2003; Foner 2009; Foner and Dreby 2011; Hirsch 2003; Hondagneu-Sotelo 1994; Kibria 1993; Menjívar 2000; Smith 2006.

6 Thorne 1987.

7 Kasinitz et al. 2009; Portes and Rumbaut 2001, 2006; Waters 2001; Zhou and Bankston 1998.

8 Dreby 2015; Yoshikawa 2011; Zayas 2015.

9 See, e.g., work by feminist scholars such as Bianchi et al. 2000; Hartmann 1981.

10 Gonzales and Chavez 2012; Gonzales 2016.

11 Dreby 2012, 2015.

12 Ibid.

13 Súarez-Orozco et al. 2011; Yoshikawa 2011; Yoshikawa, Súarez-Orozco, and Gonzales 2016.

14 Passel and Cohn 2009.

15 Yoshikawa 2011.

16 Ibid.

17 These stories come from families I interviewed in two studies. The first (2003–2006) focused on members of Mexican transnational families living in Mexico (children and caregivers) and the United States (migrant parents). Data consisted of interviews and observations with sixty children living in Mexico, ages five and up; thirty-seven of their caregivers; and forty-five migrant mothers and fathers living and working in the United States. See Dreby 2010. The second (2009–2012) specifically explored children's experiences being raised in Mexican migrant families (one or both parents were Mexican foreign-born) in northeast Ohio and central New Jersey. See Dreby 2015.

18 Orellana 2001.

19 Katz 2014; Orellana, Dorner, and Pulido 2003; Orellana 2009.

20 Ibid.

21 Dreby 2015.

22 Bernando is referring here to the cultural practice of only women who are virgins being able to get married dressed in white.

23 Sharman and Sharman 2008.

24 Smith 2006 has called this particular negotiation between parents and children "the immigrant bargain." See also Dreby 2010 for further discussion of the immigrant bargain in transnational households.

25 For more on family and immigration policy, see Strach 2007.

26 For just one example of a household approach to understanding family migration patterns, see Nakano Glenn 1987.

27 Boehm 2008, 2012; Dreby 2010.

28 Boyd and Grieco 2003; Hondagneu-Sotelo 1994; Kibria 1994; Pessar 1999.

29 George 2005; González-López 2005; Parrado and Flippen 2005.

REFLECTIONS: ENTERING MULTIPLE SYSTEMS

1 We have changed the names and other critical details of our clients' histories to protect their privacy. We also obtained their consent to include them in this essay. We are grateful for their willingness to allow us to share their experiences here.

2 See, e.g., Guralnick, Ludwig, and Englander 2014.

3 Under California law, juvenile court case information is confidential. See California Welfare and Institutions Code-WIC, Article 22, 827. However, Leslie's information has entered the public record. See *Leslie H. v. Superior Court*, 224 Cal. App. 4th 340 (2014).

4 OCPD's conduct in Leslie's case was routine. See University of California, Irvine School of Law 2013.

5 See Jackson 2012.

6 *Leslie H.*, 224 Cal. App. 4th at 350.

7 See Assemb. 899, 2015 Sess. (Cal. 2015); Western State College of Law Immigration Clinic, www.wsulaw.edu (accessed April 30, 2017).

CHAPTER 4. THE POST-1996 IMMIGRANT UNDERCLASS

1 Pseudonyms have been used for all interviewees.

2 See Morawetz 2000; Kanstroom 2007; Eagly 2010; Chacón 2007.

3 See Terrio 2015; Young and McKenna, this volume.

4 "Extreme and exceptional hardship" is a legal term and is one of the elements that must be proved in a cancellation of removal case. See 8 U.S. Code § 1229b.

5 See Chacón 2009.

6 See Myrdal 1964; Aponte 1990.

7 See Baker-Cristales 2004; Schiller, Basch, and Szanton Blanc 1995.

8 See Chacón 2007.

9 See Perea 1997; Inda 2008; Chavez 2013; Rios 2006.

10 See Gonzales and Chavez 2012.

11 See Wallerstein 1974; Harvey 2007; Galeano 2004.

12 See De León 2015.

13 See ibid., 36.

14 See Abrego and Gonzales 2010.

15 See Dreby 2012:829.

16 See Terrio 2015; Coutin 2016.

17 See Lofgren 2005.

18 See Kubrin 2014:329.

19 See Portes and Zhou 1993.

20 In this case, known as *US v. Texas*, Texas and twenty-five other states challenged President Obama's authority to issue deferred action by executive order. The case was heard in the Fifth Circuit, which placed an injunction on the president's pro-

gram. The injunction was appealed to the US Supreme Court, which in June 2016, in a deadlocked opinion, allowed the lower court's decision to stand. As of this writing, the injunction remains intact, and the Trump administration rescinded Obama's executive order, making further legal action moot. See *United States v. Texas* 579 U.S. (2016).

21 See Nicholls 2013.
22 See Seif 2011.

CHAPTER 5. YOUTH ON THEIR OWN

1 On September 5, 2017, the Trump administration announced that DACA would end in six months, in March 2018. See Memorandum from Acting Secretary Elaine C. Duke, US Department of Homeland Security, *Rescission of Deferred Action for Childhood Arrivals (DACA)* (September 5, 2017). At the time the program was enacted, its details were laid out in a memorandum from the secretary of the Department of Homeland Security; see Napolitano 2012:1222.

2 To identify participants for this study, we worked with a nonprofit organization that serves homeless youth in Pima County, Arizona. We contacted students in the program who had selected on their intake forms "immigration problems" as one of the causes of their homelessness, and offered them the opportunity to speak with a researcher about their experiences. After obtaining informed consent, we conducted a semistructured interview that ran from twenty to thirty minutes. This research was approved by the Institutional Review Board of the University of Arizona. All participants received a twenty-dollar gift card to amazon.com at the conclusion of their participation.

3 See Boehm 2011, 2016; Coutin, 2016; Terrio 2015.
4 For an overview, see Katzmann 2008.
5 See, e.g., Wong et al. 2014; Shannon 2014:165.
6 See Menjívar and Lakhani 2016.
7 Lakhani 2013.
8 Coutin 2000.
9 Menjívar 2000.
10 Coutin, 2000; Menjívar and Lakhani, 2016; Menjívar 2006.
11 Corcoran 2012:643; Shannon 2014:200.
12 Menjívar and Kanstroom 2014.
13 See Buriel and de Ment 1998; Katz 2014; Menjívar, 2000.
14 For an overview of the scholarship on the concept of immigrant youth as "brokers," see Lee, 2015:1405.
15 See Immigration and Nationality Act, Section 201(b), 8 U.S.C. 1151(b).
16 See Thronson 2015. Thronson writes, "Immigration law values families in which a family member has status, but not all such families. Those in which an adult holds status are privileged, and those in which children hold status are excluded" (41).
17 The allocation of family-based visas is set forth in the Immigration and Nationality Act, Section 203(a), 8 U.S.C. § 1153(a).

18 As of October 2017, the government reported that it was processing petitions for Mexican siblings of US citizens that were filed in 1997. A visa bulletin, which reports all processing times for family-based petitions, is posted monthly online. For the visa bulletin from October 2017, see "Visa Bulletin for October 2017," Travel.State.Gov, https://travel.state.gov. For an overview of the caps on family preference visas, see Enchautegui and Menjívar 2015.

19 The ten-year bar is in the Immigration and Nationality Act, Section 212(a)(9)(ii), 8 U.S.C. § 1182(a)(9)(ii).

20 Immigrants must show that they are not "inadmissible" in order for the government to approve a family-based petition. Certain domestic violence convictions trigger grounds of inadmissibility if they are considered "crimes of moral turpitude." This is a legal term of art set forth in the Immigration and Nationality Act, Section 212(a)(2)(A)(ii)(II), 8 U.S.C. § 1182(a)(2)(A)(ii)(II). A waiver of these crimes is available in some circumstances. Immigration and Nationality Act, Section 212(h), 8 U.S.C.A. § 1182(h). For an overview of the reentry bar and waivers available, see Enchautegui and Menjívar 2015:40–43.

21 This interview was conducted in Spanish. This is a translated version of her words.

22 Undocumented immigrant youth have taken this name for themselves as part of their social movement to push for legislation that would grant them legal status, entitled the Development, Relief, and Education for Alien Minors Act," or the "DREAM Act." See Nicholls 2013. Since 2001, at least twenty-five versions of the bill have been introduced. Although the versions vary in their particulars, they all provide a pathway to legal status for immigrant students based on their long presence in the United States and their educational accomplishments. See Bruno 2012:2. At the time of this writing, the Trump administration is calling on Congress to pass a version of a Dream Act that is conditioned on aggressive enforcement measures such as the building of a wall at the southern border and the elimination of protections for Central American youth seeking asylum in the United States. See Shear 2017.

23 See Napolitano 2012.

24 See supra notes 1, 23.

25 The requirements of the program are specified in the DHS memo (Napolitano 2012) as well as on the website of the US Citizenship and Immigration Services, the agency charged with implementation of the program. Individuals can apply for this relief if they (1) were between fifteen and thirty years of age as of June 15, 2012; (2) came to the United States before the age of sixteen; (3) were physically present in the United States on June 15, 2012; (4) have lived continuously in the United States since June 15, 2007; (5) are currently in school, have graduated or obtained a certificate of completion from high school (GED), or are an honorably discharged veteran of the Coast Guard or Armed Forces of the United States; and (6) have not been convicted of a felony, significant misdemeanor, or three or more other misdemeanors, and do not otherwise pose a threat to national security or public safety.

26 Many of these intricacies are addressed in the "Frequently Asked Questions" portion of the USCIS website (www.uscis.gov). They have also been summarized and discussed in practice advisories for immigration law practitioners that are available online.

27 See Singer, Svajlenka, and Wilson 2015.

28 See Hipsman, Gómez-Aguiñaga, and Capps 2016.

29 See Singer, Svajlenka, and Wilson 2015.

30 Ibid.; see also Gonzales et al. 2016.

31 These efforts are described in Singer, Svajlenka, and Wilson 2015.

32 In fact, Sara also appears to qualify for a special visa for immigrant children who have been abandoned by their parents. Her case exemplifies the fact that many immigrants do not have the legal information necessary to realize they are in fact eligible to apply for various forms of lawful immigration status. See Wong et al. 2014.

33 Taylor 2011.

CHAPTER 6. IMMIGRATION COURTS

1 The White House 2014.

2 EOIR, Office of the Chief Immigration Judge, Case Processing Priorities, January 31, 2017.

3 *PBS Newshour*, November 8, 2015, 2:15 p.m. "With few lawyers, child migrants fight alone in court to stay in the United States."

4 US Department of Health and Human Services Report 2008.

5 Cavendish and Cortazar 2011; Gonzalez-Barrera, Krogstad, and Lopez 2014.

6 Vogt 2013.

7 Frydman, Dallam, and Bookey 2014; Kids in Need of Defense 2016; United Nations High Commissioner on Refugees 2014; Women's Refugee Commission 2012.

8 Muzaffar and Hipsman 2014.

9 Rogers 2015.

10 Case 2:14-cv-01026 Document 1 Filed July 9, 2014, in US District Court, Seattle, Washington, by the American Immigration Council, American Civil Liberties Union, Northwest Immigration Rights project, Public Counsel and K & L Gates LLP against the Office of Refugee Resettlement, Immigration and Customs Enforcement, and the Departments of Justice and Homeland Security.

11 Counsel Complaint, case 2:14-cv-01026: 2–3; three former immigration judges filed an amicus brief in support of the lawsuit, J.E.F.M. v. Lynch, Case: 15-35738, March 14, 2016.

12 TRAC Immigration 2014a, 2014b, 2016a, 2016b.

13 Deposition, Judge Jack Weil, October 15, 2015, Washington, DC, pp. 69, 161.

14 Markham 2016a; *New York Times* Editorial Board 2016.

15 Krogstad 2016.

16 Johnson 2016.

17 Brodzinsky 2015.

208 | NOTES

18 Bhabha 2014a.

19 Thronson 2010–2011.

20 Neal 2007.

21 Slavin and Marks 2015:90.

22 Solis 2014.

23 Slavin and Marks 2015:91–92.

24 Telephone interview, immigration judge, November 28, 2011.

25 Telephone interview, immigration judge October 21, 2010.

26 Telephone interview, Judge John Gossart, July 15, 2016.

27 Telephone interview, immigration judge, June 11, 2009.

28 Telephone interview, Judge Harry Gastley, August 3, 2011.

29 Telephone interview, Judge Chris Grant, April 3, 2009; Judge Paul Schmidt, August 23, 2016.

30 Telephone interview, Judge Bruce Solow, September 22, 2016.

31 Telephone interview, Judge Paul Schmidt, August 23, 2016.

32 Preston 2017.

33 Paul Schmidt, e-mail communication, August 15, 2016.

34 TRAC Immigration 2017.

35 Preston 2017.

36 ICE made fifty-three arrests of unauthorized persons in New York state courts since January 2017, compared with eleven in 2016. Robbins 2017.

37 *Washington Post* Editorial Board 2017.

38 Ibid.

39 J.E.F.M. v. Lynch, D.C. no. 2:14-01026-TSZ, September 20, 2016.

40 Kerwin 2014.

REFLECTIONS: REPRESENTING UNACCOMPANIED CHILDREN

1 Children's names have been changed to protect their identity.

2 Markham 2016b.

3 TRAC Immigration 2016.

4 Ibid.

5 Homeland Security Act of 2002, Public Law 107-296, November 25, 2002, 116 STAT. 2135, www.dhs.gov.

6 Homeland Security Act of 2002, Section 462(b)(1)(A).

7 US Department of Health and Human Services 2017.

8 TRAC Immigration 2014a.

9 Mulcahy n.d.

10 In fiscal year 2014, about 90 percent of children were released from Office of Refugee Resettlement custody; in FY 2015, about 80 percent were released. In FY 2016, 88 percent of children were released (US Department of Health and Human Services 2016).

11 Ibid.

12 TRAC Immigration 2014 (November 25).

NOTES | 209

13 *Flores v. Reno* Stipulated Settlement Agreement, Case No. CV 85-4544-RJK(Px).

14 Homeland Security Act of 2002, Public Law 107-296, November 25, 2002.

15 William Wilberforce Trafficking Victims Protection Reauthorization Act of 2008, Public Law 110-457, December 23, 2008, www.gpo.gov.

16 TVPRA Section 235(c)(5).

17 Terrio 2014.

18 Byrne and Miller 2012.

19 US Department of Justice 2014.

20 O'Leary 2014.

21 The problem with *notarios,* or immigration consulting fraud, is so endemic that the American Bar Association has established national initiatives to combat these practices. See American Bar Association Commission on Immigration 2017.

22 Linthicum 2015.

23 Hausman and Srikantiah 2016.

24 Ibid.

25 US Department of Justice 2016a.

26 US Department of Justice 2017a.

27 Explanatory statement submitted by Mr. Rogers of Kentucky, Chairman of the House Committee on Appropriations regarding the House amendment to the Senate amendment on HR 3547, Consolidated Appropriations Act of 2014 160 Congressional Record No. 19 Book II at H511 (January 15, 2014). www.congress. gov.

28 KIND has been referred more than 15,000 children since 2009; has successfully trained more than 20,000 pro bono attorneys from law firms, corporations, bar associations, and law schools to represent unaccompanied children; and has leveraged $187 million in pro bono hours from 2009 to 2016.

29 None of the bills gained much, if any, traction. The only bills to spur limited interest were H.R. 1153, The Asylum Reform and Border Protection Act of 2015, introduced February 27, 2015, by Representative Jason Chaffetz (R-UT), and Protection of Children Act of 2015, introduced by Representative John Carter (R-TX), February 27, 2015, www.congress.gov.

30 Letter by child advocacy law professors to Senate majority leader Harry Reid and House Speaker John Boehner, "Appropriate Treatment and Processes for Unaccompanied Immigrant Children, July 21, 2014, on file with KIND; Alliance to End Slavery and Trafficking, letter, "Fair Treatment of Unaccompanied Children," July 21, 2014, signed by seventy-six NGOs, on file with KIND.

31 Each bill was reintroduced in the 115th Congress in 2017 by Representative Chaffetz and Representative Carter, respectively.

32 S. 310—EGO Act.

33 US Department of Justice 2017b.

34 White House Immigration Principles and Policies, October 8, 2017, www.politico. com.

35 Bonello 2015.

210 | NOTES

36 US Customs and Border Protection, U.S. Border Patrol Apprehensions FY2017 YTD (October 1–August 31), unaccompanied children, www.cbp.gov.

37 UNHCR, International Protection of Children in Guatemala, June 2017.

38 Ibid.

39 TRAC Immigration 2016b.

REFLECTIONS: JUDGING CHILDREN

1 Disclaimer: This chapter has been written by Judge Marks in her capacity as president of the National Association of Immigration Judges. The views expressed here do not necessarily represent the official position of the US Department of Justice, the attorney general, or the Executive Office for Immigration Review. The views represent the author's personal opinions, which were formed after extensive consultation with the membership of NAIJ.

2 US Department of Justice 2016b.

3 Neal 2007 (rescinded December 20, 2017).

4 Marks 2015.

5 National Center for State Courts 2012.

CHAPTER 7. YOUTH NEGOTIATE DEPORTATION

1 Byrne and Miller 2012.

2 While juridical terms such as "Voluntary Departure" and "repatriation" have important legal distinctions, in this chapter, I follow young participants' use of the term "deportation" in describing their complex and varied experiences of removal.

3 Boehm 2016; Coutin 2016.

4 I am profoundly grateful to those who welcomed me into their work and family lives. I also wish to thank the National Science Foundation (SES 1456889) for its generous support.

5 This chapter emerged from an ongoing study of the migration and deportation of children and youth in Guatemala. Over three years (2014–2016), I conducted multiple one-on-one interviews with fifty deported youth and their families, tracing the ways migration and removal shape kinship relationships and remake sentiments of home and belonging. These youths are between the ages of thirteen and twenty-one, have experienced removal within the previous three years, and have principally resided in the departments of Quetzaltenango, San Marcos, and Totonicapán, where the statistical majority of young Guatemalans migrate from and return to.

6 "Unaccompanied alien children" are individuals under the age eighteen who have no lawful immigration status in the United States and who have no parent or legal guardian to provide care and custody. Internationally, the more prevalent term is "separated children," which in many ways more accurately reflects the temporary or contingent nature of travel or living arrangements of many young people.

7 For a discussion of de facto deportation, see Kanstroom 2012.

8 Heidbrink 2014.

9 For an analysis of popular portrayals of migrant youth, see www.youthcirculations.com.

10 Linthicum 2016.

11 See Hamann, Zúñiga, and Garcia 2006.

12 Registro Nacional de las Personas (RENAP) is the Guatemalan National Registry of Persons responsible for issuing identity documents and for the registry of birth, marriage, and death certificates.

13 Dirección General de Evaluación e Investigación Educativa 2010.

14 Ibid.

15 Heidbrink forthcoming.

16 US Customs and Border Protection 2016.

17 Villegas and Rietig 2015.

18 Heidbrink and Statz 2017.

CHAPTER 8. YOUTH ACTIVISM

1 Nicholls 2013:74.

2 Olivas 2012:1.

3 Gonzales 2011:608.

4 Office of the Legislative Counsel, "Higher Education Act of 1965," http://legcounsel.house.gov.

5 National Immigrant Law Center 2016.

6 Abrego 2006:223.

7 Gonzales 2016:101.

8 Gleeson and Gonzales 2012:14.

9 Dreby 2015.

10 Chavez 1998:18.

11 Guevara 2013.

12 Nicholls 2013:74.

13 Marquez-Benitez and Pallares 2016:13.

14 Enriquez 2014:161; Escudero 2013:49.

15 United We Dream, "About Us," www.unitedwedream.org.

16 Biddix and Park 2006:872.

17 Valdivia 2015:168.

18 Abrego 2008:728; Enriquez and Saguy 2015:120; Patler and Gonzales 2015:1461.

19 Gonzales et al. 2016; Wong and Valdivia 2014.

20 Nicholls 2013:74.

CHAPTER 9. DREAMING ACROSS BORDERS

1 Advance Parole is a permit that, if granted, allows migrants with temporary statuses to travel internationally and, with the approval of an agent at a US port of entry, reenter the United States.

2 There is significant discussion about which terms best describe people who immigrated to the United States without documentation at a young age, including debates among immigrants themselves. While there has been movement away from the use of "Dreamers," it was used frequently by both organizers and participants throughout the trip I describe here. Thus, I use the term, as well as several others, such as "DACAmented immigrant" and "undocumented migrant youth" throughout the chapter, but with the caveat that such language has limits and is open to debate.

3 Many thanks to the forty-two young people who traveled to Mexico for generously sharing their stories with me, and to the Mexican Ministry of Foreign Affairs for allowing me to join the trip and events. All names of those on the trip are pseudonyms.

4 Gonzales 2016.

5 Boehm 2011.

6 Coutin 2000:27.

7 Abrego 2011.

8 Menjívar 2006.

9 Ibid., 1016.

10 De Genova 2010.

11 See Anderson and Solis 2014.

REFLECTIONS: LOOKING FORWARD

1 The proposed legislation would allow undocumented residents to qualify as DC residents, thereby accessing both in-state tuition and financial aid. (Currently, undocumented residents pay the international student rate and are barred from DC student aid.)

2 "A Proposed Resolution in the Council of the District of the Columbia," submitted by council member Vincent Orange, lims.dccouncil.us.

COMMENTARY: THE BEST MANKIND HAS TO GIVE?

1 Geneva Declaration on the Rights of the Child 1924.

2 For an early authoritative account of the transition from earlier perceptions of children, see Ariès 1962.

3 Zermatten 2014.

4 Zelizer 1985.

5 Rozzi 2014.

6 Shonkoff and Garner 2011.

7 See note 9 in the introduction to this volume.

8 National Academy of Science 2017.

9 *"New York Declaration for Refugees and Migrants"* 2016; Bhabha and Dottridge 2017.

BIBLIOGRAPHY

Abrego, Leisy J. 2006. "'I Can't Go to College Because I Don't Have Papers': Incorporation Patterns of Latino Undocumented Youth." *Latino Studies* 4:212–231.

———. 2008. "Legitimacy, Social Identity, and the Mobilization of Law: The Effects of Assembly Bill 540 on Undocumented Students in California." *Law and Social Inquiry* 33:709–734.

———. 2011. "Vulnerable Stability: Benefits and Disadvantages of Temporary Protected Status for Salvadoran Transnational Families." Paper presented at the annual meeting of the Law and Society Association, San Francisco, CA, May 30.

———. 2014. *Sacrificing Families: Navigating Laws, Labor and Love across Borders.* Stanford, CA: Stanford University Press.

Abrego, Leisy J., and Roberto G. Gonzales. 2010. "Blocked Paths, Uncertain Futures: The Postsecondary Education and Labor Market Prospects of Undocumented Latino Youth." *Journal of Education for Students Placed at Risk* 15 (1–2): 144–157.

Agar, Michael. 1996. *The Professional Stranger: An Informal Introduction to Ethnography.* San Diego: Academic Press.

American Bar Association Commission on Immigration. 2017. "Fight Notario Fraud." www.americanbar.org.

American Medical Association. 2017. "Press Release: AMA Adopts New Policies to Improve Health of Immigrants and Refugees." June 12. www.ama-assn.org.

Anderson, Benedict. 1983. *Imagined Communities: Reflections on the Origin and Spread of Nationalism.* New York: Verso.

Anderson, Jill, and Nin Solis. 2014. *Los Otros Dreamers.* Mexico City: Offset Santiago.

Andreas, Peter. 2000. *Border Games: Policing the U.S.-Mexico Divide.* Ithaca, NY: Cornell University Press.

Anti-Drug Abuse Act of 1988. 7 U.S.C. §§ 7341–7349.

Aponte, R. 1990. "Definitions of the Underclass: A Critical Analysis." In *Sociology in America*, edited by Herbert J. Gans, 117–137. Newbury Park, CA: Sage.

Ariès, Philippe. 1962. *Centuries of Childhood: A Social History of Family Life.* New York: Knopf.

Baker, Bryan, and Christopher Williams. 2017. "Immigration Enforcement Actions: 2015." Office of Immigration Statistics, U.S. Department of Homeland Security.

Baker-Cristales, Beth. 2004. *Salvadoran Migration to Southern California: Redefining El Hermano Lejano.* Gainesville: University Press of Florida.

Barrick, Leigh. 2016. "Divided by Detention. Asylum-Seeking Families' Experience of Separation." Washington, DC: American Immigration Council.

Batalova, Jeanne, Ariel G. Ruiz Soto, and Michelle Mittelstadt. 2017. "Fact Sheet— Protecting the Dream: The Potential Impact of Different Legislative Scenarios for Unauthorized Youth." Washington, DC: Migration Policy Institute. www.migrationpolicy.org.

Benton, Josiah Henry. 1911. *Warning Out in New England*. Boston: W. B. Clarke.

Bhabha, Jacqueline. 2014a. *Child Migration and Human Rights in a Global Age*. Princeton, NJ: Princeton University Press.

———, ed. 2014b. *Human Rights and Adolescence*. Philadelphia: University of Pennsylvania Press.

Bhabha, Jacqueline, and Mike Dottridge. 2017. "Child Rights in the Global Compacts: Recommendations for Protecting, Promoting and Implementing the Human Rights of Children on the Move in the Proposed Global Compacts." Paper presented at the "Global Conference on Children on the Move," Berlin, June 12–13.

Bianchi, Suzanne M., Melissa A. Milkie, Lina C. Sayer, and John P. Robinson. 2000. "Is Anyone Doing the Housework? Trends in the Gender Division of Household Labor." *Social Forces* 79 (1): 191–228.

Biddix, J. Patrick, and Han Woo Park. 2008. "Online Networks of Student Protest: The Case of the Living Wage Campaign." *New Media Society* 10 (6): 871–891.

Boehm, Deborah A. 2008. "'For My Children': Constructing Family and Navigating the State in the U.S.-Mexico Transnation." *Anthropological Quarterly* 81 (4): 777–802.

———. 2011. "Here/Not Here: Contingent Citizenship and Transnational Mexican Children." In *Everyday Ruptures: Children, Youth, and Migration in Global Perspective*, edited by Cati Coe, Rachel Reynolds, Deborah A. Boehm, Julia Meredith Hess, and Heather Rae-Espinoza, 161–173. Nashville, TN: Vanderbilt University Press.

———. 2012. *Intimate Migrations: Gender, Family, and Illegality among Transnational Mexicans*. New York: New York University Press.

———. 2016. *Returned: Going and Coming in an Age of Deportation*. Berkeley: University of California Press.

Bonello, Deborah. 2015. "Mexico's Deportations of Central Americans Are Rising." *Los Angeles Times*, September 4.

Boyd, Monica, and Elizabeth Grieco. 2003. "Women and Migration: Incorporating Gender into International Migration Theory." Washington, DC: Migration Policy Institute. www.migrationpolicy.org.

Brabeck, Kalina M., and Qingwen Xu. 2010. "The Impact of Detention and Deportation on Latino Immigrant Children and Families: A Quantitative Exploration." *Hispanic Journal of Behavioral Science* 32 (3): 341–361.

Brodzinsky, Sibylla. 2015. "U.S. Government Deporting Central Americans to Their Deaths." *Guardian*, October 12.

Brotherton, David C., and Luis Barrios. 2009. "Displacement and Stigma: The Social-Psychological Crisis of the Deportee." *Crime, Media, Culture* 5 (1): 29–55.

Bruno, Andorra. 2012. "Unauthorized Alien Students: Issues and 'DREAM Act' Legislation." Congressional Research Service, RL33863.

Buriel, Raymond, and Terri de Ment. 1998. "Immigration and Sociocultural Change in Mexican, Chinese, and Vietnamese American Families." In *Immigration and the Family*, edited by Alan Booth, Ann Crouter, and Nancy Landale, 165–200. Mahwah, NJ: Erlbaum.

Byrne, Olga, and Elise Miller. 2012. "The Flow of Unaccompanied Children: Through the Immigration System. A Resource for Practitioners, Policy Makers, and Researchers." New York: Vera Institute of Justice.

Cacho, Lisa Marie. 2012. *Social Death: Racialized Rightlessness and the Criminalization of the Unprotected*. New York: New York University Press.

Cantor, Guillermo, Mark Noferi, and Daniel Martínez. 2015. "Enforcement Overdrive: A Comprehensive Assessment of ICE's Criminal Alien Program." Washington, DC: American Immigration Council.

Capps, Randy, Michael Fox, and Jie Zong. 2016. "A Profile of U.S. Children with Unauthorized Parents." Washington, DC: Migration Policy Institute. www.migrationpolicy.org.

———. 2017. "The Education and Work Profiles of the DACA Population." Washington, DC: Migration Policy Institute. www.migrationpolicy.org.

CARA Family Detention Pro Bono Project. 2016. "Update on Recent ICE Enforcement Actions Targeting Central American Families." www.aila.org.

Carens, Joseph H. 2013. *The Ethics of Immigration*. New York: Oxford University Press.

Cavendish, Betsy, and Maru Cortazar. 2011. "Children at the Border: The Screening, Protection and Repatriation of Unaccompanied Mexican Minors." Washington, DC: Appleseed Network. appleseednetwork.org.

Chacón, Jennifer M. 2007. "Unsecured Borders: Immigration Restrictions, Crime Control, and National Security." *Connecticut Law Review* 39:1827–1891.

———. 2009. "Managing Migration through Crime." *Columbia Law Review* 109:138–148.

———. 2013. "The Security Myth: Punishing Immigrants in the Name of National Security." In *Governing Immigration through Crime*, edited by Julie A. Dowling and Jonathan Xavier Inda, 77–94. Stanford, CA: Stanford University Press.

Chavez, Jorge M., Analyeli Lopez, Christine Englebrecht, and Ruben Viramontez Anguiano. 2012. "Sufren Los Niños: Exploring the Impact of Unauthorized Immigration Status on Children's Well-Being." *Family Court Review* 50 (4): 638–649.

Chavez, Leo. R. 1998. *Shadowed Lives: Undocumented Immigrants in American Society*. Orlando, FL: Harcourt Brace College Publishers.

———. 2007. "The Condition of Illegality." *International Migration* 45 (3): 192–195.

———. 2013. *The Latino Threat: Constructing Immigrants, Citizens, and the Nation*. Stanford, CA: Stanford University Press.

Chavez, Lilian, and Cecilia Menjívar. 2010. "Children without Borders: A Mapping of the Literature on Unaccompanied Migrant Children to the United States." *Migraciónes Internacionales* 5 (3): 71–111.

Chávez-García, Miroslava. 2012. *States of Delinquency: Race and Science in the Making of California's Juvenile Justice System*. Berkeley: University of California Press.

Child Trends. 2014. "Immigrant Children: Indicators of Child and Youth Well-Being." www.childtrends.org.

Coe, Cati, Rachel R. Reynolds, Deborah A. Boehm, Julia Meredith Hess, and Heather Rae-Espinoza, eds. 2011. *Everyday Ruptures: Children, Youth, and Migration in Global Perspective*. Nashville, TN: Vanderbilt University Press.

Contreras, Randol. 2013. *The Stickup Kids: Race, Drugs, Violence, and the American Dream*. Berkeley: University of California Press.

Corcoran, Erin B. 2012. "Bypassing Civil Gideon: A Legislative Proposal to Address the Rising Costs and Unmet Legal Needs of Unrepresented Immigrants." *West Virginia Law Review* 115:643–685.

Cornelius, Wayne A. 2001. "Death at the Border: Efficacy and Unintended Consequences of US Immigration Control Policy." *Population and Development Review* 27 (4): 661–685.

Coutin, Susan Bibler. 2000. *Legalizing Moves: Salvadoran Immigrants' Struggle for U.S. Residency*. Ann Arbor: University of Michigan Press.

———. 2011. "Robbed of a Different Life: Alternative Stories, Interrupted Futures." In *Storied Communities: Narratives of Contact and Arrival in Constituting Political Community*, edited by Hester Lessard, Rebecca Johnson, and Jeremy Webber, 245–267. Vancouver: University British Columbia Press.

———. 2013. "In the Breach: Citizenship and Its Approximations." *Indiana Journal of Global Legal Studies* 20 (1): 109–140.

———. 2016. *Exiled Home: Salvadoran Transnational Youth in the Aftermath of Violence*. Durham, NC: Duke University Press.

De Genova, Nicholas. 2002. "Migrant 'Illegality' and Deportability in Everyday Life." *Annual Review of Anthropology* 31:419–447.

———. 2010. "The Deportation Regime: Sovereignty, Space, and the Freedom of Movement." In *The Deportation Regime: Sovereignty, Space, and the Freedom of Movement*, edited by Nicholas De Genova and Nathalie Peutz, 33–65. Durham, NC: Duke University Press.

De Genova, Nicolas, and Nathalie Peutz, eds. 2010. *The Deportation Regime: Sovereignty, Space, and the Freedom of Movement*. Durham, NC: Duke University Press.

Del Castillo, Adelaida R. 2002. "Illegal Status and Social Citizenship: Thoughts on Mexican Immigrants in a Postnational World." *Aztlán* 27 (2): 11–32.

De León, Jason. 2013. "Undocumented Use-Wear and the Materiality of Habitual Suffering in the Sonoran Desert." *Journal of Material Culture* 18 (4): 1–32.

———. 2015. *The Land of Open Graves: Living and Dying on the Migrant Trail*. Berkeley: University of California Press.

Dingeman-Cerda, Katie, and Rubén G. Rumbaut. 2015. "Unwelcome Returns: The Alienation of the New American Diaspora in Salvadoran Society." In *The New Deportation Delirium: Interdisciplinary Responses*, edited by Daniel Kanstroom and M. Brinton Lykes, 227–250. New York: New York University Press.

Dingeman-Cerda, M. Kathleen, and Susan Bibler Coutin. 2012. "The Ruptures of Return: Deportation's Confounding Effects." In *Punishing Immigrants: Policy, Politics, and Injustice*, edited by Charis E. Kubrin, Marjorie S. Zatz, and Ramiro Martínez, 113–137. New York: New York University Press.

Dirección General de Evaluación e Investigación Educativa. 2010. "Reporte General: Primaria 2010." Guatemala City: Ministerio de Educación. www.mineduc.gob.gt.

Donato, Katharine M., and Blake Sisk. 2015. "Children's Migration to the United States from Mexico and Central America: Evidence from the Mexican and Latin American Migration Projects." *Journal of Migration and Human Security* 3 (2): 58–79.

Doty, Roxanne. 2011. "Bare Life: Border-Crossing Deaths and Spaces of Moral Alibi." *Environment and Planning D: Society and Space* 29:599–612.

Dowling, Julie A., and Jonathan Xavier Inda, eds. 2013. *Governing Immigration through Crime: A Reader*. Stanford, CA: Stanford University Press.

Dreby, Joanna. 2010. *Divided by Borders: Mexican Migrants and Their Children*. Berkeley: University of California Press.

———. 2012. "The Burden of Deportation on Children in Mexican Immigrant Families." *Journal of Marriage and Family* 74 (4): 829–845.

———. 2015. *Everyday Illegal: When Policies Undermine Immigrant Families*. Berkeley: University of California Press.

Drotbohm, Heike. 2011. "On the Durability and Decomposition of Citizenship: The Social Logics of Forced Return Migration in Cape Verde." *Citizenship Studies* 15 (3–4): 381–396.

Dunn, Timothy J. 1996. *The Militarization of the U.S.-Mexico Border, 1978–1992: Low-Intensity Conflict Doctrine Comes Home*. Austin: CMAS Books, University of Texas.

———. 2009. *Blockading the Border and Human Rights: The El Paso Operation That Remade Immigration Enforcement*. Austin: University of Texas Press.

Eagly, Ingrid V. 2010. "Prosecuting Immigration." *Northwestern University Law Review* 104:1281–1360.

Enchautegui, Maria, and Cecilia Menjívar. 2015. "Paradoxes of Family Immigration Policy: Separation, Reorganization, and Reunification of Families under Current Immigration Laws." *Law and Policy* 37 (1–2): 32–60.

Enriquez, Laura E. 2014. "'Undocumented and Citizen Students Unite': Building a Cross-Status Coalition through Shared Ideology." *Social Problems* 61 (2): 155–174.

Enriquez, Laura E., and Abigail C. Saguy. 2015. "Coming Out of the Shadows: Harnessing a Cultural Schema to Advance the Undocumented Immigrant Youth Movement." *American Journal of Cultural Sociology* 4 (1): 107–130.

Ensor, Marisa, and Elżbieta M. Goździak, eds. 2010. *Children and Migration: At the Crossroads of Resiliency and Vulnerability*. New York: Palgrave Macmillan.

Escudero, Kevin A. 2013. "Organizing While Undocumented: The Law as a 'Double Edged Sword' in the Movement to Pass the DREAM Act." *the crit—A Critical Legal Studies Journal* 6 (2): 31–52.

Espiritu, Yen Le. 2003. *Home Bound. Filipino American Lives across Cultures, Communities and Countries*. Berkeley: University of California Press.

Ettinger, Patrick W. 2009. *Imaginary Lines: Border Enforcement and the Origins of Undocumented Immigration, 1882–1930.* Austin: University of Texas Press.

Ewing, Walter A., Daniel E. Martínez, and Rubén G. Rumbaut. 2015. *The Criminalization of Immigration in the United States.* Washington, DC: American Immigration Council.

Faier, Lieba, and Lisa Rofel. 2014. "Ethnographies of Encounter." *Annual Review of Anthropology* 43:363–377.

Faist, Thomas. 1995. *Social Citizenship for Whom? Young Turks in Germany and Mexican Americans in the US.* Aldershot, UK: Avebury.

Fleisher, Mark. 1998. *Dead End Kids: Gang Girls and the Boys They Know.* Madison: University of Wisconsin Press.

Foner, Nancy, ed. 2009. *Across Generations: Immigrant Families in America.* New York: New York University Press.

Foner, Nancy, and Joanna Dreby. 2011. "Relations between the Generations in Immigrant Families." *Annual Review of Sociology* 37:545–564.

Frydman, Lisa, Elizabeth Dallam, and Blaine Bookey. 2014. "A Treacherous Journey: Child Migrants Navigating the U.S. Immigration System." Center for Gender and Refugee Studies and Kids in Need of Defense. www.uchastings.edu.

Galeano, Eduardo. 2004. *Las venas abiertas de América Latina.* Mexico City: Siglo Veintiuno Editores.

GAO (Government Accountability Office). 1997. "Illegal Immigration: Southwest Border Strategy Results Inconclusive; More Evaluation Needed." www.gao.gov.

———. 2001. "INS's Southwest Border Strategy: Resource and Impact Issues Remain after Seven Years." www.gao.gov.

———. 2006. "Illegal Immigration: Border Crossing Deaths Have Doubled since 1995; Border Patrol's Efforts Have Not Been Fully Evaluated." www.gao.gov.

———. 2012. "Border Patrol: Key Elements of New Strategic Plan Not Yet in Place to Inform Border Security Status and Resource Needs." www.gao.gov.

García, M. Cristina. 2006. *Seeking Refuge: Central American Migration to Mexico, the United States, and Canada.* Berkeley: University of California Press.

Geneva Declaration on the Rights of the Child. 1924. www.un-documents.net.

George, Sheba. 2005. *When Women Come First: Gender and Class in Transnational Migration.* Berkeley: University of California Press.

Gerken, Christina. 2013. *Model Immigrants and Undesirable Aliens: The Cost of Immigration Reform in the 1990s.* Minneapolis: University of Minnesota Press.

Gleeson, Sharon, and Roberto G. Gonzales. 2012. "When Do Papers Matter? An Institutional Analysis of Undocumented Life in the United States." *International Migration* 50 (4): 1–19.

Glenn-Levin Rodriguez, Naomi. 2017. *Fragile Families: Foster Care, Immigration, and Citizenship.* Philadelphia: University of Pennsylvania Press.

Golash-Boza, Tanya. 2014. "From Legal to Illegal: The Deportation of Legal Permanent Residents from the United States." In *Constructing Immigrant "Illegality": Critiques, Experiences, and Responses*, edited by Cecilia Menjívar and Daniel Kanstroom, 203–222. New York: Cambridge University Press.

———. 2015. *Deported: Immigrant Policing, Disposable Labor and Global Capitalism*. New York: New York University Press.

Goldstein, Daniel M. 2012. *Outlawed: Between Security and Rights in a Bolivian City*. Durham, NC: Duke University Press.

Gomberg-Muñoz, Ruth. 2017. *Becoming Legal: Immigration Law and Mixed-Status Families*. New York: Oxford University Press.

Gonzales, Roberto G. 2011. "Learning to Be Illegal: Undocumented Youth and Shifting Legal Contexts in the Transition to Adulthood." *American Sociological Review* 76 (4): 602–619.

———. 2016. *Lives in Limbo: Undocumented and Coming of Age in America*. Berkeley: University of California Press.

Gonzales, Roberto G., and Leo R. Chavez. 2012. "'Awakening to a Nightmare'— Abjectivity and Illegality in the Lives of Undocumented 1.5-Generation Latino Immigrants in the United States." *Current Anthropology* 53 (3): 255–281.

Gonzales, Roberto G., Benjamin Roth, Kristina Brant, Jaein Lee, and Carolina Valdivia. 2016. "DACA at Year Three: Challenges and Opportunities in Accessing Higher Education and Employment." American Immigration Council. www.americanimmigrationcouncil.org.

Gonzales, Roberto G., Carola Suárez-Orozco, and Maria Cecilia Dedios-Sanguineti. 2013. "No Place to Belong. Contextualizing Concepts of Mental Health among Undocumented Immigrant Youth in the United States." *American Behavioral Scientist* 57 (8): 1174–1199.

Gonzalez-Barrera, Ana, Jens Manuel Krogstad, and Mark Hugo Lopez. 2014. "Many Mexican Child Migrants Caught Multiple Times at the Border." Pew Research Center. www.pewresearch.org.

González-López, Gloria. 2005. *Erotic Journeys. Mexican Immigrants and Their Sex Lives*. Berkeley: University of California Press.

Goździak, Elżbieta M. 2015. "What Kind of Welcome? Integration of Central American Unaccompanied Children into Local Communities." Institute of International Migration, Georgetown University.

Guevara, Diana. 2013. "San Marcos Undocumented Father of Five Fighting Deportation." NBC San Diego. www.nbcsandiego.com.

Guralnick, Susan, Stephen Ludwig, and Robert Englander. 2014. "Domain of Competence: Systems-Based Practice." *Academic Pediatrics* 14:S70–S79.

Haddal, Chad C. 2010. "Border Security: The Role of the U.S. Border Patrol." Congressional Research Service Report for Congress. www.fas.org.

Hamann, Edmund T., Víctor Zúñiga, and Juan Sanchez Garcia. 2006. "Pensando en Cynthia y su Hermana: Educational Implications of United States–Mexico Transnationalism for Children." *Journal of Latinos and Education* 5 (4): 253–274.

Harlan, Chico. 2016. "Inside the Administration's One Billion Deal to Detain Central American Asylum Seekers." *Washington Post*, August 14.

Hartmann, Heidi. 1981. "The Family as the Locus of, Class, and Political Struggle: The Example of Housework." *Signs* 6 (3): 366–394.

Harvey, David. 2007. *A Brief History of Neoliberalism*. New York: Oxford University Press.

Hausman, Daniel, and Jayashri Srikantiah. 2016. "Time, Due Process, and Representation: An Empirical and Legal Analysis of Continuances in Immigration Court." *Fordham Law Review* 84:1823–1843.

Heidbrink, Lauren. 2014. *Migrant Youth, Transnational Families, and the State: Care and Contested Interests*. Philadelphia: University of Pennsylvania Press.

———. Forthcoming. "The Coercive Power of Debt: Migration and Deportation of Guatemalan Indigenous Youth." *Journal of Latin American and Caribbean Anthropology*.

Heidbrink, Lauren, and Michele Statz. 2017. "Parents of Global Youth: Contesting Debt and Belonging." *Children's Geographies* 15 (5): 545–557.

Henderson, Schuyler, and Charles D. R. Bailey. 2013a. "Parental Deportation, Families and Mental Health." *Journal of the American Academy of Child and Adolescent Psychiatry* 52 (5): 451–453.

———. 2013b. "The Psychosocial Impact of Detention and Deportation on U.S. Migrant Children and Families. A Report for the Inter-American Human Rights Court." www.bc.edu.

Herndon, Ruth Wallis. 2001. *Unwelcome Americans: Living on the Margin in Early New England*. Philadelphia: University of Pennsylvania Press.

Hess, Julia Meredith, and Dianna Shandy. 2008. "Kids at the Crossroads: Global Childhood and the State." *Anthropological Quarterly* 81 (4): 765–776.

Heyman, Josiah McC. 1995. "Putting Power into the Anthropology of Bureaucracy: The Immigration and Naturalization Service at the Mexico–United States Border." *Current Anthropology* 36 (2): 261–287.

———. 1999. *States and Illegal Practices*. Oxford: Berg.

Hipsman, Faye, Bárbara Gómez-Aguiñaga, and Randy Capps. 2016. "DACA at Four: Participation in the Deferred Action Program and Impacts on Recipients." Washington, DC: Migration Policy Institute. www.migrationpolicy.org.

Hirsch, Jennifer S. 2003. *A Courtship after Marriage: Sexuality and Love in Mexican Transnational Families*. Berkeley: University of California Press.

Hirschfeld Davis, Julie. 2017. "Storm Complicates a Decision on Whether to Keep 'Dreamers' Program." *New York Times*, September 2.

Hoffman, Jan. 2017. "Sick and Afraid, Some Immigrants Forgo Medical Care." *New York Times*, June 26.

Hondagneu-Sotelo, Pierrette. 1994. *Gendered Transitions*. Berkeley: University of California Press.

Immigrant Legal Resource Center. 2017. "Unaccompanied Minors and New Executive Orders." www.irlc.org.

Inda, Jonathan Xavier. 2008. *Targeting Immigrants. Government, Technology, and Ethics*. Hoboken, NJ: Wiley.

Jackson, Kristen. 2012. "Special Status Seekers." *Los Angeles Lawyer*, February.

Johnson, Jeh C. 2016. "Statement on Southwest Border Security." March 9. US Department of Homeland Security. www.dhs.gov.

Kandel, William A. 2017. "Unaccompanied Alien Children: An Overview." Congressional Research Service R43599.

Kanstroom, Daniel. 2007. *Deportation Nation: Outsiders in American History*. Cambridge, MA: Harvard University Press.

———. 2012. *Aftermath: Deportation Law and the New American Diaspora*. New York: Oxford University Press.

Kanstroom, Daniel, and M. Brinton Lykes, eds. 2015. *The New Deportations Delirium: Interdisciplinary Responses*. New York: New York University Press.

Kasinitz, Philip, Mary C. Waters, John H. Mollenkopf, and Jennifer Holdaway. 2009. *Inheriting the City: The Children of Immigrants Coming of Age*. New York: Russell Sage Foundation.

Katz, Vikki S. 2014. *Kids in the Middle: How Children of Immigrants Negotiate Community Interactions for Their Families*. New Brunswick, NJ: Rutgers University Press.

Katzmann, Robert A. 2008. "The Legal Profession and the Unmet Needs of the Immigrant Poor." *Georgetown Journal of Legal Ethics* 21:3–29.

Kennedy, Elizabeth. 2014. "No Childhood Here: Why Central American Children Are Fleeing Their Homes." Washington, DC: American Immigration Council. www. immigrationpolicy.org.

Kerwin, Donald M. 2014. "'Illegal' People and the Rule of Law." In *Constructing Immigrant Illegality: Critiques, Experiences and Responses*, edited by Cecilia Menjívar and Daniel Kanstroom, 327–352. New York: Cambridge University Press.

Kettner, James H. 1978. *The Development of American Citizenship 1608–1870*. Durham, NC: University of North Carolina Press.

Kibria, Nazli. 1993. *Family Tightrope*. Princeton, NJ: Princeton University Press.

———. 1994. "The Intersection of Race, Ethnicity and Class: The Multiple Identities of Second-Generation Filipinos." *Identities* 2–3:249–273.

Kids in Need of Defense. 2016. "Improving the Protection and Fair Treatment of Unaccompanied Children." https://supportkind.org.

Kim, Seung Min. 2014. "Evangelicals Address Migrant Crisis." *Politico*, July 22.

King, Ryan D., Michael Massoglia, and Christopher Uggen. 2012. "Employment and Exile: U.S. Criminal Deportations, 1908–2005." *American Journal of Sociology* 117 (6): 1786–1825.

Klebaner, Benjamin J. 1958. "State and Local Immigration Regulation in the United States before 1882." *International Review of Social History* 3 (2): 269–295.

Krogstad, Jens Manuel, 2016. "U.S. Border Apprehensions of Families and Unaccompanied Children Jump Dramatically." Pew Research Center. May 4. www.pewresearch.org.

Kubrin, Charis E. 2014. "Secure or Insecure Communities?" *Criminology and Public Policy* 13 (2): 323–338.

Lakhani, Sarah Morando. 2013. "Producing Immigrant Victims' 'Right' to Legal Status and the Management of Legal Uncertainty." *Law and Social Inquiry* 38 (2): 442–473.

Lee, Stephen. 2015. Growing Up Outside the Law." *Harvard Law Review* 128 (5):1405–1451.

Levitt, Peggy, and Nina Glick Schiller. 2004. "Conceptualizing Simultaneity: A Transnational Social Field Perspective on Society." *International Migration Review* 38 (3): 1002–1039.

Linthicum, Kate. 2015. "7,000 Immigrant Children Deported without Going to Immigration Court." *Los Angeles Times*, March 6.

———. 2016. "Nearly Half a Million U.S. Citizens Are Enrolled in Mexican Schools. Many of Them Are Struggling." *Los Angeles Times*, September 16.

Lofgren, Zoe. 2005. "A Decade of Racial Change in Immigration Law: An Inside Perspective." *Stanford Law and Policy Review* 16:349–378.

Lowenstein, Antony. 2016. "Private Prisons Are Cashing In on Refugees' Desperation." *New York Times*, February 25.

Maddali, Anita Ortiz. 2016. "Left Behind: The Dying Principle of Family Reunification under Immigration Law." *University of Michigan Journal of Law Reform* 50 (1): 107–173.

Magaña, Rocío. 2011. "Dead Bodies: The Deadly Display of Mexican Border Politics." In *Aesthetics: A Companion to the Anthropology of the Body and Embodiment*, edited by Frances E. Mascia-Lees, 157–171. Malden, MA: Blackwell.

Manning, Stephen. 2015. "The Artesia Report." Innovation Law Lab. https://innovationlawlab.org.

Markham, Jerry. 2016a. "Can a 3 Year Old Represent Herself in Immigration Court?" *Washington Post*, March 5.

———. 2016b. "Former Judges Challenge Official Who Said 3-Year-Olds Can Represent Selves in Immigration Court." *Washington Post*, March 15.

Marks, Dana Leigh. 2015. "Who Me? Am I Guilty of Implicit Bias?" *Judges' Journal* 54 (4). American Bar Association. www.americanbar.org.

Marquez-Benitez, Gabriela, and Amalia Pallares. 2016. "Not One More: Linking Civil Disobediences and Public Anti-deportation Campaigns." *North American Dialogue* 19:13–22.

Marshall, Thomas Humphrey. 1950. *Citizen and Social Class and Other Essays*. Cambridge: Cambridge University Press.

Menjívar, Cecilia. 2000. *Fragmented Ties: Salvadoran Immigrant Networks in America*. Berkeley: University of California Press.

———. 2006. "Liminal Legality: Salvadoran and Guatemalan Immigrants' Lives in the United States." *American Journal of Sociology* 111 (4): 999–1037.

Menjívar, Cecilia, and Daniel Kanstroom, eds. 2014. *Constructing Immigrant "Illegality": Critiques, Experiences, and Responses*. Cambridge: Cambridge University Press.

Menjívar, Cecilia, and Sarah Lakhani. 2016. "The Transformative Effects of Immigration Law: Migrants' Personal and Social Metamorphoses through Regularization." *Academic Journal of Sociology* 121 (6): 1818–1855.

Migration Policy Institute. 2016. "Deferred Action for Childhood Arrivals (DACA) Data Tools." Washington, DC: Migration Policy Institute. www.migrationpolicy.org.

———. 20018. "Profile of the Unauthorized Population: United States." Washington, DC: Migration Policy Institute. www.migrationpolicy.org.

Molina, Natalia. 2014. *How Race Is Made in America: Immigration, Citizenship, and the Historical Power of Racial Scripts*. Berkeley: University of California Press.

Morawetz, Nancy. 2000. "Understanding the Impact of the 1996 Deportation Laws and the Limited Scope of Proposed Reforms." *Harvard Law Review* 113 (8): 1936–1962.

Moreno, Caroline. 2012. "Border Crossing Deaths More Common as Illegal Immigration Declines." *Huffington Post*, August 17.

Mulcahy, Anne Marie. n.d. "Legal Services for Unaccompanied Children." Vera Institute of Justice. www.vera.org.

Muzaffar, Chishti, and Faye Hipsman. 2014. "Unaccompanied Minor Crisis Has Receded from Headlines but Major Issues Remain." September 25. Washington, DC: Migration Policy Institute. www.migrationpolicy.org.

Myrdal, Gunnar. 1964. "The War on Poverty." *New Republic* 150 (6): 14–16.

Nakano Glenn, Evelyn. 1987. "Racial Ethnic Women's Labor: The Intersection of Race, Gender and Class Oppression." In *Hidden Aspects of Women's Work*, edited by Christine Bose, Roslyn Feldberg, and Natalie Sokoloff, 46–73. New York: Praeger.

Napolitano, Janet. 2012. "Exercising Prosecutorial Discretion with Respect to Individuals Who Came to the United States as Children." DHS Memorandum. https://www.dhs.gov.

National Academy of Sciences. 2017. "Report on the Integration of Immigrants into American Society." www.nap.edu.

National Center for State Courts. 2012, "Race and Ethnic Fairness in the Courts: Strategies to Reduce the Influence of Implicit Bias." www.ncsc.org.

National Immigration Law Center. 2016. "Toolkit: Access to Postsecondary Education." www.nilc.org.

Neal, David. 2007. "Operating Policies and Procedures Memorandum 07–01: Guidelines for Immigration Court Cases Involving Unaccompanied Alien Children." May 22. US Department of Justice, Executive Office for Immigration Review. www.usdoj.gov.

Nevarez, Griselda. 2017. "Arizona Woman Deported to Mexico Despite Complying with Immigration Officials." *Guardian*, February 9.

Nevins, Joseph. 2002. *Operation Gatekeeper: The Rise of the "Illegal Alien" and the Making of the U.S.-Mexico Boundary*. New York: Routledge.

"New York Declaration for Refugees and Migrants." 2016. http://refugeesmigrants.un.org.

New York Times Editorial Board. 2016. "Migrant Children Deserve a Voice in Court." *New York Times*, March 8.

Ngai, Mae M. 2004. *Impossible Subjects: Illegal Aliens and the Making of Modern America*. Princeton, NJ: Princeton University Press.

Nicholls, Walter. 2013. *The DREAMers: How the Undocumented Youth Movement Transformed the Immigrant Rights Debate*. Palo Alto, CA: Stanford University Press.

Nordstrom, Carolyn. 2007. *Global Outlaws: Crime, Money, and Power in the Contemporary World*. Berkeley: University of California Press.

O'Leary, Brian. 2014. "Docketing Practices Relating to Unaccompanied Children Cases in Light of the New Priorities." September 10. US Department of Justice, Executive Office for Immigration Review. www.justice.gov.

Olguín, Ben V. 2010. *La Pinta: Chicano/a Prisoner Literature, Culture, and Politics.* Austin: University of Texas Press.

Olivas, Michael A. 2012. *No Undocumented Child Left Behind: Pyler v. Doe and the Education of Undocumented Schoolchildren.* New York: New York University Press.

Orellana, Marjorie F. 2001. "The Work Kids Do: Mexican and Cultural American Children's Contributions to Households and Schools in California." *Harvard Educational Review* 71:366–390.

———. 2009. *Translating Childhoods: Immigrant Youth, Language and Culture.* New Brunswick, NJ: Rutgers University Press.

Orellana, Marjorie, F. Lisa Dorner, and Lucila Pulido. 2003. "Accessing Assets: Immigrant Youth as Family Interpreters." *Social Problems* 50 (5): 505–524.

Orozco, Anthony. 2017. "Attorney Hails Mother and Son's Release from Berks County Residential Center." *Reading Eagle*, August 12.

Parenti, Christian. 1999. *Lockdown America: Police and Prisons in the Age of Crisis.* London: Verso.

Park, Lisa Sun-Hee. 2005. *Consuming Citizenship: Children of Asian Immigrant Entrepreneurs.* Palo Alto, CA: Stanford University Press.

Parrado, Emilio A., and Chenoa A. Flippen. 2005. "Migration and Gender among Mexican Women." *American Sociological Review* 70:606–632.

Parrado, Emilio A., Chenoa A. Flippen, and Chris McQuiston. 2005. "Migration and Relationship Power among Mexican Women." *Demography* 42 (3): 347–372.

Passel, Jeffrey S., and D'Vera Cohn. 2009. "A Portrait of Unauthorized Immigrants in the United States." Pew Hispanic Center. www.pewhispanic.org.

Patler, Caitlin, and Roberto G. Gonzales. 2015. "Framing Citizenship: Media Coverage of Anti-deportation Cases Led by Undocumented Immigrant Youth Organizations." *Journal of Ethnic and Migration Studies* 41 (9): 1453–1474.

Perea, Juan F., ed. 1997. *Immigrants Out!—The New Nativism and the Anti-immigrant Impulse in the United States.* New York: New York University Press.

Pessar, Patricia. 1999. "Engendering Migration Studies: The Case of New Immigrants in the United States." *American Behavioral Scientist* 42 (4): 577–600.

Peutz, Nathalie. 2010. "'Criminal Alien' Deportees in Somaliland: An Ethnography of Removal." In *The Deportation Regime: Sovereignty, Space, and the Freedom of Movement*, edited by Nicolas Genova and Nathalie Peutz, 371–409. Durham, NC: Duke University Press.

Portes, Alejandro, and Rubén G. Rumbaut. 2001. *Legacies: The Story of the Immigrant Second Generation.* Berkeley: University of California Press.

———. 2006. *Immigrant America: A Portrait.* 3rd ed. Berkeley: University of California Press.

Portes, Alejandro, and Min Zhou. 1993. "The New Second Generation: Segmented Assimilation and Its Variants." *Annals of the American Academy of Political and Social Science* 530 (1): 74–96.

Preston, Julia. 2017. "Migrants in Surge Fare Worse in Immigration Court Than Other Groups." *Washington Post*, July 30.

Rabin, Nina. 2011. "Disappearing Parents: Immigration Enforcement and the Child Welfare System." Southwest Institute for Research on Women, College of Social and Behavioral Sciences and Bacon Immigration Law and Policy Program, James E. Rogers College of Law at the University of Arizona. https://law2.arizona.edu.

Rios, Victor M. 2006. "The Hyper-Criminalization of Black and Latino Male Youth in the Era of Mass Incarceration." *Souls* 8 (2): 40–54.

———. 2011. *Punished: Policing the Lives of Black and Latino Boys*. New York: New York University Press.

Robbins, Liz. 2017. "A Game of Cat and Mouse with High Stakes: Deportation." *New York Times*, August 3.

Rogers, David. 2015. "Under 16 and Ordered Deported—Without a Lawyer." *Politico*, November 18.

Rosas, Gilberto. 2015. "The Border Thickens: In-securing Communities after IRCA." *International Migration* 54 (2): 119–130.

Rozzi, Elena. 2014. "Transitions to Adulthood in Contemporary Italy: Balancing Sociocultural Differences and Universal Rights." In *Human Rights and Adolescence*, edited by Jacqueline Bhabha, 39–58. Philadelphia: University of Pennsylvania Press.

Rubio-Goldsmith, Raquel, M. Melissa McCormick, Daniel Martinez, and Inez Magdalena Duarte. 2006. "The 'Funnel Effect' and Recovered Bodies of Unauthorized Migrants Processed by the Pima County Office of the Medical Examiner, 1990–2005." Tucson: Binational Migration Institute, Mexican American Studies and Research Center, University of Arizona. www.derechoshumanosaz.net.

Rumbaut, Rubén G., and Kenji Ima. 1988. "The Adaptation of Southeast Asian Refugee Youth: A Comparative Study." Washington, DC: US Office of Refugee Resettlement.

Sakuma, Amanda. 2014. "Human Rights Groups Outraged over Obama's Deportation Proposal." MSNBC. www.msnbc.com.

Santos, Carlos E., Cecilia Menjívar, and Erin Godfrey. 2013. "Effects of SB 1070 on Children." In *Latino Politics and Arizona's Immigration Law SB1070*, edited by Lisa Magaña and Eric Lee, 79–92. New York: Springer.

Schiller, Nina Glick, Linda Basch, and Cristina Szanton Blanc. 1995. "From Immigrant to Transmigrant: Theorizing Transnational Migration." *Anthropological Quarterly* 68 (1): 48–63.

Schmidt, Samantha, and Peter Holley. 2017. "A 'Dreamer' Claims He Was Secretly Deported. The Government Claims It Never Happened." *Washington Post*, April 19.

Seif, Hinda. 2011. "'Unapologetic and Unafraid': Immigrant Youth Come Out from the Shadows." *New Directions for Child and Adolescent Development* 134:59–75.

Shannon, Careen. 2014. "Immigration Is Different: Why Congress Should Guarantee Access to Counsel in All Immigration Matters." *University of the District of Columbia Law Review* 17:165–219.

Sharman, Russell Leigh, and Cheryl Harris Sharman. 2008. *Nightshift NYC*. Berkeley: University of California Press.

Shear, Michael D. 2017. "White House Makes Hard-Line Demands for Any 'Dreamers' Deal." *New York Times*, October 8.

Shonkoff, Jack P., and Andrew S. Garner. 2011. "The Lifelong Effects of Early Childhood Adversity and Toxic Stress." *Pediatrics* 129 (1): 232–248.

Sigona, Nando. 2012. "'I Have Too Much Baggage': The Impacts of Legal Status on the Social Worlds of Irregular Migrants." *Social Anthropology/Anthropologie Sociale* 20 (1): 50–65.

Singer, Audrey, and Douglas S. Massey. 1998. "The Social Process of Undocumented Border Crossing among Mexican Migrants." *International Migration Review* 32 (3): 561–592.

Singer, Audrey, Nicole P. Svajlenka, and Jill H. Wilson. 2015. "Local Insights from DACA for Implementing Future Programs for Unauthorized Immigrants." Brookings Metropolitan Policy Program. www.brookings.edu.

Slavin, Denise Noonan, and Dana Leigh Marks. 2015. "You Be the Judge: Who Should Preside over Immigration Cases, Where, and How?" In *The New Deportations Delirium: Interdisciplinary Responses*, edited by Daniel Kanstroom and M. Brinton Lykes, 89–112. New York: New York University Press.

Smith, Robert C. 2006. *Mexican New York: Transnational Lives of New Immigrants*. Berkeley: University of California Press.

Solis, Dianne. 2014. "Judges' Union Calls for Change in the Nation's Immigration Courts, Separation from the Justice Department." *Dallas Morning News*, August 27.

Stephen, Lynn. 2007. *Transborder Lives: Indigenous Oaxacans in Mexico, California, and Oregon*. Durham, NC: Duke University Press.

Stevens, Jacqueline. 2011. *States without Nations: Citizenship for Mortals*. New York: Columbia University Press.

St. John, Rachel. 2011. *Line in the Sand: A History of the Western U.S.-Mexico Border*. Princeton, NJ: Princeton University Press.

Strach, Patricia. 2007. *All in the Family. The Private Roots of American Public Policy*. Palo Alto, CA: Stanford University Press.

Stumpf, Juliet. 2006. "The Crimmigration Crisis: Immigrants, Crime, and Sovereign Power." *American University Law Review* 56:367–419.

Súarez-Orozco, Carola, Hirokazu Yoshikawa, Robert T. Teranishi, and Marcelo Súarez-Orozco. 2011. "Growing Up in the Shadows: The Developmental Implications of Unauthorized Status." *Harvard Educational Review* 81 (3): 438–472.

Taylor, Paul. 2011. "Unauthorized Immigrants: Length of Residency, Patterns of Parenthood." Pew Research Center. www.pewhispanic.org.

Terrio, Susan J. 2008. "New Barbarians at the Gates of Paris? Prosecuting Undocumented Minors in the Juvenile Court—The Problem of the 'Petits Roumains.'" *Anthropological Quarterly* 81 (4): 873–901.

———. 2009. *Judging Mohammed: Juvenile Delinquency, Immigration, and Exclusion at the Paris Palace of Justice*. Palo Alto, CA: Stanford University Press.

———. 2014. "Life Ended Here." *Politico*, July 10.

———. 2015. *Whose Child Am I? Unaccompanied, Undocumented Children in U.S. Immigration Custody*. Berkeley: University of California Press.

Thorne, Barrie. 1987. "Revisioning Women and Social Change: Where Are the Children?" *Gender and Society* 1 (1): 85–109.

Thronson, David B. 2006. "You Can't Get There from Here: Toward a More Child-Centered Immigration Law." *Virginia Journal of Social Policy and the Law* 14:58–86.

———. 2010–2011. "Entering the Mainstream: Making Children Matter in Immigration Law." *Fordham Urban Law Journal* 38:393–413.

———. 2015. "Unhappy Families: The Failings of Immigration Law for Families That Are Not All Alike." In *The New Deportations Delirium: Interdisciplinary Responses*, edited by Daniel Kanstroom and M. Brinton Lykes, 33–56. New York: New York University Press.

TRAC Immigration. 2014a. "New Data on Unaccompanied Children in Immigration Court." http://trac.syr.edu.

———. 2014b. "Representation for Unaccompanied Children in Immigration Court." http://trac.syr.edu.

———. 2016a. "Handling of Juvenile Cases." http://trac.syr.edu.

———. 2016b. "Juveniles—Immigration Court Deportation Proceedings." http://trac.syr.edu.

———. 2017. "Children: Amid a Growing Court Backlog Many Still Unrepresented." http://trac.syr.edu.

Uehling, Greta. 2008. "The International Smuggling of Children: Coyotes, Snakeheads and the Politics of Compassion." *Anthropological Quarterly* 81 (4): 833–871.

United Nations High Commissioner on Refugees (UNHCR). 2014. "Children on the Run: Unaccompanied Children Leaving Central America and Mexico and the Need for International Protection." www.unhcr.org.

University of California, Irvine School of Law. 2013. "Second Chances for All: Why Orange County Probation Should Stop Choosing Deportation over Rehabilitation for Immigrant Youth." www.law.uci.edu.

USBP (United States Border Patrol). 1994. "Border Patrol Strategic Plan 1994 and Beyond."

US Customs and Border Protection 2016. "United States Border Patrol Southwest Family Unit Subject and Unaccompanied Alien Children Apprehensions Fiscal Year 2016." Washington, DC: US Customs and Border Protection. www.cbp.gov.

US Department of Health and Human Services. 2008. "Efforts to Serve Children." Office of the Inspector General, Department of Unaccompanied Alien Children's Services. http://oig.hhs.gov.

———. 2016. "Administration for Children and Families." Office of Refugee Resettlement. www.acf.hhs.gov.

———. 2017. "Administration for Children and Families—Fiscal Year 2017." www.acf.hhs.gov.

US Department of Homeland Security. 2013. "FY 2013 ICE Immigration Removals: ERO Annual Report." Washington, DC: US Immigration and Customs Enforcement.

228 | BIBLIOGRAPHY

———. 2015. "ICE Enforcement and Removal Operations Report: Fiscal Year 2015." Washington, DC: Office of Immigration Statistics.

US Department of Justice. 1982. "Sourcebook of Criminal Justice Statistics, 1981" (Bureau of Justice Statistics). Washington, DC: US Government Printing Office.

———. 1997. "Sourcebook of Criminal Justice Statistics, 1996" (Bureau of Justice Statistics). Washington, DC: US Government Printing Office.

———. 1999. "Sourcebook of Criminal Justice Statistics, 1998" (Bureau of Justice Statistics). Washington, DC: US Government Printing Office.

———. 2014. "Department of Justice Announces New Priorities to Address Surge of Migrants Crossing into the U.S." July 9. www.justice.gov.

———. 2016a. "EOIR to Revise Docketing Practices Relating to Certain Priority Cases." February 4. Executive Office for Immigration Review. www.justice.gov.

———. 2016b. "FY 2015 Statistics Yearbook." April. Executive Office for Immigration Review. www.justice.gov.

———. 2017a. "Department of Justice Memorandum." January 31. www.justice.gov.

———. 2017b. "Legal Opinion re: EOTR's Authority to Interpret the Term Unaccompanied Alien Child for Purposes of Applying Certain Provisions of TVPRA." September 19. Executive Office for Immigration Review.

Valdivia, Carolina. 2015. "DREAMer Activism: Challenges and Opportunities." In *Undocumented Latino Youth: Navigating Their Worlds*, edited by Marisol Clark-Ibáñez, 163–178. Boulder, CO: Lynne Rienner.

Vigil, James Diego. 2007. *The Projects: Gang and Non-Gang Families in East Los Angeles*. Austin: University of Texas Press.

Villegas, Domínguez, and Victoria Rietig. 2015. "Migrants Deported from the United States and Mexico to the Northern Triangle. A Statistical and Socioeconomic Profile." Washington, DC: Migration Policy Institute. www.migrationpolicy.org.

Vogt, Wendy A. 2013. "Crossing Mexico: Structural Violence and the Commodification of Undocumented Central American Migrants." *American Ethnologist* 40 (4): 764–780.

Wallerstein, Immanuel. 1974. "The Rise and Future Demise of the World Capitalist System: Concepts for Comparative Analysis." *Comparative Studies in Society and History* 16 (4): 387–415.

Washington Post Editorial Board. 2017. "America's Immigration Courts Are a Diorama of Dysfunction." *Washington Post*, January 9.

Waters, Mary C. 2001. *Black Identities: West Indian Immigrant Dreams and American Realities*. Cambridge, MA: Harvard University Press.

Welch, Michael. 2012. "Panic, Risk, Control: Conceptualizing Threats in a Post-9/11 Society." In *Punishing Immigrants: Policy, Politics, and Injustice*, edited by Charles E. Kubrin, Marjorie Zatz, and Ramiro Martinez Jr., 19–41. New York: New York University Press.

Western, Bruce. 2006. *Punishment and Inequality in America*. New York: Russell Sage Foundation.

The White House. 2014. "Fact Sheet: Immigration Accountability Executive Action." November 20. Office of the Press Secretary. www.obamawhitehouse.archives.gov.

———. 2017. "Executive Order: Border Security and Immigration Enforcement Improvements." January 25. www.whitehouse.gov.

Wildes, Leon. 1976. "The Nonpriority Program of the Immigration and Naturalization Service: The Litigative Use of the Freedom of Information Act." *San Diego Law Review* 14:42–75.

Women's Refugee Commission. 2009. "Halfway Home: Unaccompanied Children in Immigration Custody." https://womensrefugeecommission.org.

———. 2012. "Forced from Home: The Lost Boys and Girls of Central America." https://womensrefugeecommission.org.

Women's Refugee Commission, Lutheran Immigration and Refugee Service, and Kids in Need of Defense. 2017. "Betraying Family Values. How U.S. Immigration Policy at the Border Is Separating Families." https://supportkind.org.

Wong, Tom K., Donald Kerwin, Jeanne M. Atkinson, and Mary Meg McCarthy. 2014. "Paths to Lawful Immigration Status: Results and Implications from the PERSON Survey." *Journal on Migration and Human Security* 2 (4): 287–304.

Wong, Tom K., with Carolina Valdivia. 2014. "In Their Own Words: A Nationwide Survey of Undocumented Millennials." Center for Comparative Immigration Studies. http://unitedwedream.org.

Yarris, Kristin E., and Heide Castañeda. 2015. "Discourses of Displacement and Deservingness: Interrogating Distinctions between 'Economic' and 'Forced' Migration." *International Migration* 53 (3): 64–69.

Yoshikawa, Hirokazu. 2011. *Immigrants Raising Citizens. Undocumented Parents and Their Young Children.* New York: Russell Sage Foundation.

Yoshikawa, Hirokazu, Carola Suárez-Orozco, and Roberto Gonzales. 2016. "Unauthorized Status and Youth Development in the United States: Consensus Statement of the Society for Research on Adolescence." *Journal of Research on Adolescence* 27 (1): 4–19.

Young, Wendy, and Megan McKenna. 2010. "The Measure of a Society: The Treatment of Unaccompanied Refugee and Immigrant Children in the United States." *Harvard Civil Rights–Civil Liberties Law Review* 45:247–260.

Zatz, Marjorie S., and Nancy Rodriguez. 2015. *Dreams and Nightmares: Immigration Policy, Youth, and Families.* Berkeley: University of California Press.

Zavella, Patricia. 2011. *I'm Neither Here nor There: Mexicans' Quotidian Struggles with Migration and Poverty.* Durham, NC: Duke University Press.

Zayas, Luis H. 2015. *Forgotten Citizens: Deportation, Children, and the Making of American Exiles and Orphans.* New York: Oxford University Press.

Zayas, Luis H., Sergio Aguilar-Gaxiola, Huynwoo Yoon, and Guillermina Natera Rey. 2015. "The Distress of Citizen Children with Detained and Deported Parents." *Journal of Child and Family Studies* 24:3213–3223.

Zelizer, Viviana. 1985. *Pricing the Priceless Child: The Changing Social Value of Children.* Princeton, NJ: Princeton University Press.

Zermatten, Jean. 2014. "Protecting and Promoting Adolescent Rights: The Contribution of International Law and Policy." In *Human Rights and Adolescence*, edited by Jacqueline Bhabha, 23–38. Philadelphia: University of Pennsylvania Press.

Zhou, Min, and Carl L. Bankston III. 1998. *Growing Up American: How Vietnamese Children Adapt to Life in the United States*. New York: Russell Sage Foundation.

Zilberg, Elana. 2011. *Space of Detention: The Making of a Transnational Gang Crisis between Los Angeles and San Salvador*. Durham, NC: Duke University Press.

ABOUT THE EDITORS

DEBORAH A. BOEHM is Professor of Anthropology and Women's Studies/Gender, Race, and Identity at the University of Nevada, Reno. She is the author of *Intimate Migrations: Gender, Family, and Illegality among Transnational Mexicans* (New York University Press, 2012) and *Returned: Going and Coming in an Age of Deportation* (2016), and co-editor of *Everyday Ruptures: Children, Youth, and Migration in Global Perspective* (2011). Her research has been supported through a Fulbright–García Robles Award and an American Council of Learned Societies Fellowship, as well as residencies at the School for Advanced Research, the University of Arizona School of Anthropology, and the Center for the Study of Law and Society at the University of California, Berkeley, School of Law.

SUSAN J. TERRIO is Professor of Anthropology and French Studies at Georgetown University. She holds a joint appointment in the Department of Anthropology and the Department of French. She is the author of *Crafting the Culture and History of French Chocolate* (2000), *Judging Mohammed: Juvenile Delinquency, Immigration, and Exclusion at the Paris Palace of Justice* (2009), and *Whose Child Am I? Unaccompanied, Undocumented Children in U.S. Immigration Custody* (2015). She has been awarded two National Endowment for the Humanities Summer Research Grants, a Radcliffe Institute Residential Fellowship at Harvard University, and fellowships from the Russell Sage Foundation, the Institute for Advanced Study at Princeton University, and the Woodrow Wilson International Center for Scholars.

ABOUT THE CONTRIBUTORS

JACQUELINE BHABHA is Director of Research at the FXB Center for Health and Human Rights, Professor of the Practice of Health and Human Rights at the Harvard School of Public Health, Jeremiah Smith Jr. Lecturer in Law at Harvard Law School, and Adjunct Lecturer in Public Policy at the Harvard Kennedy School. She has published extensively on issues of transnational child migration, refugee protection, children's rights, and citizenship. She is the author of *Child Migration and Human Rights in a Global Age* (2014) and editor of *Children without a State* (2011) and *Human Rights and Adolescence* (2014). She serves on the board of the Scholars at Risk Network, the World Peace Foundation, and the *Journal of Refugee Studies* and is a founder of the Alba Collective, an international NGO that works with women and girls in developing countries to enhance financial security and youth rights.

SUSAN BIBLER COUTIN is Professor in the Department of Criminology, Law, and Society and the Department of Anthropology at the University of California, Irvine. She is the author of *The Culture of Protest: Religious Activism and the U.S. Sanctuary Movement* (1993); *Legalizing Moves: Salvadoran Immigrants' Struggle for U.S. Residency* (2000); *Nations of Emigrants: Shifting Boundaries of Citizenship in El Salvador and the United States* (2007); and *Exiled Home: Salvadoran Transnational Youth in the Aftermath of Violence* (2016). She recently completed National Science Foundation–funded research regarding immigrants' efforts to secure legal status in the United States and is currently part of a collaborative project supported by the Russell Sage Foundation and the NSF about liminal legalities and pathways to citizenship.

JASON DE LEÓN is Associate Professor of Anthropology at the University of Michigan. He directs the Undocumented Migration Project, a long-term anthropological study of clandestine migration between Mexico and the United States. He has published numerous academic articles and a book, *The Land of Open Graves: Living and Dying on the Migrant Trail* (2015), and his work has been featured in a variety of popular media outlets. He was named a MacArthur Fellow in 2017 and a National Geographic Emerging Explorer in 2013, and was the Weatherhead Resident Scholar at the School for Advanced Research in Santa Fe, New Mexico, during 2013–2014. He recently joined the board of directors for the Colibri Center for Human Rights, a nonprofit family advocacy organization working to end migrant death and related suffering on the US-Mexico border.

JOANNA DREBY is Associate Professor of Sociology at the University at Albany, State University of New York. She is the author of the award-winning book *Divided by Borders: Mexican Migrants and Their Children* (2010) and *Everyday Illegal: When Policies Undermine Immigrant Families* (2015). She is co-editor of *Family and Work in Everyday Ethnography* (2013). Her research projects, conducted in both Mexico and the United States, have prioritized child-centered approaches, and her written work explores the themes of gender, work-family balance, child care, transnational ties, context-specific settlement patterns, and return migration.

RACHEL GITTINGER is Director of Citizenship and Civic Engagement at CARECEN, joining the organization in that role in November 2012. She began volunteering with CARECEN in July 2012 as a bilingual civics teacher. Gittinger has extensive experience directing international civic engagement programs for youth in the Americas and worked with a microfinance agency serving female entrepreneurs in Costa Rica. Prior to joining CARECEN, she worked at the Polaris Project as a bilingual trafficking specialist in the National Human Trafficking Resource Center. Gittinger holds a BA in Spanish and International Studies from the University of Kansas.

WILLIAMS GUEVARA MARTÍNEZ migrated to the United States from El Salvador in 2012. He joined his brother and sister in Maryland, learned English, graduated from a public high school in Maryland, and is now working and taking classes in engineering at a community college near Baltimore. He left home to escape violence and to seek better opportunities; thanks to his attorney, he was awarded Special Immigrant Juvenile Status by a Maryland circuit court. He is currently a legal permanent resident who plans to naturalize as a US citizen. He has publicly shared his migration story, testifying before the Maryland General Assembly in the context of hearings to determine if eligibility for the juvenile visa should be extended from eighteen to twenty-one years of age for petitioners. He also shared his story at a special panel held at the Kennedy Center after the performance of the play *Shelter* in June 2016.

TOBIN HANSEN is a doctoral candidate in cultural anthropology at the University of Oregon. His ethnographic research with former drug traffickers on the US-Mexico border produced co-authored articles published in the *Bulletin of Latin American Research* and the *International Journal of Drug Policy*. He is currently studying the implications of deportation to northern Mexico among longtime authorized and unauthorized US residents. His research has been supported by a Social Science Research Council International Dissertation Research Fellowship with funds from the Andrew W. Mellon Foundation; a Wenner-Gren Foundation Dissertation Fieldwork Grant; and funding from the University of Oregon's Center for Latina/o and Latin American Studies, Global Oregon Initiative, Center for the Study of Women in Society, and Center for Diversity and Community.

LAUREN HEIDBRINK is an anthropologist and Assistant Professor of Human Development at the California State University at Long Beach. Her research and teaching interests include childhood and youth, transnational migration, performance and identity, law at the margins of the state, and Latin America. She is the author of *Migrant Youth, Transnational Families, and the State: Care and Contested Interests* (2014) and has published in *Children's Legal Rights Journal*; *Transnational Migration, Gender and Rights*; and *Children's Geographies*. She is Principal Investigator on a multiyear National Science Foundation grant that studies the deportation of youth in Guatemala, is cofounder and editor of the blog "Youth Circulations" (www.youthcirculations.com), and serves as Board President for the Anthropology of Childhood and Youth Interest Group of the American Anthropological Association.

KRISTEN JACKSON is a Senior Staff Attorney at Public Counsel in Los Angeles and has taught the Asylum Clinic at UCLA School of Law for the past decade. She has expertise in asylum and children's immigration issues, including Special Immigrant Juvenile Status (SIJS), and the intersection of immigration and juvenile justice. She is a frequent speaker at national, state, and local conferences. Jackson has litigated SIJS issues in state and federal court and has authored numerous publications, including a practice advisory on suppression and termination strategies in children's immigration court cases. She is cocounsel on *F.L.B. v. Sessions* and *C.J.L.G. v. Sessions*, two federal court cases seeking to establish a right to government-appointed counsel for children in removal proceedings, and clerked on the US Court of Appeals for the Ninth Circuit after receiving her JD from Yale Law School in 2002.

DANA LEIGH MARKS has presided as an Immigration Judge since January 1987. She is President Emeritus of the National Association of Immigration Judges (NAIJ), the recognized collective bargaining unit for the national Immigration Judge corps. She has published numerous articles and testified to Congress regarding the need to restructure US immigration courts to safeguard judicial independence. She has taught immigration law to judges, lawyers, and law students in academic settings and seminars and testified before Congress. Prior to taking the bench, she spent ten years engaging in the private practice of immigration law and served as lead counsel, successfully arguing the landmark case *INS v. Cardoza-Fonseca*, 480 U.S. 421 (1986), which established that asylum applicants need only meet the more generous reasonable possibility standard.

MEGAN McKENNA is Communications Director at KIND-Kids in Need of Defense. She has been writing about and working on humanitarian issues for nearly two decades. In addition to managing and implementing KIND's communications, she led the organization's advocacy in Congress and among federal agencies for more than five years. She is a co-author of *The Translator* (2008), a memoir about the life of a refugee from Darfur who risked his life to translate for journalists and nongovernmental organizations. Previously, she worked at the Women's Refugee Commission, Doctors Without Borders, the US Fund for

UNICEF, and the Robin Hood Foundation. She started her career with CNN International in London. McKenna has an MA from Columbia University's School of International and Public Affairs and a BA from the University of Michigan.

CECILIA MENJÍVAR holds the Dorothy L. Meier Chair in Social Equities at the University of California, Los Angeles, where she is a Professor in the Department of Sociology. Her research focuses on immigration from Central America to the United States; technologies of state terror, political violence, and gender and violence; and the effects of immigration laws and different legal statuses on various aspects of immigrants' lives. She is author of *Fragmented Ties: Salvadoran Immigrant Networks in America* (2000) and *Enduring Violence: Ladina Women's Everyday Lives in Guatemala* (2011); co-author of *Immigrant Families* (2016); editor of *Through the Eyes of Women: Gender, Social Networks, Family and Structural Change in Latin America and the Caribbean* (2003); and co-editor of several collections, including *Constructing Immigrant Illegality: Critiques, Experiences, and Responses* (2014).

ABEL NÚÑEZ is Executive Director of CARECEN. He has a background in nonprofit management and fund-raising, as well as a history of community activism. Prior to holding his position at CARECEN, Núñez was Associate Director of Centro Romero in Chicago. Before he moved to Chicago, he worked in Washington, DC, for the Latino Civil Rights Center. From 1998 to 2000, he was also on the staff of CARECEN, serving first as its Citizenship and Civic Participation Project Coordinator and later as its Deputy Director. Núñez has served since 2008 on the board of the Salvadoran American National Network (SANN). He is one of the founding members of the Residency Now campaign, which seeks to obtain lawful permanent residency for immigrants from El Salvador, Honduras, and Nicaragua under Temporary Protected Status. Núñez serves on the board of La Clinica del Pueblo and is a Commissioner for the Town of Cottage City.

JOSÉ ORTIZ-ROSALES is a Social Worker at Public Counsel in Los Angeles. He received his master's degree in social work from the University of Southern California and is certified in mental health first aid and motivational interviewing. He collaborates with immigration attorneys to provide client-centered legal services that focus on client understanding and ensure that the client has a voice in all decision making. He has worked with undocumented youth who have endured trauma in their country and the United States, and have encountered the criminal justice and child welfare systems. Ortiz-Rosales has worked with unaccompanied youth across the country in various capacities: as a postrelease case manager for unaccompanied youth released from the Office of Refugee Resettlement, conducting home studies for detained youth awaiting reunification, and as a Child Advocate for youth undergoing immigration proceedings.

NINA RABIN is Director of the Immigrant Family Legal Clinic at UCLA School of Law, where she runs a school-based legal clinic serving immigrant children and families in Los Angeles. She was previously Clinical Professor of Law at the University of Arizona James E. Rogers College of Law, where she directed two clinics serving low-wage immigrant workers and immigration detainees in Southern Arizona. In each of the legal clinics she has developed and directed, Rabin has worked in partnership with community organizations and local institutions to best serve the multi-faceted needs of mixed-status families. At the same time, she has undertaken policy research and advocacy to study and document the impact of immigration enforcement on women and families in the border region. Rabin graduated from Harvard College in 1998, from Yale Law School in 2003, and after law school, clerked for Judge Dorothy W. Nelson on the Ninth Circuit Court of Appeals.

MARGARITA SALAS-CRESPO is a graduate of the University of Nevada, Reno, with degrees in Anthropology and Women's Studies. Born in Tepic, Nayarit, Mexico, she immigrated to the United States at the age of ten. She lived in fear of deportation due to her undocumented status for more than fourteen years before receiving deportation relief through DACA in 2012. Salas-Crespo has worked tirelessly in Nevada to better the conditions of the Latino immigrant community. She has volunteered with multiple immigrant rights organizations and assisted in coordinating various workshops and forums, including those addressing citizenship, driver authorization cards, Know Your Rights, and DACA.

In 2014, Salas-Crespo was selected by the Mexican Consulate and the Mexican Ministry of Foreign Affairs to join students from across the country to travel to Mexico City. Salas-Crespo is the first in her family to graduate from high school and college.

CAROLINA VALDIVIA is a doctoral student and Ford Foundation Predoctoral Fellow at the Harvard University Graduate School of Education. Her work explores the ways through which immigrant status impacts the lives of immigrant youth and their families, including their educational trajectories, as well as their civic and political participation. She has conducted research on online and offline activism among undocumented immigrant youth, political incorporation of undocumented youth, educational experiences of undocumented students, undocumented youth-led organizations, and more. Most recently, she served as Senior Research Fellow at United We Dream, where she contributed to the establishment of the network's research institute and implementation of the research project "In Their Own Words: A Nationwide Survey of Undocumented Millennials."

WENDY YOUNG is President of KIND-Kids in Need of Defense. Previously she served as Chief Counsel on Immigration Policy in the Senate Judiciary Subcommittee on Immigration, Border Security and Refugees for Senator Edward M. Kennedy and also held immigration policy positions with the United Nations High Commissioner for Refugees, the Women's Refugee Commission, the United States Conference of Catholic Bishops, and the National Council of La Raza. She has written articles, reports, and op-eds on the plight of unaccompanied children and has received a number of honors for her work on immigration rights, including Harvard Law School's Women Inspiring Change Award, Foreign Policy's Leading Global Thinker Award, and the American Immigration Lawyers Association's Human Rights Award. Young earned a joint JD and MA in International Relations from American University and a BA from Williams College.

INDEX

Advance Parole, 9, 83, 133, 148, 159–60, 162–63, 164, 169, 211n1. *See also* international travel

Arulanantham, Ahilan, 105–6

border controls, 15, 24, 191. *See also* Prevention Through Deterrence

border crossings, 3, 15, 16, 19–31, 45, 47, 82, 83, 133, 160, 164, 169–70. *See also* US-Mexico border

border enforcement, 2, 23–26, 80, 82, 87. *See also* Customs and Border Protection

Border Patrol, 1, 7, 16, 21–31, 82

Central American Resource Center (CARECEN), 174–75, 176, 178–80

children, 45–58, 189–95; adult responsibilities, 45–46, 48–57, 93, 192; adult status, 3, 75, 114, 125; asylum, 106, 110–11, 113, 125; attorneys, 108, 110, 112–13, 114–19, 126; barriers, 82; behavioral modifications, 9, 144; borders, 1, 3, 7, 16, 45, 47, 83, 191; citizenship, 3–4, 56–57, 106, 191; communities, 6–7, 16, 73; courts/judges, 3, 7, 73, 100, 105–6, 108–10, 112–13, 118, 123–30; criminalization, 6, 194–95; Deferred Action for Childhood Arrivals, 83; deportations, 2, 5, 7, 9, 11, 45, 56, 64, 82, 84, 104, 107, 109, 114, 135, 141, 178, 192, 194; detention, 1, 3, 5, 7, 8–9, 10, 11, 16, 45, 116–17, 194–95; domestic violence, 125; due process, 73, 74–75, 108, 113, 114; enforcement, 3, 6, 10, 16, 57, 74–75, 194; facilities, 1, 3, 7, 10, 117; fair hearings, 108, 113; families, 3–4, 5, 10, 11, 45–58, 82, 189–91, 192, 194, 195, 203n17; fears, 11, 57, 82; foster care, 5, 61, 65; global inequalities, 82, 191; government, 2, 3, 7, 15, 73; health, 45, 93, 191; humanitarian crises, 174; human rights, 12, 189, 190–91, 193; Immigration and Customs Enforcement, 7; illegality, 7, 14, 17, 45–57, 82, 191; laws, 2, 3, 7, 8–11, 15, 47–48, 73, 74, 106–7, 109, 125–27, 189, 195; legal/pro bono representation, 73, 75, 100, 105–10, 114–19, 122, 192; legal rights, 3, 12, 74–75, 82, 106–7, 109–10; legal status, 3, 6–7, 17, 47–48, 106, 108, 191–94, 205n16; liminality/marginalization, 3, 7; migration, 2–5, 45, 141, 171, 173, 191, 195; naturalized citizenship, 83; policies, 3, 5, 10, 11, 15, 45, 57, 73, 189, 191, 195; politics, 3, 73, 75, 171–72, 189, 194; poverty, 48; power, 57, 189; refugees, 195; removals, 115, 125, 194; resources, 46, 189; risks, 194–95; schools, 48, 82, 93, 191; security, 192, 194; separations, 46–47, 190, 192, 210n6; smugglers, 5; social mobility, 46; social services, 8, 48; Special Immigrant Juvenile Status, 106–7; sponsors, 5, 8–9; states, 3–4, 6–8, 17, 103; systems, 3, 6–7, 11–14, 15, 45, 55, 60, 73, 74–75, 93, 114, 191, 192; trauma, 83, 107, 128–29, 190, 192–95; unauthorized status, 3, 5, 8, 48–49, 56–57; underclass, 73–74, 80, 82, 86; undocumented, 3, 101, 195; United States, 15, 75, 190; US-Mexico border, 16; violence, 73–74, 190; well-being, 57, 125, 178, 189, 191, 194. *See also* girls; unaccompanied minors; US citizen children; *individual countries*

241

children's rights, 64, 106–7, 189–95. *See also* children: legal rights

child welfare systems, 3, 8, 17, 58, 59–60, 103, 194

Congress, 10, 26, 97, 107, 109, 119, 120, 122, 153, 171, 206n22, 209n27. *See also* legislation

Contreras, Oliver, 176

criminal justice systems, 3, 11, 15, 34, 61, 65, 78–79, 81

Crouch, V. Stuart, 112

Customs and Border Protection (CBP), 60, 62, 117

Deferred Action for Childhood Arrivals (DACA), 96–100; age, 97, 200n31, 206n25; barriers, 98–99; belonging/ exclusions, 162, 170; borders, 167; childhood arrivals, 206n25; children, 83; citizenship, 10, 83, 160; communities, 97, 98; Congress, 10, 171; crimes, 35, 97, 200n31, 206n25; Department of Homeland Security, 205n1, 206n25; deportations, 9–10, 35, 83, 90, 97, 148, 160, 200n31; detention, 200n31; documents, 99, 200n31; driver's licenses, 9, 158, 200n31; economics, 100; education, 9, 35, 97, 158, 163, 200n31, 206n25; eligibility, 97, 200n31, 206n25; enforcement agents, 169; executive actions, 9, 158, 171, 200n31, 204n20; extreme and exceptional hardship, 97, 100; families, 94, 162–65; family-based petitions, 94; finances/poverty, 98–100, 200n31; government/policies, 10, 169, 170; health, 200n31; heritage trip, 159–70; home countries, 133, 163, 167; illegality, 148; immigrant rights movement, 87, 158; legal assistance/information, 98, 99, 207n26; legal status, 9–10, 97, 160, 163–64, 187, 200n31; liminality/marginality, 160–69; Mexico and, 133; other Dreamers, 168; removals, 164; *Rescission of*

Deferred Action for Childhood Arrivals, 205n1; residence length, 97, 206n25; resources, 98; security, 206n25; unaccompanied minors, 96–100; undocumented youth, 9, 13, 90, 96–100, 131, 170; United States Citizenship and Immigration Services, 97, 206n25, 207n26; United We Dream, 153; waivers, 97; work, 9, 35, 83, 148, 160, 163, 200n31; youth activism/empowerment, 12, 158. *See also* Advance Parole; international travel

deportations, 15–18; absentia deportation orders, 77, 112, 113, 118; Acts, 42–43, 77; age, 106; attorneys/legal representation, 92–93, 105, 114; belonging, 140, 146; border security, 106; Central America, 106, 143, 178; checkpoints, 152; childhood arrivals, 34–35, 41, 79; children, 2, 5, 7, 9, 11, 45, 56, 64, 82, 84, 104, 107, 109, 114, 135, 141, 178, 192, 194; communities, 136; countries, 16, 34, 41, 42, 79–80, 104, 132, 136–37, 141, 142, 146; courts/judges, 6, 38, 42–43, 105; crimes, 42–43, 78–79, 84, 111; DC Council, 176; de facto, 135–37, 140; definitions, 199n8; Department of Homeland Security, 13, 109; detention centers, 179; driver's licenses, 151; due process, 105; education, 136, 140, 145; enforcement, 42, 79; failure to appear, 77; families, 5, 6, 11, 41, 42, 45, 82, 89, 91, 109, 135, 136–37, 156, 162, 192, 194; fears, 82, 113; finances, 137; gender, 80, 141; government/legislation, 6, 132; health, 145; hearings, 127; history, 5–6; Immigration and Customs Enforcement, 113; laws, 109; legal-illegal binary, 193; legal permanent residents, 34–35; migrant deaths, 106, 124; noncitizens, 34, 42, 79; nonpriority status, 42; online tools, 156, 157; organization, 155; other Dreamers, 168–69; policies, 7–8; Prevention Through Deterrence,

26; race, 5–6; reentries, 79; removals, 210n2; resilience, 146; returnees, 141–46; risks, 132, 135; schools, 106; social citizenship, 33, 34; social values, 144; states, 5–6; systems, 11, 12, 15, 34, 38, 64; ten-year bar, 95, 206n19; transnationalism, 136; unaccompanied minors, 7, 11, 75, 91, 105, 106, 107, 121, 122, 135, 141; United We Dream, 153; US citizen children, 5, 6, 135–37; violence, 145; work, 145; youth, 2, 5, 11, 12, 15–16, 45, 74, 83–84, 97, 104, 131, 132, 135–46, 148, 151, 158, 210n2. *See also* Deferred Action for Childhood Arrivals: deportations

Department of Health and Human Services (DHHS), 104, 115, 119, 120. *See also* Office of Refugee Resettlement

Department of Homeland Security (DHS), 8, 13, 106, 107, 109, 127, 176, 205n1, 206n25, 207n10

Department of Justice (DOJ), 107–8, 112, 117, 118, 119, 207n10

Dream Act, 10, 153, 154, 206n22. *See also* University of the District of Columbia (UDC) Dream Act

Dreamers, 12, 96–97, 133, 159–70, 193, 206n22, 212n2

Dunn, Timothy, 22

Ecuador, 19, 29–30

education systems, 3, 17, 58, 93

El Salvador, 17–18, 66, 67, 76, 79–82, 84–86, 103–4, 116, 120–21, 135, 141, 174–75, 178–79

enforcement, 15–18; Border Patrol, 24, 27; border security, 106; children/youth, 3, 6, 8, 10, 16, 57, 74–75, 100–103, 122, 131, 194; courts/judges, 74, 102–3, 107; crimes, 42; deportations, 42, 79; deterrence, 10; Department of Homeland Security, 107; due process, 74–75; ethnicities/race, 80, 201n12; families, 3, 6, 10, 45, 56, 89, 194; fears, 57; girls,

46; human rights, 194; illegality, 2, 113; laws, 113, 194; migrant deaths, 26–27; migration, 6, 43; natural environments, 23–25, 27; policies, 7–8, 79, 100, 106; priority enforcement program, 84; public safety, 43; social citizenship, 43, 44; states, 194; well-being, 194. *See also* border enforcement; Immigration and Customs Enforcement

enforcement agents, 13, 39–40, 68–69, 169

Executive Office for Immigration Review (EOIR), 102–3, 105, 118, 119, 120–21

Esperanza, 70, 71

Ettinger, Patrick, 24

Fair Day in Court for Kids Act (2016), 120

families, 45–58; belonging/social citizenship, 35–38, 194; borders, 6, 169; childhood arrivals, 79; children, 3–4, 5, 45–58, 189–91, 192, 194; citizenship, 191; courts, 112–13, 117; Deferred Action for Childhood Arrivals, 162–65; deportations, 5, 6, 41, 42, 45, 136, 156, 162, 192; detention, 6, 10, 11; Dreamers, 159–60, 168; enforcement, 6, 10, 45, 56, 89, 194; finances/poverty, 145, 179, 181; human rights, 190–91; illegality, 6, 17, 45–57; immigrant rights movement, 87; international travel, 164–65; laws, 8–11, 57, 89, 100, 205n16; legal assistance/information, 91–92, 100–101; legal status, 6, 11; Mexico, 100; migration, 3, 45, 46, 143, 195; online tools, 156; policies, 45, 46, 73, 87, 89; politics, 73, 194; power, 57; removals, 16, 135; resources, 46; separations, 6, 46–47, 100, 192; states, 3; systems, 3, 11, 73, 91–92; unaccompanied minors, 104–5, 142; undocumented youth, 16, 74, 87, 89, 93, 146, 194; violence, 145, 179; visas, 82, 93–94, 205n17; youth summit, 177. *See also* Mexican migrant families; mixed-status families; parents; transnational families

244 | INDEX

family reunification, 11, 47, 57, 70, 89, 90, 100, 136, 141, 159, 163, 177
Flores Settlement Agreement (1997), 116, 121

girls, 16–17, 45–57, 141, 142, 203n24. *See also* children
Gossart, John, 109
government: advocacy, 105; asylum, 124; attorneys/pro bono/legal representation, 9, 105, 119–21; Central America, 102, 112; children/youth, 2, 3, 7, 10, 12, 15, 73, 103, 105, 113, 131, 175; citizenship, 166; courts/judges, 108, 112; Deferred Action for Childhood Arrivals, 170; deportations, 6, 132; Dreamers, 12; family-based petitions, 206n20; family reception centers, 10; illegality, 2, 6; legal systems, 113; migrant deaths, 27; migration, 5–6; policies, 3, 133; power, 74–75, 103; unaccompanied minors, 75, 114, 119–21, 142, 178; underclass, 80; US citizen children, 2
Guatemala, 67, 81, 104, 116, 120, 121–22, 132, 135–46, 175, 210n5, 211n12

Higher Education Act (1965), 149
Hirono, Mazie, 120
Homeland Security Act (2002), 115, 116
Honduras, 1, 81, 104, 116, 120, 121, 135, 141, 175
humanitarian visas, 9, 92

Illegal Immigration Reform and Immigrant Responsibility Act (1996), 6, 43, 77, 80, 83
immigrant rights, 64, 178–79. *See also* children's rights; legal rights
immigrant rights movement, 87, 132, 147, 152, 153, 158, 206n22
Immigration Act (1990), 42–43
Immigration and Customs Enforcement (ICE), 1–2, 7, 32–33, 37, 64, 84, 113, 207n10, 208n36

Immigration and Nationality Act (1965), 205n15, 205n17, 206n19, 206n20
Immigration and Naturalization Services (INS), 22, 23–24, 85
international travel, 9, 83, 84, 87, 90, 131–33, 147–48, 150, 156, 163–65, 169, 211n1. *See also* Advance Parole

Johnson, Jeh, 106
judges, 6, 42–43, 64, 74, 80, 102–13, 118, 120, 123–30, 207n11
juvenile detention systems, 102, 104
juvenile justice systems, 58, 61, 63–65, 110, 126–27, 172–73, 204n3. *See also* rocket dockets

KIND-Kids In Need Of Defense, 114, 115, 209n28, 209n30
King, Carole, 111
Klein, Eliza, 112

laws, 8–11, 73–75; American Civil Liberties Union (ACLU), 105; adult status, 125; age, 107; antiterrorism laws, 6; asylum, 110; attorneys/legal representation, 74, 75, 92–93; children, 2, 3, 7, 8–11, 15, 47–48, 73, 74, 106–7, 109, 125–27, 195; complexity, 124; Congress, 109; courts, 75, 106–7, 113, 130; deportations, 109; enforcement, 113, 194; ethnic exclusion laws, 201n12; families, 8–11, 57, 89, 100, 205n16; family law, 127; girls, 46; global inequalities, 82; hearings, 125; illegality, 2, 5; international, 13, 173, 178, 189; judges, 103, 107, 108, 110–12; legal status, 12, 205n16; legal systems, 113; migrant deaths, 124; migration, 8–11, 79; minors, 125; naturalized citizenship, 83; noncitizens, 79; nonviolent misdemeanors, 126–27; resistance, 131; states, 2, 194; Supreme Court, 124; ten-year bar, 95, 206n19; trauma, 107; unaccompanied minors, 11, 103, 106–

107, 114; undocumented youth, 9, 10, 89; visas, 93–94; youth, 8–11, 12, 14, 15, 73, 94, 109; youth activism, 131

lawsuits, 22, 86, 105–6, 112, 204n20, 207n10, 207n11

legal information, 10, 91–93, 99, 100, 207n26, 207n32

legal representation, 74, 75, 103, 104–5, 113, 114–22, 124–26, 129, 177, 207n3, 209n27

legal rights, 3, 12, 64, 74–75, 82, 103, 105–7, 109–10, 113, 115, 117, 119, 125–26, 160, 163, 178–79, 189–95. *See also* immigrant rights movement

legal status: childhood arrivals, 34–35; children/youth, 3, 6–7, 11, 12, 17, 47–48, 73, 106, 108, 191–94, 205n16; Deferred Action for Childhood Arrivals, 9–10, 97, 160, 200n31; Dream Act, 10, 206n22; families, 6, 47; family-based petitions, 95; identities, 44; immigrant rights movement, 153; judges, 108; legal permanent residents, 34; migrants, 12, 44, 207n32; noncitizens, 79; peers, 48; policies, 80; politics, 154–55; removals, 135; security, 17; ten-year bar, 95; transnationalism, 160; unaccompanied minors, 9, 102–3; underclass, 73, 79; undocumented youth, 59, 65, 149, 150–51; United States, 65; work, 47

legal systems, 3, 6–7, 11–14, 17, 38, 58, 59, 73–75, 81, 89–93, 113, 124, 192, 195. *See also* legal information; youth: systems

legislation, 2, 6, 7–8, 57, 65, 71, 83, 97, 120, 122, 153, 156, 176, 209n29, 209n31. *See also individual acts*

Lofgren, Zoe, 120

Mexican migrant families, 46–49, 82, 203n17

Mexico: Advance Parole, 159–60, 169; Central America, 141, 169, 179; checkpoints, 151–52; childhood arrivals, 159; children/youth, 91, 104, 203n17;

crimes, 182; Deferred Action for Childhood Arrivals, 133; deportations, 16, 34, 41, 104, 141; detention centers, 179; Dreamers, 159–70; economics, 43, 166, 182; families, 16–17, 100, 162–63; government, 112; illegality, 55; marginalization, 16; migration, 3; poverty, 182; unaccompanied minors, 7, 102, 141; United States, 43, 50, 81, 94, 158, 159, 165–66; US citizen children, 136; violence, 102, 143; visas, 82, 94, 206n18. *See also* US-Mexico border

migrant deaths, 15–16, 24–27, 82, 104, 106, 115, 121, 124–25, 201n12

migrants, 5, 11–14, 44, 46, 49, 74–75, 83, 91–93, 123–30, 187, 207n32

migration: age, 143; anti-immigrant sentiments, 102; attorneys, 124; Central America, 3, 173; children's rights, 195; children/youth, 2–5, 15–16, 45, 73, 131, 141, 171, 173, 191, 195; countries, 3, 65, 135, 143, 173, 195, 210n5; crimes, 43, 80; criminalization, 6, 173, 179; economics, 56; education, 8, 58; enforcement, 6, 43; exclusions, 5–8; families, 3, 45, 46, 143, 195; finances, 143, 145; gender, 46, 57, 143; girls, 55–57; global inequalities, 173; government, 5–6; home countries, 81; illegality, 2; languages, 143; laws, 8–11, 79; legal-illegal binary, 195; media, 3; natural environments, 23–26; Non Governmental Organizations, 3; policies, 3, 4, 43, 133, 173, 179, 191; politics, 3, 13–14, 173; refugees, 195; risks, 143; states, 2, 15; Supreme Court, 6; systems, 3, 8, 13–14, 58, 64, 173; transnationalism, 3, 174, 178; underclass, 81; violence, 5, 25; work, 54, 141, 143

mixed-status families, 10, 11, 17, 46, 194. *See also* transnational families

noncitizens, 34, 42, 43, 75, 79, 84, 192, 202n2

246 | INDEX

Non Governmental Organizations (NGOs), 3, 105, 112, 117, 122, 209n30. *See also individual organizations*

Obama, Barack, 9, 10, 13, 86, 90, 97, 102, 113, 119, 171–74, 176, 185, 204n20
Office of Refugee Resettlement (ORR), 60, 62, 64–65, 104, 105, 115–19, 120, 207n10, 208n10

parents: border crossings, 47; childhood arrivals, 165; children/youth, 5, 45, 46–47, 48, 56–57, 60, 74, 82, 89, 136, 190, 194, 195; Deferred Action for Childhood Arrivals, 94; deportations, 11, 45, 82, 89, 91, 109, 135, 136–37, 194; detention, 45; economics, 56; enforcement, 3; family-based petitions, 95; family reception centers, 10; girls, 56–57; international travel, 164–65; laws, 11; legal status, 47; mixed-status families, 46; parental rights, 127; poverty, 48; prosecutions, 13; removals, 136–37, 194; separations, 46–47; Special Immigrant Juvenile Status, 127; systems, 59; unaccompanied minors, 5, 89, 91, 121; unauthorized status, 48–49; undocumented, 6, 7, 101, 152, 195; US citizen children, 89, 135–37; visas, 93–94; work, 5, 47, 141. *See also* families
Plyer v. Doe (1982), 149
policies, 8–11; advocacy, 4; anti-immigrant sentiments, 157, 179; barriers, 83; borders, 80, 169, 191; Central America, 173; childhood arrivals, 97; child protections, 122; children, 45, 57, 73, 189, 191, 195; citizenship,160, 191; controls, 5–8; courts, 102–3; crimes, 43, 80, 84; criminal aliens, 84; criminalization, 179; Deferred Action for Childhood Arrivals, 10, 169; deportations, 7–8; deterrence, 23, 102, 106,

173; enforcement, 79, 100, 106; entry, 7; families, 45, 46, 73, 87, 89; girls, 46; humanitarianism, 146, 179; human rights, 173; judges, 64, 80; migrant deaths, 24–27; migration, 43, 133, 173, 179, 191; politics, 133; poverty, 133, 136; presidents, 13–14, 79, 90–91, 100, 102, 179; restrictions, 5–8; unaccompanied minors, 91, 105, 132, 178; underclass, 78, 80; undocumented youth, 5, 7–8, 10–11, 14, 15, 59, 73, 87, 89, 100, 131, 136, 147, 152; United States, 3, 80, 173; US-Mexico border, 3; violence, 25, 26, 133, 145
political systems, 3, 110
Prevention Through Deterrence, 15–16, 22–27, 173, 201n9
pro bono representation, 9, 75, 104–5, 110, 113, 115, 117–18, 119, 124, 126, 177, 209n28. *See also* legal representation
Public Counsel, 58, 62–63, 64–65

reforms, 4, 6, 8, 43, 77, 80, 83, 100, 153, 160
refugees, 176, 179, 195. *See also* Office of Refugee Resettlement
Reyes, Silvestre, 22–24
rocket dockets, 9, 74, 102–3, 105, 107, 112, 117–19
Rose, Scott, 70
Rysavy, Charles F., 114

Schmidt, Paul, 110, 112
Secure the Northern Triangle Act (2016), 120
Sessions, Jeff, 113, 170
Slavin, Denise Noonan, 107
Smith, Robert C., 203n24
social citizenship, 16, 32–44, 202n4, 202n5
Solow, Bruce, 110
Special Immigrant Juvenile Status (SIJS), 9, 62–63, 64, 70, 71, 106–7, 121, 127
Supreme Court, 6, 124, 149, 204n20

Thorne, Barrie, 46
Thronson, David B., 205n16
tourist visas, 168–69, 181
Temporary Protected Status (TPS), 86
transnational families, 6, 11, 16–17, 46,
47, 57, 100, 160, 162–63, 168, 203n17,
203n24. *See also* mixed-status families
transnationalism, 3, 76, 80, 86, 132–33, 136,
160–66, 169, 174, 178–80
Trump, Donald, 9–10, 13–14, 43, 79, 87,
90–91, 100, 102, 113, 120–21, 147, 148,
170, 179, 204n20, 205n1, 206n22
T visa, 60

Unaccompanied Alien Children. *See*
unaccompanied minors
unaccompanied minors, 89–101, 104, 111,
112–113, 120, 210n6; 114–22; absentia
deportation orders, 118; Acts, 115,
120; advocacy, 135, 171, 178; asylum,
104, 120, 121; attorneys/legal/pro
bono representation, 75, 103, 104–5,
106, 113, 114–22, 207n3; behavioral
modifications, 144; borders, 116,
121–22; Central America,102; child
abuse, 121; child advocacy, 104, 120,
209n30; child protections/democracy,
103, 120–22; communities, 142, 178;
Congress, 120, 122; continuances, 118;
countries, 7, 102, 104, 115–16, 121–22,
141–46; courts/judges, 89, 102–3, 107,
121, 122; crimes, 142–43; Deferred Action for Childhood Arrivals, 96–100;
detention, 75, 104, 121, 142; detention
centers, 116–17, 144; Department of
Justice, 119; domestic violence, 104;
due process, 75, 103, 112, 114, 121;
enforcement, 102–3; Executive Office
for Immigration Review, 118, 120–21;
families, 89, 91, 104–5, 121, 141, 142;
family-based petitions, 93–96; fears,
116; federal funds, 115–16, 119–20,
122; Flores Settlement Agreement

(1997), 121; girls, 141; government,
75, 114, 119–21, 142, 178; hearings,
103, 105, 118–19; DHHS, 115; home
countries, 104; humanitarianism,
104; human trafficking, 121; laws, 103,
107, 114; legal rights, 103; legislation,
120, 209n29; media, 103, 106, 207n3;
migrant deaths, 115, 121; notifications,
118; Office of Refugee Resettlement,
115–19, 120, 208n10; policies, 91, 132,
178; politics, 171–72; poverty, 116, 141;
power, 103; presidents, 102, 119, 120–
21, 174–75; prosecutions, 114; refuge,
7; removals, 113, 117, 120; resources,
119; returnees, 141–46; rocket dockets,
102–3, 117–19; smugglers, 5; social
values, 144; sponsors, 102–3, 118–19;
surges, 102, 104, 106; systems, 89,
93, 102–3, 104; trauma, 118; United
States Citizenship and Immigration
Services, 120; US-Mexico border,102;
violence, 102, 104; work, 141
UndocuBlack Network, 158
undocumented youth, 58–60, 147–58;
Advance Parole, 164; advocacy, 132,
171; attorneys, 58–60; barriers, 59,
83–84, 149, 158; belonging, 132, 148–49,
152, 153, 157, 158; border crossings, 133;
childhood arrivals, 73–74, 79, 150;
citizenship, 160, 161; communities,148,
161; crimes, 84; Deferred Action for
Childhood Arrivals, 90, 96–97; deportations, 83–84, 97, 132, 148, 151, 158;
detention, 10, 151; Dream Act, 153, 154,
206n22; driver's licenses, 80–81, 82–83,
84, 132, 148, 151; education, 59, 79, 80,
82–83, 84, 149–51, 153; exclusions, 132,
147, 149–52, 158, 161–62; families, 59,
60, 89, 194; fears, 132, 148, 151; financial
aid, 79, 82–83, 149, 150, 185, 212n1;
health, 80; identities, 148, 153, 158; illegality, 147–48, 178; immigrant rights
movement, 87, 132, 152, 153;

248 | INDEX

undocumented youth (*cont.*)
  international travel, 83, 84, 132, 147–48, 150; languages, 58, 59; laws, 89; legal rights, 160; legal status, 59, 65, 132, 148, 149, 150–51, 155; legislation, 156; liminality, 161–62; marginalization, 149–50, 161; media, 154; online tools, 148–49, 155–57; organization, 132, 147–49, 153–58; policies, 10, 59, 89, 147, 152; politics, 132, 147–48, 152–55, 158, 171–72; reforms, 153; resilience, 158; resistance, 132, 157, 158; resources, 59; risks, 84, 194; schools, 59, 80, 149; Supreme Court, 149; systems, 58–60, 65, 89; terms, 212n2; transnationalism, 132–33, 160, 161–62; trauma, 58; underclass, 73–74; United States, 58, 147; unlawful presence, 83; work, 80–81, 82–83, 84, 150, 151; youth empowerment, 153. *See also* Dreamers; unaccompanied minors; youth
United States: Advance Parole, 133, 159–60, 169; childhood arrivals, 41, 166, 167; children/youth, 58, 75, 122, 133, 147, 190; deportations, 42, 132, 136–37, 141; deterrence, 23, 102, 173; Dreamers, 159–60, 165, 166; humanitarianism, 173; illegality, 55; international laws, 173; legal rights, 119; legal status, 65; migration, 65, 173, 195; organization, 153; policies, 80, 173; reentries, 83, 133; security, 81; unaccompanied minors, 102, 115–16, 121–22, 141; UWD, 153; visas, 60, 82. *See also* government; *individual countries*
United States Citizenship and Immigration Services (USCIS), 64, 97, 120, 159, 164, 206n25, 207n26
United States v. Texas (2016), 86, 204n20
United We Dream, 153, 157
University of the District of Columbia Dream Act, 175–76, 212n1

US citizen children, 2, 5, 6–7, 11–12, 89, 91, 135–37, 194, 195. *See also* families
US-Mexico border, 3, 8, 16, 23, 60, 102, 144, 151–52, 173, 174. *See also* border crossings
U visa, 148

waivers, 25, 92, 96, 97, 100, 206n20
Weil, Jack, 105–6
women, 1, 10, 47, 57, 77, 80, 91, 110, 124, 143

youth: adult status, 125; advocacy, 79–80, 175; asylum, 9, 206n22; attorneys/legal representation, 4, 9, 17, 73–75, 105, 113; barriers, 87; belonging, 73–74, 136–37, 140, 146; borders, 2, 3, 15, 16, 87–88; citizenship, 2, 3, 11, 12, 140; communities, 16, 73, 131, 133, 142, 175–76; courts, 2, 3, 9, 73–75, 131; creative arts, 176; crimes, 142–43; criminalization, 6; cultures, 146; Deferred Action for Childhood Arrivals, 13, 97–100, 131, 170; Department of Homeland Security, 8, 109; deportations, 2, 5, 11, 12, 15–16, 45, 74, 84, 104, 131, 132, 135–46, 210n2; detention, 2, 3, 5, 6, 15, 16, 18, 142–43; due process, 73; education, 8, 17, 73–74, 94, 140, 145, 149–51; enforcement, 6, 8, 10, 16, 74, 100, 101, 131; exclusions, 131–34, 175–76; failures, 141–46; families, 7, 10, 16, 74, 87, 89, 93, 94, 136, 140, 146; family-based petitions, 92, 94–96; fears, 87; finances/poverty, 73–74, 145, 179; global inequalities, 191; health, 17, 145; home countries, 3, 132, 136; human rights, 180, 192, 193; identities, 146; illegality, 2, 5–8, 14, 15, 17, 45, 132, 193; interdisciplinary teams, 65; international travel, 87, 131; languages, 146; laws, 8–11, 12, 14, 15, 73, 94, 109; legal assistance, 100–101; legal information, 92, 93, 100; legal status, 2, 3, 10–11, 12, 17, 73; legislation, 7–8, 65; liminality,

3, 4; marginalization, 7, 16, 17–18, 131; migration, 2–5, 15–16, 73, 131; online tools, 192–93; organization, 12, 193; peers, 136–37; policies, 5, 7–8, 10–11, 14, 15, 73, 87, 100, 131, 136; politics, 73; race, 73–74; reentries, 83; removals, 131, 135, 145; resilience, 86, 94, 146; resistance, 131; resources, 175; returnees, 141–46; risks, 73, 135; schools, 73, 101; security, 17; smugglers, 5, 16; social mobility, 7; social services, 8, 101; sponsors, 5, 8–9; states, 2, 7–8, 14, 15; systems, 2–5, 11, 12, 14–18, 45, 65, 73–74, 81, 89, 92, 100, 131–32, 175; trauma, 65, 94, 177, 192; unauthorized status, 3, 192; violence, 5, 145, 179; well-being, 7; work, 7, 73–74, 136, 145, 177, 190. *See also* Deferred Action for Childhood Arrivals; government: children/youth; unaccompanied minors; undocumented youth; youth activism; *individual countries*

youth activism, 131, 147–58, 175–78, 185–87, 193

youth empowerment, 7–8, 12, 153–54, 157, 192, 193. *See also* immigrant rights movement, youth activism

Zelizer, Viviana, 190

Printed in the United States
By Bookmasters